ANDRE GINGRICH AND SIEGFRIED HAAS (EDS.)

SOUTHWEST ARABIA ACROSS HISTORY: ESSAYS TO THE MEMORY OF WALTER DOSTAL

thanks ever so much for your 2014-16 term in our Scientific Advisory Board!

With gratitude + respect + admiration,

05-11-2016 Andre

ÖSTERREICHISCHE AKADEMIE DER WISSENSCHAFTEN
PHILOSOPHISCH-HISTORISCHE KLASSE
DENKSCHRIFTEN, 472. BAND

SAMMLUNG EDUARD GLASER XVI

Verlag der
Österreichischen Akademie
der Wissenschaften

ÖAW

Wien 2014

ÖSTERREICHISCHE AKADEMIE DER WISSENSCHAFTEN
PHILOSOPHISCH-HISTORISCHE KLASSE
DENKSCHRIFTEN, 472. BAND

Andre Gingrich and Siegfried Haas (eds.)

SOUTHWEST ARABIA ACROSS HISTORY: ESSAYS TO THE MEMORY OF WALTER DOSTAL

Verlag der
Österreichischen Akademie
der Wissenschaften

Wien 2014

ÖAW

Vorgelegt von w. M. Andre Gingrich in der Sitzung vom 27. Juni 2014

Die Forschungen und die Drucklegung der Publikation wurden durch Mittel aus dem SFB F42 VISCOM des FWF der Wissenschaftsfonds ermöglicht.

Diese Publikation wurde einem anonymen, internationalen Peer-Review-Verfahren unterzogen.
This publication has undergone the process of anonymous, international peer review.

Die verwendete Papiersorte ist aus chlorfrei gebleichtem Zellstoff hergestellt, frei von säurebildenden Bestandteilen und alterungsbeständig.

ISBN 978-3-7001-7603-9

Satz: Andrea Sulzgruber
Druck: Ferdinand Berger & Söhne Ges.m.b.H., 3580 Horn

http://hw.oeaw.ac.at/7603-9
http://verlag.oeaw.ac.at
Printed and bound in the EU

TABLE OF CONTENTS

ACKNOWLEDGMENTS

The present volume is the outcome of a conference held on October 8th 2012 at the Diplomatic Academy in Vienna, Austria. The conference was convened on the occasion of commemorating Walter Dostal's untimely death fourteen months earlier, in August 2011, and was co-hosted by the three institutions where Walter Dostal had been active throughout his academic career since his return from Switzerland in 1975. These include the University of Vienna's Department for Social and Cultural Anthropology (in 1975 still bearing the old name Institut für Völkerkunde) where he became department chair, the Austrian Society for the Middle East (Österreichische Orient-Gesellschaft Hammer-Purgstall) which Dostal himself had founded in the 1950s and whose Honorary President he remained until the end, and the Austrian Academy of Sciences' (AAS) Institute for Social Anthropology (ISA) whose precursor units Dostal chaired since the late 1970s, acting first as an Associate and then as a Full Academy Member.

The editors thus gratefully acknowledge the good services and assistance provided by these three host institutions, together with the Diplomatic Academy, for making the event possible that preceded this volume. The presence and support of members of the Dostal family was appreciated with gratitude, in particular that of his nephew Prof. Dr. Michael Roden. Moreover, the presence of several high-ranking scholars from the Republic of Yemen, including epigrapher Dr. Yusuf Abdallah and historian Dr. Husayn al-Amri, testified to the great respect and affection that scholarly communities engaging with the study of Arabia continue to hold for Walter Dostal, and share with significant segments of public life in southwest Arabia where he carried out the greatest and most extensive part of a lifetime of research.

Beyond that original commemorative conference, the editors wish to express their gratitude to the academic contributors to the event and to this volume for their commitment to demonstrate the fertility of combining anthropological approaches in a cross- and transdisciplinary manner with expertise in epigraphy, archaeology, philology, history, geography, and other related fields for the advancement of South Arabian studies.

Finally, our respect and gratitude are expressed to all those who were involved in the process of producing this volume including Lisbeth Triska, Herwig Stöger and Robert Püringer at the AAS publishing house (Verlag der ÖAW); Rosemarie Willi for her translation into English of Roswitha Stiegner's contribution; Sarah Kwiatkowski, David Mihola, and Andrea Sulzgruber for their assistance in adapting the manuscript according to the publisher's specific technical style. We also are thankful for the permissions given by the European Association of Social Anthropologists' "*EASA Newsletter*" and by the "*Anthropos*" journal's editor to reprint revised sections of the respective obituaries and Dostal's list of academic print and film publications for the present context. In addition, the editors wish to praise the valuable insights, advice and feedback provided by the publishing house's two anonymous international academic reviewers.

A substantial amount of the financial expenses that were required for this book manuscript's preparation were paid through the Austrian Science Fund (FWF) and its grant SFB F42 VISCOM. This grant allows for comparative research on the medieval histories of Asia and Europe through a cooperative project between the Austrian Academy of Sciences and the University of Vienna. The FWF's substantial support in making this intermediate result of the VISCOM SFB in Yemeni studies available is hereby acknowledged and appreciated.

Vienna, Spring 2014

Siegfried Haas and Andre Gingrich

WALTER DOSTAL | 1928-2011

Walter Dostal was one of the most eminent representatives of German-speaking socio-cultural anthropology between the 1960s and the turn of the 20th/21st centuries. His family's experience as bilingual citizens of Czechoslovakia (or: Bohemia) before and during World War II, their anti-Nazi orientation and the communist takeover at the end of the war profoundly shaped Dostal's engagement as a student and scholar. Born in Grulich near Brno (Moravia, today: Czech Republic), Dostal moved to Vienna in 1945 where he began his university studies in a field still called "Voelkerkunde" during the 1950's. Those formative years in Dostal's career resulted in his clear rejection of speculative historicism and diffusionism, and in his preference for ethnographic fieldwork and solid historical evidence. In spite of his critical stand regarding his teachers' approaches, they decisively promoted and encouraged him during the early phases of his career – in particular Robert Heine Geldern as a leading expert in the archaeology and historical anthropology of Asia, and Joseph Henninger as the Arabia expert among the Vienna culture circle theory group.

After his doctoral thesis on groups of Semitic languages Dostal soon embarked upon fieldwork in the Arab-speaking parts of the Middle East. His early empirical studies in the Arab Gulf countries during the 1950's, and in southern Yemen (early 1960's) – both regions still under indirect British control at the time – in fact made Dostal the world's first professional socio-cultural anthropologist to carry out ethnographic fieldwork in eastern and southern Arabia.

He established his reputation as an excellent analyst of ethnography and history already through his first book (submitted as his Venia Docendi thesis) on the Bedouins in Southern Arabia. In 1965, he left his position as curator of the Vienna Museum for Ethnology's Middle Eastern Department to become the founding professor in Switzerland's capital at the Bern University's Seminar for Ethnology, which he helped to build up throughout the subsequent decade. In 1975, he returned from Switzerland to Vienna to take over Chair I of what today is that University's Department of Social and Cultural Anthropology.

His study of the market of San'a, and his co-editorship (with Georg Gruenberg) of the results from the first Barbados conference on native Americans' rights highlighted his growing interest in socio-economic topics, and in what then were relevant new issues such as local markets, indigenous struggles, gender issues, and questions of political power. – During the 1970s, Dostal also initiated together with Eugen Wirth, the leading head of the German school of cultural geographers at Erlangen University, the "Geographers' and Anthropologists' Working Group on Contemporary Islam". Throughout the subsequent two decades, that working group and its annual conferences functioned as one of the most relevant forces across German-speaking academia for promoting, orienting and inspiring interdisciplinary research in the Middle East. As chair of the Vienna department, Dostal further elaborated these interests through his publications on the intersection between environment and society, his edited volume "On Social Evolution", and his studies on tribal organization and development in Arabia. Those years also showed that in several important ways, Dostal for some time pursued a German-speaking version of what was contemporary neo-evolutionism in North America and Western Europe.

After becoming a corresponding (1977) and a full member (1993) of the Austrian Academy of Sciences, Dostal re-invigorated the field's institutional unit there as well. Through the Academy's Commission for Social Anthropology, he promoted new fieldwork projects in Tibet and the Himalayan areas, in South East Asia, and in South Arabia. Several generations of contemporary socio-cultural anthropologists in Vienna, Bern, Germany, and elsewhere were his doctoral students, benefitting from his wide ethnographic expertise and his competent reading of the disciplinary production in several languages other than German – comprising English, French, Italian, Russian and Arabic. During his later years, Dostal continued his prolific publication activities, which included his book on equality and hierarchy in Arabia, his two volumes on the famous Austrian 19th century Yemeni scholar Eduard Glaser (born in what today is the Czech Republic), and his two edited books on the southwestern provinces of Saudi-Arabia. After his retirement from the University of Vienna Department in 1996, Dostal continued at the Austrian Academy of Sciences in helping to build the current Institute for Social Anthropology's precursor unit there. Walter Dostal will be remembered as one of the pioneers in post-1945 German-speaking socio-cultural anthropology who decisively contributed to its re-connection and integration into today's global discipline, and as an eminent ethnographer of South Arabia.

Andre Gingrich and Helmut Lukas

Adapted after obituaries for Walter Dostal by Andre Gingrich, published in Almanach der Österreichischen Akademie der Wissenschaften 2012, 607-612 (with Helmut Lukas); Anthropos 107/1/2012, 167-169; EASA Newsletter 54, September 2011, 18.

LIST OF ACADEMIC PRINT & FILM PUBLICATIONS BY WALTER DOSTAL

Compiled by Verena Baldwin, Silvia Haas, Wolfgang Kraus

Print Publications

1949 Kriminologie und Ethnologie. *Archiv für Völkerkunde* 4: 214–218.

1955 Die Zigeuner in Österreich. Monographische Zusammenfassung der Ergebnisse meines Studienaufenthaltes unter Zigeunern (1954). *Archiv für Völkerkunde* 10: 1–15.

1956 Die Ṣolubba und ihre Bedeutung für die Kulturgeschichte Arabiens. Monographische Zusammenfassung der Ergebnisse meines Studienaufenthaltes in Kuwēt (1956). *Archiv für Völkerkunde* 11: 15–42.

1957a Ein Beitrag zur Frage des religiösen Weltbildes der frühesten Bodenbauer Vorderasiens. *Archiv für Völkerkunde* 12: 54–109.

1957b Das Museum für Völkerkunde, seine Aufgaben und Probleme im Rahmen der Volksbildung. *Archiv für Völkerkunde* 12: 230–241.

1957c Personality and Culture Conflict of the Austrian Gypsies. *Journal of the Gypsy Lore Society* 36: 53–56.

1958a Arabia. *Bulletin of the International Committee on Urgent Anthropological and Ethnological Research* 1: 42–45.

1958b Ethnographische Notizen über die el-Äzēridj. *Wiener völkerkundliche Mitteilungen* 6/1–4 (N. F. 1): 93–99.

1958c Felsmalereien in al-Kuwait. *Archivio Internazionale di Etnografia e Preistoria* 1: 57–68.

1958d Zum Problem der Mädchenbeschneidung in Arabien. *Wiener völkerkundliche Mitteilungen* 6/1–4 (N. F. 1): 83–90.

1958e Zur Frage der Entwicklung des Beduinentums. *Archiv für Völkerkunde* 13: 1–14.

1959 The Evolution of Bedouin Life. *Studi Semitici* 2: 1–34.

1960a Bemerkungen über meine Südarabien-Reise (Oktober bis Dezember) 1960. *Archiv für Völkerkunde* 15: 1–6.

1960b Some Remarks Concerning the Baṭāḥira, a Social Inferior Tribe in Southern Arabia. *Archiv für Völkerkunde* 15: 7–9.

1962a Über Jagdbrauchtum in Vorderasien. *Paideuma* 8: 85–97.

1962b Vorderasien. In: A. Lommel und O. Zerries (Hrsg.), JRO-Völkerkunde. Afrika – Amerika – Asien – Australien – Ozeanien; pp. 47–69. München: JRO-Verlag.

1964a Paria-Gruppen in Vorderasien. *Zeitschrift für Ethnologie* 89: 190–203.

1964b Zur Frage der Konstanz von Kulturformen. In: E. Haberland, M. Schuster und H. Straube (Hrsg.), Festschrift für Ad. E. Jensen. Teil 1; pp. 91–101. München: Klaus Renner Verlag.

1965 Vorläufige Ergebnisse einer Untersuchung zur Feststellung der politischen Meinungsbildung in Südarabien. *Mitteilungen der Anthropologischen Gesellschaft in Wien* 95: 1–21.

1967 Die Beduinen in Südarabien. Eine ethnologische Studie zur Entwicklung der Kamelhirtenkultur in Arabien. Horn: Berger. (Wiener Beiträge zur Kulturgeschichte und Linguistik, 16)

1968 Zur Megalithfrage in Südarabien. In: E. Gräf (Hrsg.), Festschrift Werner Caskel. Zum 70. Geburtstag gewidmet von Freunden und Schülern; pp. 53–64. Leiden: Brill.

1968/69 Zum Problem der Stadt- und Hochkultur im Vorderen Orient. Ethnologische Marginalien. *Anthropos* 63/64: 227–260.

1969 Umsturz und Verschwörung. Dargestellt an drei Beispielen aus dem islamischen Raum – ein ethnologischer Beitrag zur Phänomenologie der Macht. *Mitteilungen der Anthropologischen Gesellschaft in Wien* 99: 13–43.

1970a Erfahrungen mit einem Situationsbilder-Test in Südarabien. (Ein Beitrag zur Methodik der ethnographischen Datenerhebung.) *Mitteilungen der Anthropologischen Gesellschaft in Wien* 100: 380–387.

1970b The Significance of Semitic Nomads in Asia. In: Proceedings of the VIIIth International Congress of Anthropological and Ethnological Sciences, 1968, Tokyo and Kyoto. Vol. 3: Ethnology and Archaeology; pp. 312–316. Tokyo: Science Council of Japan.

1971 Dorfstruktur – Soziale Ordnung – Subcultures. In: Alacahöyük. Ethnographische Skizzen eines Anatolischen Dorfes. Ergebnisse einer Feldübung des Seminars für Ethnologie der Universität Bern. *Jahrbuch des Bernisch Historischen Museums* 47/48 (1967/68): 215–231.

1972a Handwerker und Handwerkstechniken in Tarîm (Südarabien, Hadramaut). Göttingen: Institut für den Wissenschaftlichen Film. (Publikationen zu wissenschaftlichen Filmen, Sektion Völkerkunde – Volkskunde; Ergänzungsband, 3)

1972b The Shiḥūḥ of Northern Oman. A Contribution to Cultural Ecology. *Geographical Journal* 138/1: 1–7.

1973 Islam ükelerinde etnografi arastirmalari ve özellike etnografie Filim. *Avusturya kültür yayainlari 3, Etnografya ve Bilimsel Filimler* (Istanbul): 11–14.

1974a Nomaden. In: K. Kreiser, W. Diem und H. G. Majer (Hrsg.), Lexikon der islamischen Welt. Bd. 2: Gram–Nom; pp. 206–212. Stuttgart: Verlag W. Kohlhammer.

1974b Quellenkritische Bemerkungen zum "Ethnographic Atlas". *Mitteilungen der Anthropologischen Gesellschaft in Wien* 104: 44–55.

1974c Sozio-ökonomische Aspekte der Stammesdemokratie in Nordost-Yemen. *Soziologus* 24: 1–15.

1974d Theorie des öko-kulturellen Interaktionssystems. *Anthropos* 69: 409–444.

1975 Two South Arabian Tribes: al-Qarā and al-Ḥarāsīs. *Arabian Studies* 2: 33–41.

1976 Zur Kooperation zwischen Ethnologen, Kameramann und einheimischen Mitarbeitern bei der ethnologischen Filmdokumentation. *Wissenschaftlicher Film* 17: 24–32.

1978 Taṭawwur ḥayāt al-badw fī 'l-djazīra 'l-ʿarabīya fī ḍauw al-mādda 'l-atharīya (Entwicklungen des Beduinenlebens im Lichte des archäologischen Materials). *Fikrun wa Fann* 15/31: 20–43.

1979a The Development of Bedouin Life in Arabia Seen from Archaeological Material. In: Abd al-Rahman T. al-Ansary (ed.), Studies in the History of Arabia. Vol. 1, part 1; pp. 125–157. al-Riyāḍ: Jāmiʿat al-Riyāḍ.

1979b Der Markt von Ṣanʿāʾ. Wien: Österreichische Akademie der Wissenschaften. (Österreichische Akademie der Wissenschaften, Veröffentlichungen der Arabischen Kommission 1; Sitzungsberichte der Phil.-Hist. Kl., 354)

1979c Towards an Ethnographic Atlas of Arabia. *Proceedings of the Seminar for Arabian Studies* 9: 45–52.

1980 [Together with J. Salat] Arabic, English, Turkish, and German Questionnaire for Crafts in Western Asia. *Bulletin of the International Committee on Urgent Anthropological and Ethnological Research* 22: 9–109.

1981a [Zusammen mit Leo Reisinger] Ein Modell des öko-kulturellen Interaktionssystems. *Zeitschrift für Ethnologie* 106: 43–50.

1981b Mulāḥaẓāt ḥawla 'l-handasa 'l-taqlīdīya fī djunūb shibh al-djazīra 'l-ʿarabīya (Notes on the Traditional Architecture in the South of the Arabian Peninsula). *Fikrun wa Fann* 35: 56–84.

1983a Analysis of the Ṣanʿāʾ Market Today. In: R. B. Serjeant and R. Lewcock (eds.), Ṣanʿāʾ. An Arabian Islamic City; pp. 241–275. London: World of Islam Festival Trust.

1983b The Development of Bedouin Life in Arabia Seen from Archaeological Material. *Studies in the History of Arabia* 1: 125–158.

1983c Ethnographic Atlas of ʿAsīr: Preliminary Report. (With Contributions by A. Gingrich and H. Riedl.) Wien: Österreichische Akademie der Wissenschaften. (Österreichische Akademie der Wissenschaften, Phil.-Hist. Kl.; Sitzungsberichte, 406)

1983d Die geschlechtliche Arbeitsteilung in ethnologischer Sicht. In: B. Sitter (Hrsg.), Menschliches Verhalten. Seine biologischen und kulturellen Komponenten, untersucht an den Phänomenen Arbeitsteilung und Kleidung, bzw. Tracht; pp. 61–86. Freiburg: Universitätsverlag. (Kolloquien der Schweizerischen Geisteswissenschaftlichen Gesellschaft, 1)

1983e Interpretation der sozio-ökonomischen Verhältnisse südarabischer Beduinen. In: P. Snoy (Hrsg.), Ethnologie und Geschichte. Festschrift für Karl Jettmar; pp. 112–127. Wiesbaden: Franz Steiner Verlag. (Beiträge zur Südasien-Forschung, 96)

1983f Some Remarks on the Ritual Significance of the Bull in Pre-Islamic South Arabia. In: R. L. Bidwell and G. R. Smith (Hrsg.), Arabian and Islamic Studies. Articles presented to R. B. Serjeant on the Occasion of His Retirement from the Sir Thomas Adam's Chair of Arabic at the University of Cambridge; pp. 196–213. London: Longman.

1983g The Traditional Architecture of Rās al-Kẖaimah (North). Wiesbaden: Reichert. (Tübinger Atlas des Vorderen Orients, Beihefte, B, 54)

1984a Editor's Preface. In: W. Dostal (ed.), On Social Evolution; pp. 5–11.

1984b Socio-Economic Formations and Multiple Evolution. In: W. Dostal (ed.), On Social Evolution; pp. 170–183.

1984c Squire and Peasant in Tarim. A Study of "Rent Capitalism" in Southern Arabia. In: W. Dostal (ed.), On Social Evolution; pp. 228–252.

1984d [ed.] On Social Evolution. Contributions to Anthropological Concepts. (Proceedings of the Symposium Held at the Occasion of the 50th Anniversary of the Wiener Institut für Völkerkunde in Vienna, 12th–16th December, 1979.) Horn: Verlag Ferdinand Berger & Söhne. (Vienna Contributions to Ethnology and Anthropology, 1)

1984e Toward Ethnographic Cartography: A Case Study. *Current Anthropology* 25: 340–344.

1985a Egalität und Klassengesellschaft in Südarabien. Anthropologische Untersuchungen zur sozialen Evolution. Horn: Verlag Ferdinand Berger & Söhne. (Wiener Beiträge zur Kulturgeschichte und Linguistik, 20)

1985b Towards a Model of Cultural Evolution in Arabia. Pre-Islamic Arabia. *Studies in the History of Arabia* 2: 185–191.

1986a Bahrain and Its Position in an Eco-Cultural Classification Concept of the Gulf. Some Theoretical Aspects of Eco-Cultural Zones. In: Shaykha Haya Ali Al Khalifa and M. Price (eds.), Bahrain through the Ages; pp. 418–427. Bahrain: Distr. Routledge and Kegan Paul.

1986b Ethnographischer Film – Ethnographische Kartographie. Methodologische Überlegungen zur Datenerhebung. Beispiele aus Südarabien. In: H. Fischer (Hrsg.), Feldforschungen. Berichte zur Einführung in Probleme und Methoden; pp. 67–89. Berlin: Reimer.

1987a Auf der Suche nach der Zukunft. In: W. Daum (Hrsg.), Jemen. 3000 Jahre Kunst und Kultur des glücklichen Arabien. Erschienen aus Anlaß der gleichnamigen Ausstellung im Staatlichen Museum für Völkerkunde München; pp. 441–459. Innsbruck: Pinguin-Verlag.

1987b Landherr und Landarbeiter in Tarîm. Eine Studie über den "Rentenkapitalismus" in Südarabien. In: M. Fischer und M. Sauberer (Hrsg.), Gesellschaft. Wirtschaft. Raum. Beiträge zur modernen Wirtschafts- und Sozialgeographie. Festschrift für Karl Stiglbauer; pp. 279-293. Wien: Arbeitskreis. (AMR-Info; Mitteilungen des Arbeitskreises für neue Methoden in der Regionalforschung, 17)

1987c Traditionelle Wirtschaft und Gesellschaft. In: W. Daum (Hrsg.), Jemen. 3000 Jahre Kunst und Kultur des glücklichen Arabien. Erschienen aus Anlaß der gleichnamigen Ausstellung im Staatlichen Museum für Völkerkunde München; pp. 331–364. Innsbruck: Pinguin-Verlag.

1988 Craftsmen and Their Techniques in Tarim, Southern Arabia, Hadramawt. *Visual Anthropology* 1: 245–250.

1989a Nomad's Role in Arab Culture. In: Y. Christe (réd.), Le désert. Image et réalité. (Actes du Colloque de Cartigny 1983); Leuven: Peeters. (Les cahiers du CEOPA, 3)

1989b Mahra and Arabs in South Arabia. A Study in Interethnical Relations. In: M. Ibrahim (ed.), Arabian Studies in Honour of Mahmoud al-Ghul. (Symposium at Yarmouk University, December 8-11, 1984); pp. 27–36. Wiesbaden: Harrassowitz.

1989c The Transition from Cognatic to Unilinear Descent Systems in South Arabia. In: A. Gingrich, S. and S. Haas, and G. Rasuly-Paleczek (eds.), Kinship, Social Change, and Evolution; pp. 47–63. (Wiener Beiträge zur Ethnologie und Anthropologie, 5)

1990a Eduard Glaser – Forschungen im Yemen. Eine quellenkritische Untersuchung in ethnologischer Sicht. Wien: Österreichische Akademie der Wissenschaften. (Österreichische Akademie der Wissenschaften, Veröffentlichungen der Arabischen Kommission Nr. 4, Sitzungsberichte der Phil.-Hist. Kl., 545)

1990b "Sexual Hospitality" and the Problem of Matrilinearity in Southern Arabia. *Proceedings of the Seminar for Arabian Studies* 20: 17–30.

1990c Sūq Ṣan'ā'. (Translated by Wafiq Muhammad Ghunaym.) Riyadh: Publications of the Research Centre, College of Arts, King Saud University.

1991a Mecca before the Time of the Prophet. Attempt of an Anthropological Interpretation. *Der Islam* 61/2: 193–231.

1991b On Methods in Ethnographic Documentation. A Retrospective Consideration of Field Research in Arabia. *Folk* 33: 169–182.

1992a Al-aswāq. In: Aḥmad Jābir 'Afīf et al. (ed.), *Al-Mausū'a al-Yamanīya* (The Encyclopaedia of Yemen), Vol. 1; pp. 115–117. Ṣan'ā': Mu'assasat al'Afīf al-Thaqāfīya.

1992b Al-ḥirfa al-yadawīya. In: Aḥmad Jābir 'Afīf et al. (ed.), *Al-Mausū'a al-Yamanīya* (The Encyclopaedia of Yemen), Vol. 1; pp. 358–361. Ṣan'ā': Mu'assasat al'Afīf al-Thaqāfīya.

1992c Al-'urf. In: Aḥmad Jābir 'Afīf et al. (ed.), *Al-Mausū'a al-Yamanīya* (The Encyclopaedia of Yemen), Vol. 1; pp. 645–654. Ṣan'ā': Mu'assasat al'Afīf al-Thaqāfīya.

1992d Eric R. Wolf. Anthropologie und Weltgeschichte aus neuer Sicht. *Mitteilungen der Anthropologischen Gesellschaft in Wien* (MAGW) 122: 1–4.

1993a Ethnographica Jemenica. Auszüge aus den Tagebüchern Eduard Glasers mit einem Kommentar versehen. Wien: Verlag der Österreichischen Akademie der Wissenschaften. (Österreichische Akademie der Wissenschaften, Phil.-Hist. Kl., Sitzungsberichte, 593; Veröffentlichungen der Arabischen Kommission, 5)

1993b The Structure and Principles of Customary Law among the Tribes in Yemen. An Anthropological Interpretation. In: Abd al-Rahman T. al-Ansary and Wafik Ghoneim (eds.), Dirâsât fî al-Âthâr, Part 1. (On the Occasion of the 10th Anniversary of the Establishment of the Department of Archaeology and Museology at King Saud University.); pp. 1-33. Riyadh: King Saud University.

1993c Maria Höfner. Nachruf. In: Almanach. Österreichische Akademie der Wissenschaften. Jg. 143. 1992/93; pp. 467-472. Wien Verlag der Österreichischen Akademie der Wissenschaften

1994a Schweigen in der Finsternis. Ein Essay über die deutsche Ethnologie zur Zeit des Nationalsozialismus. In: J. Ohlemacher und H. Schultze (Hrsg.), Die Ausgrenzung des Fremden. Antisemitismus und Fremdenhaß; pp. 88–93. Loccum: RPI.

1994b Silence in the Darkness. An Essay on German Ethnology during the National Socialist Period. *Social Anthropology / Anthropologie Sociale – The Journal of the European Association of Social Anthropologists* 2/3: 251–262.

1995a Schulbuchanalyse (Geschichte 2). Das große Mißverständnis. In: S. Heine (Hrsg.), Islam zwischen Selbstbild und Klischee. Eine Religion im österreichischen Schulbuch; pp. 221–237. Köln: Böhlau Verlag. (Kölner Veröffentlichungen zur Religionsgeschichte, 26)

1995b Über den Wandel des Islambildes und seine Auswirkungen auf die Schulbücher. In: S. Heine (Hrsg.), Islam zwischen Selbstbild und Klischee. Eine Religion im österreichischen Schulbuch; pp. 267–293. Köln: Böhlau Verlag. (Kölner Veröffentlichungen zur Religionsgeschichte, 26)

1996a The Special Features of the Yemeni Weekly Market System. An Attempt at an Anthropological Interpretation. *New Arabian Studies* 3: 50–57.

1996b Anthropology in Germany and Austria (mit Andre Gingrich). In: A. Barnard and J. Spencer (eds.), Encyclopedia of Social and Cultural Anthropology; pp. 263-265. London: Routledge.

1997a Abbau des Eisenerzes und Erschmelzen des Eisens im südlichen Ḥijāz der Neuzeit. *Mare Erythraeum* 1: 163–170.

1997b Die Araber in vorislamischer Zeit. *Der Islam* 74: 1–63.

1998a Die Araber in vorislamischer Zeit. In: A. Noth und J. Paul (Hrsg.), Der islamische Orient. Grundzüge seiner Geschichte; pp. 25–44. Würzburg: Ergon-Verlag. (Mitteilungen zur Sozial- und Kulturgeschichte der islamischen Welt, 1)

1998b Some Visions on the Political and Economic Situation in Soqotra in the 19th Century from the Reports of the Austrian Marine Archive. In: H. J. Dumont, (ed.), Soqotra. (Proceedings of the First International Symposium on Soqotra Island – Present and Future.Aden, March 1996.) Vol. 1; pp. 265–269.

1999a Der Prophet Mohammed im Spiegel der europäischen Wissenschaft. In: W. Dostal, H. A. Niederle und K. R. Wernhart (Hrsg.), Wir und die Anderen. Islam, Literatur und Migration; pp. 35–56. Wien: WUV-Universitätsverlag. (Wiener Beiträge zur Ethnologie und Anthropologie, 9)

1999b [Hrsg. mit H. A. Niederle und K. R. Wernhart] Wir und die Anderen. Islam, Literatur und Migration. Wien: WUV-Universitätsverlag. (Wiener Beiträge zur Ethnologie und Anthropologie, 9)

1999c Stier und Ritual im Jemen: Fortleben antiker Traditionen in heutigen Volksbrächen. In: W. Daum, W. W. Müller, N. Nebes und W. Raunig (Hrsg.), Im Land der Königin von Saba. Kunstschätze aus dem antiken Jemen. 7. Juli 1999-9. Januar 2000; pp. 131-136. München: Staatliches Museum für Völkerkunde.

2000a The Ethnographic Atlas of Southwestern Saudi Arabia. On the Significance of Ethnographic Cartography. In: D. Balland (éd.), Hommes et terres d'Islam. Mélanges offerts à Xavier de Planhol. Vol. 1; pp.363-376. Téhéran: Institut Français de Recherche en Iran. (Bibliothèque iranienne, 53)

2000b Some Anthropological Reflections on the Cultural Transformations through the Development of High-Cultures in Pre-Islamic Times. *ADUMATU* 1: 40–46.

2001 L'univers du Mashreq. Essais d'anthropologie. Paris: Éditions de la Maison des Sciences de l'Homme.

2002a The Austrian-Saudi Arabian Collaborative Project in the South-Western Region of the Kingdom of Saudi Arabia. *Proceedings of the Seminar for Arabian Studies* 32: pp. 225–232.

2002b Die Erschließung Südarabiens durch die Portugiesen. Eine kognitiv anthropologische Betrachtung. *Mare Erythraeum* 5: 63–71.

2002c Malamih min al-thaqafah al-taqalidiyah li mantaqah `Asir (Wesenszüge der traditionellen Kultur der Provinz `Asir). (Transl. Yusuf Mukhtar al-`Awan und Sa`ad b. `Abd ul-`Aziz al-Rashid.) Riyadh: King Fahd National Library 2000/1422 H.

2002d Von der Ethnologie zur Sozialanthropologie. Das Werden einer jungen Wissenschaft. In: K. Acham (Hrsg.), Geschichte der österreichischen Humanwissenschaften. Bd. 4; pp. 415–464. Wien: Passagen-Verlag.

2002e Al-Say'ar: A Social Anthropological Sketch of a South Arabian Triab from 1960 with some additional observations collected in 1995. In: Journal of Semitic Studies Supplement 14. Studies in Arabia in Honour of G. Rex Smith; pp. 67-80. Oxford: University Press

2004 Al-Sa`idah. Bemerkungen über eine Heilige aus dem Süden des Jemen. In: Scripta Jemenica. Festschrift für M. B. Pietrowski zum 60. Geburtstag; pp. 188–196. Moskau: Russkaya Akademia Nauk.

2005a Introduction. In: W. Dostal and W. Kraus (eds.); pp. 1–19.

2005b [ed. with Wolfgang Kraus] Shattering Tradition. Custom, Law, and the Individual in the Muslim Mediterranean. London: Tauris. (The Islamic Mediterranean, 8)

2005c The Saints of Hadramawt. In: W. Dostal and W. Kraus (eds.); pp. 233–253.

2005d Tribal Customary Law of the Zahran. Confederation in Southern Hijaz (Kingdom of Saudi Arabia). In: W. Dostal and W. Kraus (eds.); pp. 122–147.

2005e Über zwei vor-islamische Heilige im Jemen. Ein Beitrag zur Frage der "Survivals" in islamischen Kulturstrukturen. In: Arabia Vitalis. Festschrift für B. B. Naumkin zum 60. Geburtstag; pp. 324–331. Moskau: Russkaya Akademia Nauk.

2005f Eduard Glaser im Jemen: Die Tragik einer Forscherpersönlichkeit. In: Jemen-Report, 2005. 36(2): pp. 19-22.

2006a The Mahra in Southern Arabia. Some Notes on Their Kinship System and Tribal Structure Based on Field Data Collected in 1960, 1995, and 2005. In: The Culture of Arabia in the Asian Context. Festschrift anläßlich des 60. Geburtstages von Michael Rodionov; pp. 49–54. St. Petersburg: Russische Akademie NAUK, Peter the Great Museum of Anthropology and Ethnography.

2006b [Hrsg.] Tribale Gesellschaften der südwestlichen Regionen des Königreiches Saudi Arabien. Sozialanthropologische Untersuchungen. (Mit Beiträgen von A. Gingrich, J. Heiss und J. Zötl.) Wien: Verlag der Österreichischen Akademie der Wissenschaften. (Österreichische Akademie der Wissenschaften, Phil.-Hist. Kl., Sitzungsberichte, 732; Veröffentlichungen zur Sozialanthropologie, 8).

2007 [A. Gingrich, S. M. Haas] An Interview with Walter Dostal. *Current Anthropology* 48: 429–437.

2008 Von Mohammed bis al-Qaida. Einblicke in die Welt des Islam. Wien: Passagen-Verlag. (Passagen – Religion und Politik, 8)

2009a Die Beduinen Südarabiens und das Meer: Sozialanthropologische Beobachtungen über den Sardinenfang. In: W. Arnold, M. Jursa, W. W. Müller, St. Procházka (Hrsg.) Philologisches und Historisches zwischen Anatolien und Sokotra. Analecta Semitica. In Memoriam Alexander Sima. pp. 17-26. Wiesbaden: Harrassowitz

2009b Über die Lebensweise der städtischen Bevölkerung vom Tarim (Wadi Hadramawt). In: Anzeiger der philosophisch-historischen Klasse, 144. Jahrgang/ 2 Halbband; pp. 5-48. Wien: Verlag der Österreichischen Akademie der Wissenschaften

2012 Riding Camels in Arabia: Outline of a Revised Cultural History. In: E.-M. Knoll and P. Burger (eds.): Camels in Asia and North Africa. Interdisciplinary perspectives on their past and present significance; pp. 123-130. Wien: Verlag der Österreichischen Akademie der Wissenschaften. (Denkschriften der philosophisch-historischen Klasse, 451; Veröffentlichungen zur Sozialanthropologie, 18).

Ethnographic Films (1)
(originally published in the "Encyclopaedia Cinematographica")

1967 Arabien, Hadramaut
Sprengen eines Steinblocks
Film E 1180

1967 Arabien, Hadramaut
Herstellen einer Handmühle
Film E 1181

1967 Arabien, Hadramaut
Behauen von Säulentrommeln; Errichten einer Säule
Film E 1182

1967 Arabien, Hadramaut
Behauen und Beschriften eines Grabsteins
Film E 1183

1967 Arabien, Hadramaut
Tonbereitung; Formen einer Steinbock-Figur
Film E 1184

1967 Arabien, Hadramaut
Formen eines Weihrauchbrenners aus Ton
Film E 1185

1967 Arabien, Hadramaut
Formen und Bemalen eines Tongefäßes
Film E 1186

1967 Arabien, Hadramaut
Formen eines Wasserrohres aus Ton
Film E 1187

1967 Arabien, Hadramaut
Herstellen von Ziegeln; Errichten einer Mauer
Film E 1188

1967 Arabien, Hadramaut
Anfertigen eines Stiftes aus Eisenblech
Film E 1189

1967 Arabien, Hadramaut
Herstellen eines Ziernagels
Film E 1190

1967 Arabien, Hadramaut
Herstellen einer Feuerzange
Film E 1191

1967 Arabien, Hadramaut
Herstellen eines Trichters
Film E 1192

1967 Arabien, Hadramaut
Herstellen einer Hakensichel
Film E 1193

1967 Arabien, Hadramaut
Schmieden einer Beilklinge
Film E 1194

1967 Arabien, Hadramaut
Schmieden eines Hackenblattes (traditionelle Technik)
Film E 1195

1967 Arabien, Hadramaut
Zersägen eines Baumstammes
Film E 1196

1967 Arabien, Hadramaut
Herstellen eines Fensters
Film E 1197

1967 Arabien, Hadramaut
Herstellen eines Kaffeemörsers
Film E 1198

1967 Arabien, Hadramaut
Anfertigen eines Wassersackes
Film E 1199

1967 Arabien, Hadramaut
Rauchen mit Wasserpfeife
Film E 1200

1967 Arabien, Hadramaut
Krankenbehandlung („Brennen“)
Film E 1201

1968 Arabien, Hadramaut
Schmieden eines Hackblattes (neue Technik)
Film E 1315

1968 Arabien, Hadramaut
Silber-Bearbeitung
Film E 1346

Ethnographic Films (2)
(not in the "Encyclopaedia Cinematographica")

1956 Schiffsbau in Kuweit.
SHB-Film C 1074

1957 Die Beduinen in Arabien.
SHB-Film CTf1080

1959 Araber (Arabien, Al-Kuwet)
Nutzung des Schafes bei Beduinen
Film E 226 des Inst. Wiss. Film, Göttingen

1959 Araber (Arabien, Al-Kuwet)
Kamelsattelung bei den Beduinen
Film E 227 des Inst. Wiss. Film, Göttingen

1959 Araber (Arabien, Al-Kuwet)
Schiffsbau
Film E 228 des Inst. Wiss. Film, Göttingen

1962 Hadhrami (Arabien, Hadhramaut)
Bewässerungsfeldbau
Film E 428 des Inst. Wiss. Film, Göttingen

1962 Al-Manahil (Arabien, Hadhramaut)
Geselliger Tanz der Frauen und Männer
Film E 429 des Inst. Wiss. Film, Göttingen

SOUTHWEST ARABIA ACROSS HISTORY: INTRODUCING INSIGHTS FROM CURRENT RESEARCH

Andre Gingrich and Siegfried Haas

In its central dimensions, the present volume discusses recent research results in South Arabian studies in the humanities and social sciences. These results are informed through disciplinary and transdisciplinary perspectives that fuse such diverse fields as socio-cultural anthropology, epigraphy, Semitic philology, archaeology, the history of Islam and of Arabia, contemporary history and the qualitatively oriented elements in the social sciences. By consequence, these contributions also address some very diverse historical periods across the pre-Islamic, Islamic, and modern and contemporary eras in their Southwest Arabian dimensions.

In a topical and thematic sense, these investigations into "Southwest Arabia across history" examine questions of language and linguistic continuities, economy and water management, settlements and fortifications, conflict and peace among local and tribal societies, and state governance and its limits. This collection therefore strives to make available a number of key insights into cutting edge research by focusing on a selected number of central topics across the major eras of Southwest Arabia's past and present.

Since this volume emerged out of a conference that celebrated Walter Dostal's life, his work and achievements, these contributions obviously do not hide that they were inspired by Dostal's work. On the contrary, all of this volume's contributors in one way or another were linked to that great scholar's research activities and institutional advances. A short obituary and Walter Dostal's list of academic print and film publications precede this introduction to provide readers with the respective background information if needed.

Yet, this is not a retrospective volume in the sense that these chapters primarily focus on past records of research. As Dostal would have wanted to see it, this is a volume dedicated to current research. These articles take one or several of Dostal's insights as their points of departure in order to unfold their own analyses according to the standards of the present and by addressing contemporary and future research agendas.

In this manner, Roswitha Stiegner, the passionate supporter of epigraphic studies in Austria, relates Dostal's ethnographic insights to lexicographic changes and continuities in Southwest Arabia's linguistic repertoires through history. She thereby demonstrates the fertility in crossing disciplinary boundaries between philology, ethnography and history, and highlights this along with important aspects of the academic record in South Arabian studies as carried out in Austria since the days of David Heinrich Mueller's prolific academic activities at this Academy, and by those of Mueller's famous, independently-minded earstwhile disciple Eduard Glaser in the late 19th and the early 20th century.

Ingrid Hehmeyer's chapter focuses on water technology and management in South Arabia and in relation to this, on aspects of continuity and change. She discusses two cases of wadi/sayl irrigation systems, i.e. that of the pre-Islamic dam of Marib, and that of Islamic mediaeval Wadi Zabid.[1] In both places water management and its related rules had to be adapted to local circumstances. The Marib dam system saw a total collapse just before the Islamic period, while Wadi Zabid has seen a continuous usage until the present time and is still in use. In both cases, the principle of upstream priority is among the most important rules of distribution, even though in Wadi Zabid this principle has at times been challenged by ideas of also securing some of the water

[1] A note on transliteration for Arabic and other languages of the region: For this introduction, the editors have used a simplified version of IJMES rules, except for terms with a fairly common Anglicized spelling. For the other contributions to this volume, the editors have decided to accept the transliteration rules chosen by each author for his/her own text, as specified in a respective footnote there.

shares for downstream users. Islamic and customary law are both invoked and used to legitimate the local rules, and Hehmeyer concludes her article with some hypotheses on their respective qualities and dynamics.

The following chapter by Eirik Hovden focuses on one specific form of water technology used for providing household and drinking water, that is the so-called birka or cistern. Usually a cistern is a storage tank of water on slopes and ridges, where little or no groundwater can be found. A birka, however, is not sunk into the ground. These are highly common in large parts of Yemen, especially in areas located on steep mountains. In addition, one of its other main purposes is to collect rainwater during heavy rain by leading local runoff through canals into the cistern. In what follows, this chapter investigates how public or community village cisterns are owned and managed by using various combinations of customary and Islamic law, and especially the institution of waqf. The exact ownership status of these cisterns often remain ambiguous (for example, to what extent they are waqf or not), although there is at the same time a strong fundamental notion that they do belong to the village as a unit. In that regard similar to one result of the subsequent chapter by Heiss, Hovden demonstrates another characteristic feature through the interrelation between customary and Zaydī (or other forms of Islamic) law – namely their mutual interaction and reciprocal penetration, which includes potentials not only for occasional tension, but for complementary adaptation and mutual support as well.

As Daniel Mahoney shows, many of our modern conceptions of culture heritage focus on the ways that places, objects, and practices aid in the formation, maintenance, and anchoring of political identities through acts of commemoration and remembering. In similar ways, Mahoney continues, the tenth century scholar al-Hamdanī promotes and legitimizes the political, cultural, and regional identity of the inhabitants of South Arabia in the eighth volume of *al-Iklīl* through descriptions of a variety of monuments located across its landscapes. In this manner, Mahoney re-examines a famous text of medieval South Arabian scholarship that was first edited and partially translated by David. H. Mueller at this Academy (1879/80). In entries organized by location, al-Hamdanī praises the exceptional workmanship of various types of structures including fortified palaces, pre-Islamic and Islamic religious buildings, and dams or other types of water management installations. Through each of these architectural types he brings out various aspects of the identity and historical experience of Southern Arabs. While the glory and prosperity of the pre-Islamic Himyarite Kingdom is often referred to, more intriguing are passages that allude to horrific events, which occurred at some of the sites as a result of invasions at various points in time in the region's history as recent as the period of al-Hamdani's childhood and adolescence. His choice to commemorate these darker aspects of their past seems to point to specific political motivations for prompting his fellow countrymen to act against their contemporary Zaydī and Fatimid invaders. In this manner, Mahoney re-emphasizes an interpretation of some of al-Hamdani's writing as contextualized in his time and his biography – in particular within his interests as a South Arabian patriot.

In his contribution about the origins of the northern Yemeni town of Sa'da, Johann Heiss continues an important aspect of his previous research. This eminent one-time student and disciple of Walter Dostal tries to show that the new town called by that name (Sa'da) grew out of the village al-Ġayl as a consequence of a tribal conflict between two factions of the (northern) Khawlān-federation and their allies. The first Zaydī imam of the Yemen and his two sons and successors on the one hand played an important part in the growth of the new town into a center for many imams in the centuries to come. On the other hand, they also became themselves part of the tribal conflicts they had aspired to solve. The old town of Sa'da gradually lost its importance and eventually disappeared altogether. Beyond its value as a contribution to the local medieval history and archaeology of a region which currently is recovering from an unfortunate civil war during the first decade of the 21st century, Heiss thereby also highlights important dimensions of the town's medieval Islamic history. In particular, Heiss summarizes and in fact moves beyond his earlier studies on the same topic, by highlighting interactions between fiqh in its Zaydī version and the built-in necessity in customary law for seeking at one point or another appeals for mediation by more or less neutral outsiders – who in some cases may include representatives of state order and Islamic law with an agenda of their own.

Marieke Brandt draws attention to the diversity and different nature of the plethora of tribal societies in Upper Yemen. Quite frequently, they are subsumed by experts and the media alike under the homogenizing notion of "the Yemeni tribes" – as if they were a uniform block. In her comparative analysis of leadership concepts among the present-day confederations of Khawlān b. ʻĀmir and Hamdān (Ḥāshid und Bakīl), she demonstrates that tribal communities of Upper Yemen have developed very different modes to "inhabit" actually homologous structures. The structures of tribes and confederations and the features making up their socio-political organization therefore need to be analytically distinguished. On the basis of her meticulous analysis of different leadership concepts she demonstrates where power and influence are located among these confederations, and elucidates the various forms of cooperation and competition as well as interpenetration and repulsion among the different tribes and the Yemeni state.

In his text for the present volume Andre Gingrich, another former student and research assistant of Walter Dostal throughout the 1970s and 1980s, continues to explore the field that some of the previous authors in this book already have inspected through their discussion of certain aspects of jurisprudence and state law. He questions which conceptual or theoretical models of historical Southwest Arabian states, including Zaydī states in particular, actually have been elaborated and tried out in the humanities' research record on this phenomenon. In his discussion of answers to this guiding question, he then singles out two major conceptual strands that have often been seen as contradictory. Gingrich proceeds to demonstrate how certain elements among each of these seemingly opposing strands could and might be combined in much more productive ways than was seen in the past. To some extent, Dostal's research in this regard may be perceived as an early innovation towards improvements in the field of conceptualizing historical states' roles for this region. Still, the argument continues, the so-called "segmentary model" with its stronger emphasis on local tensions as well as the "cumulative model" with its closer attention for external forces share a certain salient disregard for factors of pre-Ottoman Islamic states' mobility and fluidity in Southwest Arabian history. The argument concludes with the suggestion that in this respect, revised versions from a third source might be helpfully combined with existing insights – i.e. from the so-called "galactic model".

In this manner, the present volume strives to honour the memory to Walter Dostal by contributing contemporary insights for current research into questions that have always inspired that great scholar and the research traditions that informed his own biography. It therefore is no coincidence that this volume comes out in an Academy book series that is bearing the name of one of the great founding fathers of precisely that research tradition, which Dostal continued and innovated. The editors hope that the present volume, with its contributions by an international group of senior and junior scholars who in one way or another have all come to interact with Dostal's legacy, will be received with sympathy, interest and appreciation by the relevant scholarly communities of today and tomorrow.

WALTER DOSTAL AND (ANCIENT) SOUTH ARABIA

Cultural and Social Anthropology and the "ivory tower" of Regional Studies in Ancient South Arabia[1]

ROSWITHA G. STIEGNER

"One sees the flowers fade and the leaves fall, but
one also sees fruits ripen and fresh buds germinate"
(Goethe)[2]

A PIONEER AND HIS GROUP OF RESEARCH ASSOCIATES

Esteem, humility, gratitude and melancholy are only few words that shape the memory of Prof. Walter Dostal (1928 – 2011) who was one of the most distinguished and pioneering scholars of Arabian studies from the mid-20th century up to the beginnings of the new millennium.

Johann Wolfgang von Goethe's words of solace in the above quote are merely symbolic. True solace, however, can be found in Dostal's work, which can be compared to the above quote as rich, strong, prudent seeds, whose buds are still sprouting, bearing fruits and blossoming today and in the future to come. His best students are leading researchers and research associates[3] today, keeping his memory and academic achievements alive in the spirit of BNYN, *Bāniyān* (asa) = *al-Bānī* (arab.) - which means builders, architects[4]. I shall use the shorthand formula of an "ivory tower" in this text for referring to the interdisciplinary academic basic research field of studies in Ancient South Arabia.

THE VISIONARY IN THE SENSE OF RA´B AL-UMŪR[5]:

'Rescue' or revitalization of the series of papers: "Sammlung Eduard Glaser" (SEG)[6] by the Austrian Academy of Sciences, Vienna (ÖAW/AAS), as a component of the South Arabian studies legacy in Austria:

---

[1] Some notes on the title: Why use (Ancient) South Arabia in the title rather than Sabaean, Old South Arabian Languages and Cultures, or alternatively, Epigraphic South Arabic? On the one hand it would have been impossible to do justice to Dostal's extensive research, on the other hand it would be rather limiting to discuss just one specific topic in an anthology. This would surely not be what Dostal intended. Dostal's understanding of the 'ivory tower' or, more specifically, of ancient oriental studies guided him in the right direction, even without modern technological and scientific research methods that seem so indispensable today. Dostal's approach still serves and will serve as a guideline and basis of research today and in the future. For this reason this is an attempt to present a more or less chronological overview of Dostal's most important topics and concerns, his merits concerning the 'ivory tower' and all other specialist disciplines, his way of putting research results into practice, e.g. to be in touch with the people, as K. Wilhelm von Humboldt (1767-1835) had stated.

[2] Johann Wolfgang von Goethe, ‚Wilhelm Meister's Travels', chapter 2, http://oll.libertyfund.org/simple.php?id=2275)

[3] Andre Gingrich, Johann Heiss, Siegfried Haas, and their junior associates such as Eirik Hovden, Daniel Mahoney or Marieke Brandt

[4] Found as a tribe or proper name all over the Arabian Peninsula, e.g. in Ancient South Arabian (CIH 287, 7-8 = Gl 265; RES 3709, 2; Lundin 23, 1) and in central as well as in early north Arabic. Sima 1999: 7, 93f, even documents the prevalence of the Verb , bny', ,to build', by means of a Lybian inscription from Wadi al-`Udayb (near ancient Dedan, todays al-`Ula, Saudi-Arabia), 8 = Stiehl A 12 = Abu l-Hasan 56.

[5] According to Lane 993f , 'a rectifier, an amender of affairs', and ra´´b 'a man who effects reconciliation, or makes peace, between people', whereby the Sabaean r´b (/mlkn) in SD 112 is translated as 'title of functionary, laqab sahib mansib'. This is however meant in the sense of a royal dignitary's function as a mediator, as quoted by Müller 1972, 99. Wehr, in modern arabic 'ra´aba' is understood as 'to repare, to fix something, to bring about reconciliation', Lu 22,1=Graf 3 = DJE 14. Lt.

[6] See, e.g. Sienell (i. pr.).

The history of the SEG publication series was closely linked to the "South Arabian expedition" (SE, 1898/99)[7], which was linked to a number of former Academy commissions, initiated in the late imperial age and later continued by the ÖAW. Studying their shared histories is not the object of this study. The key points, however, must be addressed in order to comprehend the publication series SEG and SEGI, the first of which was published as early as 1913 and followed by SEGII/1961 and SEGIII/1981 after more than half a century.

In the SEG XIV/1981,'Sabäische Inschriften', sub-headed as the 'final edition', the author Maria Höfner lists p.46) the entire SEG series from II-XIII, missing however SEG I/1913, 'Eduard Glasers Reise nach Marib', which was edited by D.H. Müller and N. Rhodokanakis (the latter a student of D.H. Müller and the teacher of M. Höfner in Graz). Höfner also mentions SEG III/1964 by Hermann von Wissmann, 'Zur Geschichte und Landeskunde von Alt-Südarabien' under a different abbreviation. In her lectures in Graz she had mentioned that this particular publication was something like the 'bible' for subsequent research in the field.

Wissmann's fascination for Arabia and Yemen, in particular, already became apparent during his first field venture as a young geographer in 1927/28 (accompanied by Carl Rathjens). His subsequent fieldwork increased his understanding of historical-geographical regional studies, Middle Eastern archaeological problems as well as his knowledge about the Sabaeans and Sabaean, which he described as having learnt autodidactically (SEG III/7). He fruitfully collaborated with the Semitist Enno Littmann in Tübingen, an academic site still known as a stronghold of Oriental Studies in 1983 (after previous joint ventures and cooperations with Vienna). From 1944 onwards Wissmann also cooperated with Höfner (going to Graz, Vienna and from 1964 to Graz again). This is how his SEG II came to be dedicated to Eduard Glaser. Wissmann was the author of the SEG XIII from 1975 'Über die frühe Geschichte Arabiens und das Entstehen des Sabäerreiches. Die Geschichte von Saba'I'. He still managed to finalize ,Die Geschichte von Saba' II. Das Großreich der Sabäer bis zu seinem Ende im frühen 4. Jh. v. Chr.' before his untimely death in 1979. This was published by the ÖAW publishing house – though neither as a part of the SEG nor in the frame of the Academy's Arabian Commission – thanks to Walter W. Müller (presented by Prof. M. Mayrhofer as secretary of the phil.-hist. Kl. (humanities' section) meeting on 4.4.1979, and came out in 1982).

Following the South Arabian Commission (from the end of the 19th Century) the Arabian Commission was initiated by the Academy in 1943, due to the "plan of the AWW[8] to create a dictionary of ancient South Arabian that compares the vocabulary of modern day South Arabian semitic languages".[9] Viktor Christian (then Professor for Semitic Studies and Dean at Vienna University, Academy member, and director of an SS "Ahnenerbe" institute[10]) who had been one of D. H. Müller's last students but who rose to dubious prominence during the Nazi years, was behind that Academy initiative. This can also be seen by the fact that Viktor Christian took up his studies of Mehri again at that time (1944: 1). In SEG II/1961 (p. 4) Höfner as the head of the Arabian Commission thanked him especially for his "enduring" commitment to the edition of the Glaser series /SEG.

In the frame of the Arabian Commission several works were published on Dostal's own initiative (for example Dostal 1979, 1990, 1993; Behnstedt 1993). That Commission was dissolved or rather, merged with the Academy's Commission for Social Anthropology in 1992 following Höfner's death. After Höfner's retirement (Graz, 1979) Ancient Oriental Philology – or Arabic Studies – focussing on South Arabia had no longer existed in Austria. Dostal wrote her obituary in the almanac of the ÖAW in 1993 urging to keep Maria Höfner's work alive (p. 472): "Maria Höfner has left us with a great deal, and it should be our duty to keep alive her work and achievements"[11]. With the Commission for Social Anthropology of the ÖAW that Dostal had greatly advanced since 1990 he had already laid the groundwork for its gradual transformation in 2003

---

[7] See Lechleitner, Traces of the South Arabian Expedition in the Phonogrammarchiv (ÖAW), and Stiegner, Presentation 'Archives of the Austrian South Arabian Expedition and the Eduard Glaser Collection' (ÖAW) both in WOO 10/2, chap.VII.

[8] The designation "Akademie der Wissenschaften in Wien" (Academy of Sciences in Vienna) and its acronym AWW were used under Hitler Germany's rule as part of the Nazis' general policy of avoiding any reference to Austria as a separate legal, institutional or political entity (editors' note).

[9] Christian (1944: I), Translated by Rosalind Willi

[10] See Gohm and Gingrich 2010.

[11] Dostal (1993: 472). Translated by Rosalind Willi.

and the definite transformation in 2011 into today's Institute for Social Anthropology (ISA) of the ÖAW(AAS). Unfortunately, Dostal did not live to see the Institute's new facility opened in the year of his decease.

The ISA (together with IKGA, i.e. the Institute for Cultural and Intellectual History of Asia, and IfI, i.e. the Iranian Studies Institute) until 2012 was part of the Academy's Centre of Asian Cultures and Social Anthropology, and continues to closely cooperate with these two other Asian studies institutes at the Academy. They are one of several research clusters in the humanities and social sciences at the ÖAW. Apart from ISA's regional focus and expertise on Buddhist Central Asia, and Southeast Asia and adjacent island groups in the Indian Ocean, there is a strong focus on the Islamic Middle East and the Mashriq. Elaborating Dostal's vision Andre Gingrich writes in an email at the end of 2011: "The ISA will continue with its strong focus on South Arabia rather than Northern Arabia, due to the tradition of the ÖAW since D.H. Müller but also due to our staff's areas of specialisation. The 'collection Eduard Glaser' will remain one of ISA's two publication series and shall maintain its focus on the cultural history of South Arabia. Since 1.1.2012, for example, there is the possibility to 'compare medieval cultural history of South Arabia (with Europe and Tibet) at the ISA over a timeframe of four years'."[12]

After roughly a quarter of a century Gingrich (at the centre of research on Asian Cultures and Social Anthropology at the ÖAW) ventured the reanimation of the above mentioned SEG as that series new editor, by publishing Gertraud Sturm's 'Leben für die Forschung. Das Ethnologenpaar Wilhelm und Marie Hein in Südarabien'[13] as SEG XV. Gingrich presented this publication at the session on 22nd June 2007 and in the first paragraph of his foreword he conveys the following thoughts:

"The research ventures featured in this book in and about South Arabia took place at the turn of the 19th and 20th century. The works of Wilhelm and Marie Hein represent an early climax in a distinct research tradition that was continuous in Austria from the second half of the 19th century up to the present day. The main centres of this tradition were Vienna and Graz with related museums, university departments and scientific societies, very often connected to the active research department of the Academy of Sciences. The spectrum of scientific personalities ranges from David Heinrich Müller and Eduard Glaser to Maria Höfner and my teacher Walter Dostal; the academic fields involved reach from archaeology and epigraphy, to geography and humanities to Arabic Studies, ethnography and Ethnology/social anthropology."[14]

By way of comparison, an extract from the manuscript on SE IX/1909 'Mehri- and Hadrami-Texts: Collected in 1902 in Gischin by Dr. Wilhelm Hein. Edited by DAV Heinrich Müller' states the following:

"Chancellor D.H. Müller, chairman of the South Arabian Commission for the writings/inscriptions handed over the manuscript 'Mehri-texts, collected and translated by Dr. Wilhelm Hein, edited by D.H. Müller', and adds:

‚I am honoured to present the Mehri texts that were collected in Gishin in the frame of the South Arabian Commission by Dr. Wilhelm Hein who was taken out of life and research too early. [...] The texts consist of around 60 stories and a large number of poems that include sayings, games and riddles. The texts were carefully collected and greatly enrich our knowledge of the Mehri in a linguistic (lexicographically and grammatically) as well as in a folkloristic sense. I went through a number of these texts with my informants from Soqotra and Araf and could therefore assure myself of the veracity of Hein's work. [...]"[15]

In short, Walter Dostal's ideas, words and actions continue to be carried further especially by his students Heiss and Gingrich and the group of junior research associates, building upon the groundwork their teacher had laid.

Dostal was ahead of his time in many areas, partly building upon D.H. Müller's work (1846–1912). They both remain unparalleled role models to this day in the interdisciplinary fields of Southern Arabian studies. As the quotations above reveal it has always been about multi- and transdisciplinary collaborations in international networks of researchers and scientists. Thereby the 'ivory tower' was an elementary basis which together with field research is of paramount importance for research in social and cultural anthropol-

12 Andre Gingrich (personal email, 2011). Translated by Rosalind Willi.

13 See Sturm 2007, their detailed investigation of W. and M. Hein.

14 Gingrich (foreword in Sturm 2007). Translated by Rosalind Willi.

15 D. H. Müller, SE IX, 1909. Translated by Rosalind Willi.

ogy. Unfortunately, despite the significant number of research results the 'ivory tower' still has difficulties being considered influential in the field of ancient Oriental Studies, i.e. Semitist and Arabian studies.

Yet the fact that for the first time in many years 'languages of Southern Arabia' featured in the special session of the programme in the annual 'Seminar for Arabian Studies' (SAS, British Museum London, 26.–28.7.2013) gives reason for hope. In their concluding remarks the two research associates Janet C. E. Watson (Salford/U.K.) and Orhan Elmaz (St. Andrews/U.K.) mentioned: (This was) "(f)ollowed by a final meeting for discussing further questions, future research areas, and an international research network." Whether recognition and further development actually materialise remains to be seen.

Dostal had almost always attended the SAS. He would most probably have criticised the fact that the special session was held simultaneously to the regular sessions on 'Ancient Cultural Connections: Mesopotamia, Dilmun, Magan and the Indus' or 'Palaeolithic to Neolithic Arabia', 'Neolithic Arabia' or 'Archaeology of Yemen and Ethiopia'. A session on South Arabian societies as mentioned in the publications 'Typologie des Sanctuaires de l'Arabie du Sud Antique: essai de classification' (C. Darles), or 'Excavations at Jebel Faya and importance of the southern Arabian Corridor for movements of Paleolithic peoples' (Bretzke, N.J. Conrad & H.-P. Uerpmann) were not included and are of primary importance for linguists, as they were of course not isolated cultures.

The past creates the present and the present created the future is a frequently cited proverb, which could significantly contribute to scientific research if truly applied. Throughout most of his career Dostal engaged in finding answers to major questions on development and evolution.

The following section aims at presenting some details on the context of the 'ivory tower':

Today in Social and Cultural Anthropology the group of Dostal's former research associates and their junior colleagues continue and further Dostal's work at the ÖAW's ISA (See Gingrich 2012: 167f). The 'ivory tower' is also furthered by studies of (old) South Arabic/(A)SA at the Institute for Oriental Studies/IfO at the University of Vienna. It was a great achievement when a part-time lectureship for Ancient South Arabian languages was finally approved there. It will be offered starting from the academic year 2013/14. This means that there is now an official contact person on these research issues and the role of coordinator is entrusted to an expert who is officially affiliated to the university as well as the IfO. Since 2014, this is George Hatke.

By way of comparison and for a deeper insight into these issues and the reason for continuing the SEG, it is indeed important to mention the lack of publications during the many 'dark' years which included two world wars. In the foreword of SEG I/1913: 'Eduard Glasers Reise nach Mārib' (1888) the two editors D.H. Müller and N. Rhodokanakis (Vienna and Graz, October 1912, p. IIIf) state the following:

> "The fact that the South Arabian Commission decided to publish the previously unpublished inscriptions and carry on Glaser's work who was a prime researcher in the area of Sabaean Studies will hopefully be an incitement for further work in this area. [...] The publication highlights his views on Islam, Christianity and Judaism as well as on culture and technical progress.
>
> We felt that adding excerpts from his diary to the travel documentation itself and its annexes on pg. 171ff would make them more lively. [...] Dr. Adolf Grohmann completed the difficult and arduous task of converting shorthand notes in the diary written in old German shorthand. He also reworked the index of names and tribes as well as the geographical index, while the second author of this foreword completed the subject index.
>
> Regarding the cartographical and topographical annexes and dam sketches we cite Dr. Feuersteins remarks on pg. 2011ff.
>
> The acquisition of Glaser's estate by the imperial Academy of Sciences was made possible thanks to the generous donation of Dr. Horace Ritters v. Landau. [..].[16]

This text from 1912 and the text from 1909 mentioned above convey the predominant idea of interdisciplinary research and publishing. They were published under the aegis of the South Arabian Commission which was established at the end of the 19th century.

[16] Müller & Rhodokanakis (1913, IIIf). Translated by Rosalind Willi.

Figure 1: Walter Dostal and the "ivory tower": 60th birthday in Vienna 15. 5. 1988. (cf. camel statue, big and large stone head: Inv.Nr. SEM 1285–1287 in the KHMW: Hölzl 2013, image 4-6) (Photo: R. Stiegner)

Therefore, it is extremely important to keep alive the ÖAW's longstanding series - now and in future. They will be kept alive by the ASA inscriptions that can be found in diverse Viennese archives, in keeping with Höfner and W.W. Müller's vision of divulging the inscriptions in the SEG.

THE "IVORY TOWER" AS A SO-CALLED "ORCHID SUBJECT"?

To a certain degree Dostal had always understood *Völkerkunde* (former German term for ethnology) as *social and cultural anthropology* in the true sense of the subject. He was ahead of his time, given the fact that many German-speaking university institutes were still called Institutes of *Völkerkunde* in his time – and a long time thereafter. In ethnology the term 'culture' was on a whole very vague, frequently marred by incongruence and subject to manifold re-definitions and developments. Humans are social beings whose primary means of communication is language. Language is composed of sounds and words that define, name and give meaning to something. Anything may be described through language; humans and their elementary needs such as nutrition and the ways, locations, time and circumstances of its procurement; the animal kingdom; the earth, sky, sun, moon and stars.[17] There is causal thinking but also thinking across boundaries - about gods, demons and so on. In sum, language is culture. Unfortunately, the deeper meanings of ancient times and oral culture can rarely be discerned today. The continuity of traditions that have been subject to change and opportunely adapted to times and circumstances do not reveal much about their origins. This is one of the mysteries of life that troubles and fascinates humankind to this day. At this point we may return to the 'ivory tower', the exotic 'orchid subject' which was often in pursuit of these hidden mysteries.

[17] See for example, Gingrich 1997. Referring to P. Kunitzsch, 'Untersuchungen zur Sternnomenklatur der Araber' (1961) the author states "...stars which belong to the basic astrothetic inventory not only among the Arabs but in any culture ..." (p. 45).

This connects to Dostal's vision of the 'ivory tower': The 'ivory tower' represents language and writing as an integral part of culture. It is a symbol of strength and embodies a strong base composed of ‚mammoth and elephant tusks'[18]. However, only in conjunction with fieldwork and further methods can the door be opened to successful social and cultural anthropological research.

This however, was not always acknowledged in the past. For example, the disciplines in question – involving language and writing – are subordinated to the faculty of philological and cultural studies[19]. To name a further example, the *Festschrift* for the famous oriental archaeologist, P.R.S. Moorey was entitled 'Culture through Objects' (2003). Furthermore, in the cultural historical journal 'Zeitschrift für Sprach- und Sachforschung' that was founded in Graz more than 100 years ago the Sabaean scholar Nikolaus Rhodokanakis (Graz) wrote 'Zum Siedlungswesen im alten Südarabien' (1929). The main conceptual framework of this work is based on R. Meringer's statement: "Linguistics is only one part of the cultural sciences. Etymology needs to be explained by history"[20]. Another interesting example is 'Brisante Semantik. Neuere Konzepte und Forschungsergebnisse einer kulturwissenschaftlichen Linguistik' which was published in 2005 (Busse, Niehr & Wengeler 2005). While referring to Humboldt and Wittgenstein, the book describes how linguistics and semantics in particular can give valuable insights into social knowledge, departing from the traditional notion of language as a mere system of signs and as the cognitive expression of the individual. In sum, we have arrived at F. de Saussure's rule of thumb: "La langue est un fait social" (1967: 18).[21]

If these fundamental premises are not adhered to, even accredited and experienced researchers may severely misinterpret their findings. The following example illustrates how two researchers from a similar specialization came to different conclusions with sufficient and insufficient field research:

barrah: according to J. Watson 2005/06, 61: "Given incorrectly in P. Behnstedt (1987b:101) as 'to go early in the morning'" instead of: "to fetch firewood" (from a conversation with a woman). P. BEHNSTEDT 2013, 84, who was in Yemen and had been living in the Arab world for decades replied: "[...] The Verb in Behnstedt 1987b: 143 is conjugated. If the meaning were 'to fetch firewood', then we could not have had the masculine form, as women fetch firewood in this region."[22] Having been in Yemen myself, I can only second this. He continues: "This would be similar to trying to conjugate 'to give birth'. The meaning of 'to go early in the morning' has been verified in [...] many [cases], and therefore primarily means 'to leave in the morning'."

Further forms of words for 'going' depending on the time of day[23] have been documented, from classical Arabic or two modern South Arabian languages, from Šḫauri:

beʿér: 'travelling by night, leaving'; from Mehri: *bār*: 'travelling by night, leaving'.[24]

W. DOSTAL: "*VÖLKERKUNDE* AND HUMAN DIGNITY".

The next section is an attempt to gain an insight into Dostal's empirical mode of research – in his 'ivory tower'. The pillars for this mode of work are presented below:

1. STUDIES

Even his early studies (1948) were an indication of his future academic path; studying *Völkerkunde*/ethnology (with Koppers, Heine-Geldern) and Islamic studies and Arabic philology (with H.L. Gottschalk) in Vienna und Rome which were completed with his dissertation on Semites 'Eine Studie zum Semitenproblem' (Vienna 1952). During his time as curator of the Middle Eastern section at the Museum of Ethnology in Vienna

[18] Even if it is not 35000 years old - unlike the ivory workshop including mammoth tusks in Saxony-Anhalt, which was discovered by the Roman-Germanic Museum in Mainz

[19] Since October 2012 with dean Matthias Meyer, a Germanist, and vice-dean Michael Zach, from the Institute of African Sciences.

[20] Meringer (1929). Translated by Rosalind Willi.

[21] "i. e. language is a social fact."

[22] Behnstedt, 2013 (84). Translated by Rosalind Willi.

[23] See Behnstedt 1987a (101): e.g. nasaruk 'I left in the afternoon'; 1987b: 96f; 1992: 79; Behnstedt & Woidich 2005: 141.

[24] Bittner 1911: 123, 1914: 77; Jahn 1902: 171. Jahn quotes byr, and Bittner b'r as linguistic root.

Figure 2: Walter Dostal and Walter W. Müller (Interim Eduard-Glaser-Ring-owner, see Müller 2002: 220) – Wien/Sievering, 16.5.2008 (Photo R. Stiegner)

(1954–1965), he went on first fieldwork ventures (with collections) (see Steinmann 2013) and pursued smaller research assignments, for example with W. Caskel (Cologne 1960) or E. Jensen (Frankfurt/Main 1962/63). This resulted in his internationally acclaimed habilitation on Bedouins in Arabia: "Eine ethnologische Studie zur Entwicklung des Beduinentums in Arabien" (Vienna 1964/1967) (see Müller 1968: 2013). The result was his appointment as professor to a newly-founded chair for ethnology at the University of Bern (1965). His assignment included the setting up of a new seminar as well as leading the ethnographic department at the *Bernisches Historisches Museum* (Museum of History in Bern). Eventually, Dostal took over the chair for *Völkerkunde I* at the University of Vienna since March 1975.

2. Fieldwork

A brief glance at his first field work ventures further highlights his future path and deeply-rooted vision of his future career:

He intensely examined the life of so-called *"gypsies"* in Austria 'Zigeuner in Österreich' (AfV X, 1955, 1–15) and of a Pariah group in Kuwait: 'Die Sulubba und ihre Bedeutung für die Kulturgeschichte Arabiens' (AfV XI, 1956, 15–42). His fieldwork was mainly focused on social life, work and social status; in other words on cultural diversity, especially of the underprivileged. This often meant that the researcher himself faced difficult life and work situations.

3. Open ivory tower

For Dostal it was important to convey his research beyond the realm of the 'scientific community' or academia. In the spirit of an 'open ivory tower' he aimed at making his findings easy to understand and accessible for as many people as possible. He tirelessly pursued this goal throughout his career which is illustrated by the following examples:

3.1.

"*Völkerkunde und Menschenwürde*" (*Völkerkunde* and human dignity) was a seminar that Dostal devised in 1956. It largely demonstrates his understanding that *Völkerkunde* is only one branch of the 'science of the human' – which he had already dedicated his life to as a child and young adult. He liked to tell one particular experience of his which was entitled "Mein menschlichstes Erlebnis: *Das Zigeunerkind*" ('My most humane experience: the gypsy child') which was published in a newspaper in 26. 5. 1956.

3.2.

„*... Und es suchte das Leben*":

Two years earlier, in 1957, Dostal attempted the adaptation and a first literary edition of the ancient oriental epos of Gilgameš "Nachdichtung und erstmalige dramatische Bearbeitung des altorientalischen Epos von Gilgameš" as an audio book: „*Und es suchte das Leben*".[25] Unfortunately, the following excerpt from his foreword is more relevant today than ever:

> "[...] an attempt at gaining an insight into the spiritual world of the third and fourth millenia B.C. It aims at countering the somewhat antiquated views of people of the pre-antique period. Or more generally: we hope to humbly contribute to the rehabilitation of pre-historic humans. This is a necessity considering the historic events of our time. We have never more urgently needed respect for ourselves – for humankind. However, how can the human of today respect himself, if he merely sees animalistic gruesome brutes in his predecessors? [...] the relics that are left are witnesses of intellectual life and must speak for themselves without being faced by prejudice. Their inherent creative spirit will allow us to recognise the human in them. We will be free from presumptuous assumptions of our own culture and our stance towards unknown cultures will be tolerant. This is a path to direct the human towards the humane" [26]

G. Selz (2011) further developed and explained Dostal's ideas in the above quote and is a good reference to enhance their understanding; Dostal's main aim was to comprehend the situation out of which the Gilgameš-Epos arose. He predominantly underlines the chtonic character of the Sumerian religion:

> "At the centre of religious thinking and sacred acts was the eternal cycle of the dying and reincarnating god of vegetation. This god had various names, of which Tammuz is the most well-known. The fate of Tammuz is analogue to the fate of grain: sowing - harvest. The notion was supported that in earthly life each sin must be paid for. The punishments for sin were diseases, suffering and early death. The human was rooted in the mortal world. It is therefore understandable that man wished to break the eternal cycle of life and death and to overcome the power of death. He longs for absolution. The Gilgameš-Epos mirrors humanity's tragic struggle to overcome death..."[27]

3.3.

‚Austrian ambassador in the Orient'(‚Botschafter Österreichs im Orient')[28]: One of his biggest and most sustainable successes in putting theory into practice, as already mentioned above in the subchapter 'open ivory tower', was his foundation of the Hammer-Purgstall-Gesellschaft (Hammer-Purgstall Society). One of his former students, Siegfried Haas, later took over its leadership. It was re-developed as the Österreichische Orient Gesellschaft – Hammer-Purgstall (ÖOG, Austrian Society for the Middle East-Hammer Purgstall) which also includes an academy for Oriental Studies. Dostal also founded the Austrian Yemeni society which used to be associated with the ÖOG. In recent years, however, it has almost exclusively been focusing on social services and is more oriented towards the GÖAB (Society for Austro-Arab Relations). Dr. Margarete Dostal, Dostals wife, must not be forgotten in this context. She was very active in the Austrian

[25] I'd like to acknowledge architect Franz Kiener's invaluable help. He rendered invaluable documents and pieces of information. F. Kiener had been a life-long friend of both Walter Dostal and his wife Dr. Margarete Dostal.

[26] Dostal, 1954. Translated by Rosalind Willi.

[27] Selz, 2011. Translated by Rosalind Willi.

[28] Presentation of the Golden Hammer-Purgstall-Medal (1993) with the above mentioned conferment of a symbolic title by S. Haas.

Yemeni Society and was especially interested in adult education. She went on fieldwork expeditions and was an active co-worker in a wide array of different functions.

DOSTAL AND THE SEARCH FOR HISTORY IN THE PRESENT

Pre-Islamic survivals

Preliminary remark: The problems of ,seeking and finding'

Pagan, pre-Christian elements are quite commonly known in Europe, although their acknowledgment and acceptance is less widespread. In western occidental culture, ancient, pre-Christian Greece is still perceived as the cradle of civilization and our culture. More often than not the Middle Eastern areas of the Mediterranean and their influence are overlooked.

To a certain degree the Muslim world's stance towards its own pre-Islamic age (al-ǧāhīlīya) is similar. The time before 622 A.C. which is the beginning of the Islamic calendar is often seen as a time of ignorance. In recent years however, the interest and openness towards this time has been on the rise (Dostal 1983; Musée du Louvre 2010). For example, it is now known and acknowledged that Jews and Christians were (both) 'ahl al- kitāb' 'people of the Book/Scripture' and had the legal status of 'ahl al-ḏimma' 'protected non-Muslim citizens'. After receiving the scripture and proof, the two religions split (analogous to al-Qur'ān 98, 4) (See various articles in EI, from 1986).

Alternatively, the first printed version of the Koran only became known in Europe (Venice) by 1530, and two further editions towards the end of the 17th Century. Only since 1834 an official version of the Koran has been available in Europe and the first one with concordance since 1842, which was made accessible by Gustav Flügel.[29]

Ancient South Arabian inscriptions often are known to locals as pagan, pre-Islamic, or Himyar elements. They were largely destroyed, having been inscribed in houses, wells, columns and gates. According to mainly Arabic sources and records 'Quellen und Überlieferungen' (Stiegner 1986,94) first tiny fragments of these inscriptions were copied by U. Jasper Seetzen in 1810 who neither had any knowledge of the script nor of the language. Joseph von Hammer-Purgstall published these in 'Fundgruben des Orients' in 1811 (vol.2, 282). Following subsequent findings Wilhelm Gesenius managed to decode the language comprehensively for the first time in 1841 (Stein 2013: 275.). Further decodings were undertaken according to increasing discoveries, until Glaser made his major discovery (at the end of the 19th century). This led to the establishment of a new branch of research – Sabaean Studies. The first Ancient South Arabian grammar book ,Altsüdarabische Grammatik' was written by Höfner in 1943. The first Sabaean Dictionary (SD) followed in 1982. Currently Norbert Nebes and his students (cf. DOT 2013) are working on a comprehensive dictionary and grammar (according to new technical standards) in Jena, which can be seen as the new German-speaking academic stronghold for Ancient South Arabian studies.

The systematic collection (corpus) of all Ancient South Arabian inscriptions (CSAI) which encompass around 15.000 texts, their publications or exhibitions, is being carried out in Pisa since 2000 under the leadership of Alessandra Avanzini and her students. This will enable experts, specialists but also a wider audience from various disciplines (archaeologists, linguists, cultural historians etc.) to gain access to the data, a previously extremely difficult matter. This project has been growing in recent years, always in European-Arabic cooperation (MENCAWAR- Mediterranean Network for Cataloguing and Web Fruition of Ancient Artworks and Inscriptions) or Cataloguing the Inscriptions Conserved in Yemeni Museums (CASIS) since 2007. Additionally the scope of the project was expanded by a 5-year European project (DASI) in 2011: "(...) with the objective of extending the scope of the CSAI to the entire body of epigraphic documentation from pre-Islamic Arabia (...) improving its power and flexibility as a research tool (...and) excellent teaching tool (...)" [30]

---

[29] Johann Fück (1955: 36, 94f). See also de Sacy (1934).

[30] A. Avanzini, Corpus of South Arabian Inscriptions: The CSAI Project. In: WOO 10/2, Kap. IV. - http://csai.humnet.unipi.it

Nowadays we know a great deal more thanks to these initiatives. We know, for instance, that there was neither one Ancient South Arabian language nor various dialects, but that there were several Ancient South Arabian languages. Moreover, in addition to the epigraphic monumental script *musnad* the cursive form of the ancient Yemeni alphabet (Stein 2013, i. pr.) is known, and much more. From this extended knowledge, further questions and discussions have arisen.

DOSTAL'S EFFORTS IN ACADEMIC HISTORY

W. Dostal's habilitation thesis (1964/67) was an ethnological study on the development of camel pastoral culture, entitled: 'Die Beduinen in Sűdarabien: Eine ethnologische Studie zur Entwicklung der Kamelhirtenkultur in Arabien'. In a very successful manner, it also emphasized the fertility of (ethno)linguistic approaches. In a parallel way, his doctoral thesis also to an extent had been an ethno-linguistic study of Semitic languages written in 1952: 'Eine ethnologisch-linguistische Studie über das Problem der semitisch sprechenden Völker'. Furthermore, the aforementioned publication (1967) 'Wiener Beiträge zur Kulturgeschichte und Linguistik' fits into the frame of the 'ivory tower'.

The Mahra ethnic group as the basis of research:

1. – Mehri:

Mehri is one of six dialects and is the most prevalent. Mehri, along with Soqoṭrī are defined as Modern South Arabian languages, both of which are in danger of becoming extinct due to the dominance of modern standard Arabic. Mehri should not be confused with other South Arabian dialects such as Yemeni or Saudi vernacular or local languages. These are different, although the latter also are extremely rare (cf. SAS, London 2013: ‚Languages of Southern Arabia'; or Elmaz 2011a, i. pr.). Apart from the aforementioned recordings, publications in the SE or by W. Hein (Sturm 2007) and the continuation of these studies in 1944 by Christian in Vienna, a further scholar attempted to take up the study of the Mehri language. The talented young Semitist Alexander Sima set about continuing this old tradition and updating it according to the current state of research (for example, verifying the SE publications among other things). Tragically, the 35-year old scholar died in an accident in September 2004 on the way to his area of fieldwork, the Mahra-country in the Yemeni Southeast where he planned to verify some of the data for his habilitation thesis. His exceptional skills and diligence are evident through the extensive list of publications, compiled by Stefan Weninger (Arnold et al. 2009, IX-XIII). Further works by Sima have been and are still to be published posthumously. His habilitation thesis could not be published as it was not finished when he died.[31]

This explanation should help to understand Dostal's emotions after this tragedy, which seemed to jeopardise the tradition of combining ethnology and epigraphy with the 'ivory tower'. However, it was picked up again in 2008 when Ancient South Arabia became a focus at the IfO in Vienna as mentioned above.

Dostal's findings in the areas of the Mahra and further ethnic groups (Baṭharī, Ḥarsūsī, Šaḥrī, etc.; see Dostal 1967: 34, 146, 163, etc.) with a similar language and cultural history are of course not complete and may be criticised or amended in terms of certain linguistic details. However, they serve as a basis for Dostal's and other scholars' international research in terms of today's global interconnectedness of studies on the pre- and proto-historical Ancient South Arabian region. In 1990 D. T. Potts, for example, already addressed this global interconnectedness in his 'Notes on some horned buildings in Iran, Mesopotamia and Arabia'. Further work on the region led to the research question in 1997 on whether South Arabia could be seen as a bridge between Africa and Eurasia: 'Süd-Arabien. Brücke zwischen Afrika und Eur-Asien?' (Stiegner 1997: 241-366).

---

[31] See J. C. E. Watson (2012). On the cover of this extensive book is stated: „...Based on fieldwork conducted by the author and material in Sima this is one of the first studies of any non-state language to include data from new technology (SMS and e-mail)".

In addition it would be important to consider the Baluchistan region in terms of the Indus Valley Civilization (ca. 3rd century.). This region, and in fact, large parts of Central Asia have remained under-researched due to on-going political tensions in the area.

Thanks to space technology and satellite images since the 1980/90s we now know that the northern Yemeni Ǧawf valley used to be connected to the southern Yemeni Wādī Ḥaḍramawt by a river system that ran all the way down to the Indian Ocean. Today, the two areas are divided by the desert. Towards the western area of northern Africa, it has long been proven that the Ethiopian syllable script is derived from the Ancient South Arabian script.[32] However, only in 2008 following the DAI excavations (by Iris Gerlach and her team) and the involvement of other researchers (e.g. Wolbert Smidt among others) it was evident that there were substantial ties ´between Ancient South Arabia and Ethiopia as early as the 8th, 7th and 6th centuries B.C. Norbert Nebes (i. pr.) substantiated their claim and translated and interpreted an Ancient South Arabian inscription found in Tigray (Ethiopia, 7th century; also with typical bull heads).

This recalls the story of the so-called geo-botanical ‚Nubo-Sindian province' (in India, South Arabia, Northeast Africa) where changing climate phases and sea level fluctuation were scientifically proven only recently, including an ensuing battle for survival by inhabitants, which subsequently contributed to specific cultural developments and changes over centuries. Undoubtedly there were migration flows in these areas from and to more populated areas and their peripheries. The influence of autochtonous areas must also be considered, however, as W. Dostal did in his study of the Mahra.[33]

In summary we know today that Mehri and Soqoṭri, i.e. Modern South Arabian languages, are not directly derived from Ancient South Arabian. W.W. Müller described them as being daughter languages of the periphery populations in 1968: „Tochtersprachen von Randvölkern der alten Hochkulturzone". This however only says very little about the true nature of these languages. This linguistic (and etymological) problem has persisted ever since.

Figure 3: Gl A 844 + 845 as a tribute to the great Arabia-pioneer Walter Dostal (first facsimile attempt based on the original copy, R. G. Stiegner).

[32] Rainer Voigt (Berlin), Sprache, Schrift und Gesellschaft im Axumitischen Königreich. In: WOO 10/1, Kap. III.

[33] It would go beyond the scope of this article to elaborate on even a few of his most important topics, but they are discussed in more detail in my other papers, especially in 'Keynote 3', WOO10/1. See also Gebhard J. Selz, Das Verändern der Erzählungen. Zur Bedeutung der Altsüdarabienforschungen aus Altorientalistischer Perspektive. In: WOO 10/1, Keynote 2.

2. Onomastics:

The archaeologist P. Yule clearly verified the place names that Dostal (1967) mentioned. The dispersion of these place names and of Mehri (see comment nr. 23) can be traced on the basis of signs (Yule 2013: 19-22). In general these historical languages do not only stretch from south-western Saudi Arabia to Yemen/Oman to south-eastern Saudi Arabia, but have also been available on the internet since about 1980 on the NGA QuickGeo-Names server. However, they would still need to be verified by qualified Arabists.

3. Camel- (or dromedary-) saddle types:

According to Dostal (1967) ḥaulānī and šadād saddles are placed on the croup (for transporting) or on the camel hump. The Mahra used the ḥawlānī saddle as well as a special saddle for use by women and for transporting packages (cf. Yule 2013: 23).

4. Matronymica – matrolinearity – sexual hospitality

Since and especially due to the rise of monotheism in the Middle East many Arabic genealogists and kinship experts, often because of their own patrilineal leanings and stereotypes, did not like to accept the fact that the kinship systems of the Mehri and Soqoṭra ethnic groups were predominantly matrilinear. Dostal writes about these issues mainly from his own fieldwork experience but also in discussion with other well-known scholars in the annex of his publication in 1990 (137-174). His final critical thoughts on the question of kinship systems in Arabia will be published in the WOO 10/2, chapter. V (Dostal i. pr.).

5. Wild goats, ibex, gazelles – Ancient South Arabian: zbyt, Arabic ẓby

These horned animals have dominated the South Arabian regions from prehistoric times up to the present day. They were domesticated and utilized for productive livestock in the Mahra areas and on Soqoṭra along with sheep - although these had a different meaning and were of lesser importance. They were also sacred animals and symbolically represented the oldest Ancient South Arabian gods, such as Almaqah, 'Attar, SM' = Samiʿ (as the one who is hearing - *al-Samīʿ* - in the Koran in the list of 99 names of Allah) or as Sami' (Höfner 1961: 15). Around the turn from the 4th to the 3rd centuries B.C. a new Ancient South Arabian god appeared: Taʾ LaB (Ta'lab) took over all the attributes, symbols and temples of the older god SMʿ about whom there is little documentation. Höfner (1961: 13-16) notes that there are a few key documentations about SMʿ. He was one of the moon gods and was often associated with related symbolic animals, therefore also interchangeable. For example, Almaqah is symbolically and in meaning represented by a ‚bull' (*ṯwr;* cf. Dostal 1983; Gingrich 1989) as well as having the nickname "lord of the ibex". Another prominent scholar, W.W. Müller (1997) also discusses this topic.

These animals are omnipresent in mythology. Jahn (1902: 124-127) published: "Erzählung in der Mundart von Qâśän (*Qiśin*)": which was a transcription of the Mehri text, the wild goat, with a German translation (which includes among other aspects the transformation of a boy into a wild goat through other wild goats). In *Sheep and Goat in Socotran Mythology* Vitaly Naumkin und Victor Porkhomovsky close with the following comment (p. 119):

> "Goats are not the most common domestic animal in Northern Europe, yet in this rather atypical plot almost all the motifs that have been discussed are present: a pair of animals, death and rescue from death, ritual consumption of goat flesh, teeth (with particular stress on tusks, or fangs) and even a little boy." [34]

Here are a few additional comments by the author (cf. comment 28 on page 85):

> "[...]Herewith a complex system of belief emerges that described the Sumerian-Arcadian pair of gods Dumuzi (Tammuz) / Inanna (Ištar) as the 'leading goat of the land', as 'a child that provides life-giving

[34] See also Stiegner 1986: 82-85, starting from the above mentioned Taʾlab, the „rain provider", bʿl/šṣrm, bʿl/ẓbyn, and therefore 'Lord of the Animals' (Höfner 1976) which reminds of the coessential Mesopotamian Ištar, that Dostal recognised to be a 'Lady of the Animals' as early as 1962.

Figure 4: Gl A 844: Rock graffiti copy, photographed by A. Jamme (1943).

Figure 5: Gl A 845: Rock graffiti copy (small part of Gl 845), photographed by A. Jamme (1943).

water' or as a 'Virgin She-Goat'. Furthermore, the goat is described in the Artemis legend, for example, as a substitute sacrifice for a girl. In our hemisphere the ibex is perceived as a ‚walking pharmacy', and also is related to the tautological figure of the Habergeiß – the demon of vegetation."[35]

I sincerely hope that Dostal would have appreciated my first attempt at a facsimile (figure 3) in his honour. The original consisted of two copies made by locals (figures 4 and 5) which was collected by Glaser from the north-western Ǧabal Ḏabāb mountain range of the Wādī al-Sirr (around 30 km to the north-east of von Ṣanʿāʾ; it has not been exactly located).[36]

In the spirit of *murāṯad/marṯad Sāmiʿ/Samīʿ*, let us hope that the memory as well as the inherited groundwork of the Arabian pioneer (or protégée in the sense of Protegee according to SD 119) Walter Dostal will live on.[37]

REFERENCES

al-Hamdani, Abu Muhammad. *Ṣifat Ǧazīrat al-ʿArab*. (Ed. David H. Mueller, 1884-91, reprint 1968, 2 Vols., Leiden: Brill).

Arnold, Werner, Jursa, Michael, Müller, Walter W., Procházka, Stephan (Eds.) (2009). *Philologisches u. Historisches zwischen Anatolien u. Sokotra: Analecta Semitica. In Memoriam Alexander Sima*. Wiesbaden.

Behnstedt, Peter (1987a). Anmerkungen zu den Dialekten der Gegend von Ṣaʿdah. *Zeitschrift für arabische Linguistik, 16*, 93–107.

Behnstedt, Peter (1987b). *Die Dialekte der Gegend von Ṣaʿdah (Nord-Jemen)*. Wiesbaden.

Behnstedt, Peter (1992). *Die nordjemenitischen Dialekte. Teil 2*: Glossar. Jemen-Studien, Vol. 3.

Behnstedt, Peter & Woidich, Manfred (2005). *Arabische Dialektgeographie. Handbook of the Oriental Studies, Section 1: The Near and Middle East, Vol. 78*. Leiden: Brill.

Bittner, Maximilian (1911). *Studien zur Laut- u. Formenlehre der Mehri-Sprache in Südarabien*. II. Sb. KAWW ph.-h.Kl. 168. Bd., 2. Abhandlung.

Bittner, Maximilian (1914). *Studien zur Laut- u. Formenlehre der Mehri-Sprache in Südarabien*. II. Sb. KAWW ph.-h.Kl. 174. Bd., 2. Abhandlung.

Busse, Dietrich, Niehr, Thomas, Wengeler, Martin (Eds.) (2005). *Brisante Semantik. Neuere Konzepte und Forschungsergebnisse einer kulturwissenschaftlichen Linguistik. Reihe Germanistische Linguistik, Vol. 259*. Tübingen. (bes. Wengeler S.7)

Christian, Viktor (1944). *Die Stellung des Mehri innerhalb der semitischen Sprachen. 222. Band, 3. Abh.* Österreichische Akademie der Wissenschaften in Wien, 1–26.

Dostal, Walter (1957). Ein Beitrag zur Frage des religiösen Weltbildes der frühesten Bodenbauer Vorderasiens. *Archiv für Völkerkunde, 12*, 54–109.

Dostal, Walter (1967). *Die Beduinen in Südarabien. Eine ethnologische Studie zur Entwicklung der Kamelhirtenkultur in Arabien. Wiener Beiträge zur Kulturgeschichte u. Linguistik. Veröffentlichungen des Instituts für Völkerkunde der Universität Wien, XVI*. Horn–Wien.

Dostal, Walter (1979). *Der Markt von Ṣanʿāʾ*. Vienna: Verlag der Österreichischen Akademie der Wissenschaften.

Dostal, Walter (1983). Some Remarks on the Ritual Significance of the Bull in Pre-Islamic South Arabia. In: R. L. Bidwell and G. R. Smith (Eds.). *Arabian and Islamic Studies. Articles presented to R. B. Serjeant on the Occasion of His Retirement from the Sir Thomas Adam's Chair of Arabic at the University of Cambridge* (196–213). London: Longman.

Dostal, Walter (with contributions by Gingrich, Andre & Riedl, Harold (1983). *Ethnographic Atlas of ʿAsīr*. Preliminary Report. Österreichische Akademie der Wissenschaften in Wien.

Dostal, Walter (1985). *Egalität und Klassengesellschaft in Südarabien. Anthropologische Untersuchungen zur sozialen Evolution. Wiener Beiträge zur Kulturgeschichte und Linguistik XX*. Horn–Wien.

35 Translated by Rosalind Willi.

36 See Höfner 1944: 73, in „Graffiti der SEG", where she notes that these are all unsigned, mostly without mentioning the sources and predominantly unclear or even illegible. Therefore they have all remained unpublished so far.

37 See Stiegner 2009: 371. Fig. 4 shows a survey map of approximately the whole area, in which god SMʿ is attested. Unfortunately the map was published in an almost unreadable state. About the author's first facsimile attempt: it was a difficult operation considering that I did the facsimile without technical aides. I hope that my work will be furthered by colleagues from Berlin and Hamburg who were in the archive of the ÖAW in June/July 2011 with the aim of digitalising all SEG-copies. The copies that have been preserved for over 100 years will be digitalised. Special thanks to Dr. Iris Gerlach of the DAI Berlin/Yemen and Ethiopia for all her efforts.

Dostal, Walter (1990). *Eduard Glaser – Forschungen im Yemen. Eine quellenkritische Untersuchung in ethnologischer Sicht.* Österreichische Akademie der Wissenschaften in Wien.

Dostal, Walter (1992/93). Maria Höfner. Nachruf. *Almanach der Österreichischen Akademie der Wissenschaften in Wien,* 467–472.

Dostal, Walter (1993). *Ethnographica Jemenica. Auszüge aus den Tagebüchern Eduard Glasers mit einem Kommentar versehen.* Österreichische Akademie der Wissenschaften in Wien.

Dostal, Walter (2005). Eduard Glaser im Jemen. Die Tragik einer Forscherpersönlichkeit. *Jemen-Report, 36(2),* 19–22.

Dostal, Walter (2008). *Von Mohammed bis al-Qaida. Einblicke in die Welt des Islam.* Wien: Passagen Verlag.

Dostal, Walter (2009). Die Beduinen Südarabiens und das Meer. Sozialanthropologische Beobachtungen über den Sardinenfang. In: Werner Arnold, Michael Jursa, Walter W. Müller, Stephan Procházka (Eds.). *Philologisches u. Historisches zwischen Anatolien u. Sokotra: Analecta Semitica In Memoriam Alexander Sima* (17–25). Wiesbaden.

Dostal, Walter (in press) Kritische Bemerkungen zur Frage der Verwandtschaftssysteme in Arabien. *Wiener Offene Orientalistik, 10.*

Elmaz, Orhan (2011a). k͟hus͟hub musannadah (Qur'ān 63.4) and Epigraphic South Arabian ms³nd. *Proceedings of the Seminar for Arabian Studies, 41,* 83–94

Elmaz, Orhan (2011b). *Studien zu den koranischen Hapaxlegomena unikaler Wurzeln. Jenaer Beiträge zum Vorderen Orient 8.* Wiesbaden: Harrassowitz Verlag.

Elmaz, Orhan (in press). `arim – A Sabaic word in the Qur'ān? *Wiener Offene Orientalistik, 11.*

Fillitz, Thomas, Gingrich, Andre & Rasuly-Paleczek, Gabriele (Eds.) (1993). *Kultur, Identität und Macht. Ethnologische Beiträge zu einem Dialog der Kulturen der Welt.* Frankfurt: IKO Verlag.

Fück, Johann (1955). *Die Arabischen Studien in Europa bis in den Anfang des 20. Jahrhunderts.* Leipzig.

Gebel, Hans Georg K. (2013). Arabia's fifth-millennium BCE pastoral well cultures: hypotheses on the origins of oasis life. In *Proceedings of the Seminar for Arabian Studies, 43,* 111–126.

Gingrich, Andre (1987). Saba und wir. Österreichs Beitrag zur Erforschung Südarabiens. *Die Presse, 8./9. 8.1987.*

Gingrich, Andre (1989). Kalender, Regenzeit u. Stieropfer in Nordwest-Jemen. In: *Der orientalischer Mensch und seine Beziehungen zur Umwelt: Beiträge zum 2. Grazer Morgenlaendischen Symposion,* 353–370.

Gingrich, Andre (1997). Female form, evil times. Local concepts related to the Pleiades in the Ethnography of Southern Ḥijāz. In: Roswitha G. Stiegner (Ed.), *Südarabien Interdisziplinär. In Memoriam Maria Höfner. Aktualisierte Beiträge zum 1. Internationalen Südarabien-Symposium an der Universität Graz, mit kurzen Einführungen zu Sprach- und Kulturgeschichte* (45–53). Graz: Leykam Verlag.

Gingrich, Andre (2012). Walter Dostal (1928–2011). *Anthropos, 107(1),*167–172.

Gingrich, Andre, Haas, Siegfried, Haas Sylvia & Paleczek Gabriele (Eds.) (1993). Studies in Oriental Culture and History. Festschrift für Walter Dostal. Wien.

Glaser, Eduard (1885). Die Sternkunde der südarabischen Kabylen. *Sitzungsberichte der mathematisch-naturwissenschaftlichen Classe, 91(2),* 89–99.

Gohm, Julia & Gingrich, Andre (2010). Rochaden der Völkerkunde. Hauptakteure und Verlauf eines Berufungsverfahrens nach dem ‚Anschluß'. In: Mitchell Ash, Wolfram Nieß, Ramon Pils (Ed.), *Geisteswissenschaften im Nationalsozialismus: Die Universität Wien 1938–1945.* Göttingen, 167–197.

Höfner, Maria (1944). *Die Sammlung Eduard Glaser. Verzeichnis des Glaser-Nachlasses, sonstiger südarabischer Materialbestände und einer Sammlung anderer semitischer Inschriften. Sitzungsberichte der philosophisch-historischen Klasse, 222. Band, 5. Abhandlung.* Österreichische Akademie der Wissenschaften in Wien.

Höfner, Maria (1961). *Inschriften aus dem Gebiet zwischen Mârib und dem Gôf. Sitzungsberichte der philosophisch-historischen Klasse, Band 238/3.* Österreichische Akademie der Wissenschaften in Wien.

Jahn, Alfred (1902). *Die Mehri-Sprache in Südarabien. Südarabische Expedition III.* Vienna: Alfred Hölder.

Kopp, Horst (Ed.) (1993). *Glossar der jemenitischen Dialektwörter in Eduard Glasers Tagebüchern (II,III,VI,VII,VIII,X). Veröffentlichungen der Arabischen Kommission Nr. 6.* Österreichische Akademie der Wissenschaften in Wien.

Kopp, Horst (2013). Eine sagenhafte Reise in den Jabal Rāziḥ. *Zeitschrift für arabische Linguistik, 57,* 83f.

Liebhaber, Sam (in press). Acoustic Spectrum Analysis of Mahri Oral Poetry: An Empirical Approach to Bedouin Vernacular Prosody. *Wiener Offene Orientalistik, 10.*

Maraqten, Mohammed (2013). 'Umm el-Ġēṯ „Mutter des Regens" und die Volksriten der 'Istisqā' in Palästina. In: Renaud Kuty, Ulrich Seeger, Shabo Talay (Eds.). *Nicht nur mit Engelszungen. Beiträge zur Semitischen Dialektologie. Festschrift für Werner Arnold* (235–244). Wiesbaden: Harrassowitz Verlag.

Mazzini, Giovanni (2005). Ancient South Arabian Documentation and the Renconstruction of Semitic. In: P. Franzaroli & P. Marrassini, (Eds.). *Proceedings of the 10th Meeting of Hamito-Semitic (Afroasiatic) Linguistics, Univ. di Firenze* (215–238).

Meringer, Rudolf (1929). *Wörter und Sachen. Kulturhistorische Zeitschrift für Sprach- und Sachforschung XII. Festband zum 70. Geburtstag R. Meringers (Graz).* Heidelberg.

Morris, Miranda J. (2013). The use of ‚veiled language' in Soqoṭri poetry. *Proceedings of the Seminar for Arabian Studies, 43*, 239–244.

Mukarovsky, Hans G. (1981). Hamito-Semitisch, Afro-Asiatisch, Erythräisch. Zum Wandel von Begriffen u. Verständnis. *Zeitschrift für Phonetik, Sprachwissenschaft u. Kommunikationsforschung, 34(5)*, 511–526.

Müller, David Heinrich & Rhodokanakis, Nikolaus (Eds.) (1913). *Eduard Glasers Reise nach Mārib. Sammlung Eduard Glaser I.* Österreichische Akademie der Wissenschaften in Wien.

Müller, Walter W. (2002). Der böhmische Südarabienreisende Eduard Glaser und seine Bedeutung für die Erforschung des antiken Jemen. *Schriften der Sudetendeutschen Akademie der Wissenschaften u. Künste 23. Forschungsbeiträge der Geisteswissenschaftlichen Klasse.* 195–220.

Müller, Walter W. (1968). Rezension zu Walter Dostal: Die Beduinen in Südarabien. Eine ethnologische Studie zur Entwicklung der Kamelhirtenkultur in Arabien. *Zeitschrift der Deutschen Morgenländischen Gesellschaft, 118*, 399–402.

Müller, Walter W. (1993). ‚Heilige Hochzeit' im antiken Südarabien. In: Andre Gingrich et al. (Eds.) *Studies in Oriental Culture and History. Festschrift Walter Dostal* (15–28).

Müller, Walter W. (1997). Das Statut des Gottes Ta'lab von Riyām für seinen Stamm Sum`ay. Zur Interpretation der sab. Felsinschrift RES 4176 seit der Erstveröffentlichung durch N. Rhodokanakis. In: R. G. Stiegner (Ed.), *Südarabien interdisziplinär* (89–110). Graz: Leykam Verlag.

Müller, Walter W. (2013). Zum Gedenken an Walter Dostal (1928–2011). *Jemen-Report, 44(1/2),* 50f.

Musée du Louvre (2010). *Routes d'Arabie. Archéologie et Histoire du Royaume d'Arabie Saoudite. Catalogue de l'exposition.* Paris: Musée du Louvre.

Naumkin, Vitaly & Prokhomovsky, Victor (1996). Sheep and Goat in Socotran Mythology. *Proceedings of the Seminar for Arabian Studies, 1996*, 115–124.

Nebes, Norbert (1999). Vorwort des Herausgebers. In: Norbert Nebes (Ed.), *Tempus und Aspekt in den semitischen Sprachen. Jenaer Kolloquium zur semitischen Sprachwissenschaft.* (5). Wiesbaden: Harrasowitz Verlag.

Nebes, Norbert (in print). Eine altsabäische Inschrift auf einem Bronzekessel aus Färäs May (Tigray/Äthiopien). *Wiener Offene Orientalistik, 10.*

Potts, D. T. (1990). Notes on some Horned Buildings in Iran, Mesopotamia and Arabia. *Revue d'Assyriologie, 84(1)*, 33–39.

Rhodokanakis, Nikolaus (1929). Zum Siedlungswesen im alten Südarabien. *Wörter u. Sachen. Kulturhistorische Zeitschrift für Sprach- u. Sachforschung, 12*, 93–111.

Rodionov, M. (1994). The Ibex Hunt Ceremony in Hadramawt Today. In: R. L. Bidwell, G. Rex Smith, J. R. Smart (Eds.). *New Arabian Studies* (123–129). University of Exeter Press.

Rose, Jeffrey I. (in press). Ice Age Arabia: archaeology, genetics and palaeo-environments along the highway of human Evolution. *Wiener Offene Orientalistik, 10.*

de Sacy, Silvestre (1836). Rezension zu Gustav Flügel`s Corani Textus Arabicus, 1834. *Journal des Savans, 335–339.*

de Saussure, Ferdinand (1967). *Grundfragen der allgemeinen Sprachwissenschaft.* Berlin: De Gruyter.

Sienell, Stefan (in press). *Zur Geschichte der Sammlung Glaser. Wiener Offene Orientalistik, 10.*

Stein, Peter (2013). Wilhelm Gesenius, das Hebräische Handwörterbuch und die Erforschung des Altsüdarabischen. In: St. Schorch & E.-J. Waschke (Eds.). *Biblische Exegese u. hebräische Lexikographie. Das „Hebr.-deutsche Handwörterbuch" von W. Gesenius als Spiegel u. Quelle alttestamentlicher u. hebräischer Forschung, 2oo Jahre nach seiner ersten Auflage. – Beihefte zur ZS für die alttestamentliche Wissenschaft* (267–301). Berlin: De Gruyter.

Stein, Peter (in press). Südarabien im Spiegel der Minuskelinschriften. *Wiener Offene Orientalistik, 10.*

Steinmann, Axel (in press). Die Sammlungen aus der Arabischen Halbinsel im Museum für Völkerkunde Wien. *Wiener Offene Orientalistik, 10.*

Stiegner, Roswitha G. (1986). Altsüdarabien. Teil des Alten u. des Neuen Orients? In: *Grazer Morgenländische Studien* 1. 79–94.

Stiegner, Roswitha G. (1997). Süd-Arabien. Brücke zwischen Afrika und Eur-Asien? In: R. G. Stiegner (Ed). *Aktualisierte Beiträge zum 1. Internationalen Symposion Südarabien – Interdisziplinär: an der Universität Graz; mit kurzen Einführungen zur Sprach- und Kulturgeschichte;* in memoriam Maria Höfner (241–366). Graz: Leykam.

Stiegner, Roswitha G. (2009). Kulturhistorische Überlegungen zum Wādī al-Sirr im Raum Ṣanʿāʾ – Ṣirwāḥ – Mārib. In: Werner Arnold, Michael Jursa, Walter W. Müller & Stephan Procházka (Eds.). *Philologisches u. Historisches zwischen Anatolien u. Sokotra: Analecta Semitica. In Memoriam Alexander Sima* (351–371). Wiesbaden.

Stiegner, Roswitha G. (Ed.) (in press). Süd-Arabien/South Arabia. A Great ‚Lost Corridor' of Mankind. A collection of papers dedicated to the Re-Establishment of South Arabian Studies in Austria (2008–2013). *Wiener Offene Orientalistik, 10*(1–2).

Sturm, Gertraud (2007). *Leben für die Forschung: Das Ethnologenehepaar Wilhelm u. Marie Hein in Südarabien (1901/02)*. Österreichische Akademie der Wissenschaften in Wien.

Watkins, T. (2004). Building houses, farming concepts, constructing worlds. *Paléorient. Revue pluridisciplinaire de préhistoire et protohistoire de l'Asie du Sud-Ouest et de l'Asie centrale. CNRS Editions*, Vol. 30(1), 5–23.

Watson, Janet C. E. (2006). Two texts from Jabal Razih. In: Lutz Edzard & Jan Retsö (Eds.). *Current Issues in the Analysis of Semitic Grammar and Lexicon II. Oslo-Göteborg Cooperation 4th–5th Nov.2005. Abhandlungen für die Kunde des Morgenlandes LIX* (40–63). Wiesbaden: Harrassowitz Verlag.

Watson, Janet C. E. (2012). *The Structure of Mehri. Semitica Viva 52*. Wiesbaden: Harrassowitz Verlag.

Yule, Paul (2013). Late Pre-Islamic Oman: The Inner Evidence – The Outside View. In: Michaela Hoffmann-Ruf, Abdulrahman Al Salimi (Eds.). *Oman and Overseas. Studies on Ibadism and Oman, Vol. 2* (13–33). Hildesheim.

Zaborski, Andrzej (in press). South Arabian Languages in a Semitic Perspective. *Wiener Offene Orientalistik, 10.*

LIST OF ABBREVIATIONS:

ASA/asa	Altsüdarabisch / Old South Arabian
AfV	Archiv für Völkerkunde /archive for Völkerkunde (Vienna)
DAI	Deutsches Archäologisches Institut (Oriental-department), Berlin.
DOT	Deutscher Orientalistentag
EFAH	Epigraphische Forschungen auf der Arabischen Halbinsel. DAI. Hgg. von Norbert Nebes (Jena).
EI	The Encyclopaedia of Islam (New Ed. ab 1986)
Gl	Eduard Glaser
GMS	Grazer Morgenländische Studien. H.D. Galter and B. Schol (Hg.)
IfO	Institut für Orientalistik; Institute for Oriental Studies
JR	Jemen-Report. Mitteilungen der Deutsch-Jemenitischen Ges. e.V., Hg. Horst Kopp. Stuttgart/Freiburg (www.djg-ev.de)
KAWW, ph.-h.Kl.	Kaiserliche Akademie der Wissenschaften Wien, philosophisch-historische Klasse; philosophical-historical class
KHMW	Kunsthistorisches Museum Vienna.
Lu	Lundin, A.G.
NHM	Naturhistorisches Museum Vienna.
ÖAWW	Österreichische Akademie der Wissenschaften Wien; Austrian Academy of Science, Vienna
PSAS	Proceedings of the Seminar for Arabian Studies. Archaeopress, Oxford.
SB	Sitzungsberichte; session reports (ÖAW)
SD	Sabaic Dictionary. Beeston, Ghul, Müller,Ryckmans. 1982 Beyrouth.
SE	Südarabische Expedition / KAWW; South Arabian expedition
SEG	Sammlung Eduard Glaser
w.M.	Wirkliches Mitglied (der KAWW bzw. ÖAWW); official member
WBEA	Wiener Beiträge zur Ethnologie u. Anthropologie; Viennese contributions to ethnology and anthropology
WOO	Wiener Offene Orientalistik. Wiener Universitätsreihe, hgg.v. Gebhard J. Selz.
WOO 10/1+2	s.u. Stiegner (ed.) 2013 (in print)
ZAL	Zeitschrift für Arabische Linguistik. Harrassowitz Wiesbaden

WATER ENGINEERING AND MANAGEMENT PRACTICES IN SOUTH ARABIA

Aspects of Continuity and Change from Ancient to Medieval and Modern Times

INGRID HEHMEYER

Since ancient times, humans have lived and even prospered in the arid regions of South Arabia, where the pre-eminent factor limiting life is water. How did people in the past interact with a natural environment that seems so uninviting, indeed hostile towards humans? What kinds of strategies did they use in order to deal with the scarce water resources? Did their practices change over time, or did the natural conditions restrict the options severely? There are numerous sites in South Arabia that can serve as examples for skillful hydraulic engineering and water management, both from ancient and medieval Islamic times. The following considerations are based on two case studies: first, the ancient oasis of Mārib that flourished during the first millennium BCE and was abandoned around 600 CE, just before the coming of Islam; and, second, the city of Zabīd, founded in the ninth century CE, with its agricultural hinterland that has been farmed continuously since then. These two sites where the author has conducted field research since the 1980s also allow us to address the question of continuity and change from pre-Islamic to Islamic times. In order to appreciate what people in the past accomplished and still do, it is necessary to start with a brief review of what aridity means in terms of the water resources.

WĀDĪ AND *SAYL*

Following a humid period with perennial bodies of stagnant and flowing water in South Arabia, the transition from the fourth to the third millennium BCE went hand in hand with the climate gradually becoming dryer. As a result of this so-called mid-Holocene climate change, the lakes and rivers disappeared eventually. Apart from minor fluctuations, the climate has remained basically the same, and it is no different today than 3,000 years ago (Brunner 1999: 38–39). The typical water course of arid regions is the *wādī*. This Arabic term designates a dry stream bed that contains water only in direct connection with rain falling on higher ground in its catchment basin. Generally speaking, the monsoon-influenced biannual rainy seasons are pretty predictable and can be expected during a shorter period in spring (March/April) and a longer period in late summer (July/August) (Kopp 2005: 13–16). However, it is important to bear in mind that the specified cycle is based on long-term averages, and considerable variability occurs both in terms of time and volume. Every now and then the rains will be missing entirely.

The surface run-off from the rains results in short-lived spates, for which the Arabic term *sayl* is used. Depending on the intensity and continuance of the precipitation, a spate may last for a few hours or several days, even up to a couple of weeks in case of regular thundershowers. Soon after the rain in the catchment area stops, the *wādī* dries up and remains dry until the beginning of the next rainfall. Thus, the main characteristics of the *sayl* are its seasonality and limited duration.

In order to make use of the water for irrigation, the *sayl* is diverted from the *wādī* by earth barrages that reach into the flood course like a finger and direct part of the water onto the fields on either side (see Fig. 1). Eventually, such a barrage will be washed away and has to be re-built by the farmers before the start of the next rainy season in the mountains; otherwise the *sayl* will remain unused.

Typically the individual fields are irrigated once per rainy season by submerging them with water at least knee-deep in order to have enough moisture stored in the soil for the ensuing growing season.[1] This requires the heaping up of earth banks around the fields (Fig. 2). Because of the erosive force of water, the surface run-off and the *sayl* carry considerable quantities of silt. Therefore irrigation with the muddy spate results in the deposition of a thin layer of sediment. While the process provides nutrients to the cultivated plants and helps soil fertility, it also leads to a very slow, yet continuous build-up of the fields over time. Consequently, when irrigation systems operate successfully over centuries, the irrigation structures need to be raised again and again or may have to be moved further upstream in order to gain height so that the water can still reach the fields under gravity flow.

IRRIGATION IN THE ANCIENT OASIS OF MĀRIB

Mārib, first mentioned in inscriptions written in Old South Arabian in the early first millennium BCE, was the capital of the Sabaean realm, Saba', and one of the main halting places on the ancient caravan route, the so-called frankincense route that linked the regions producing incense and other aromatic substances around the Arabian Sea with those consuming them around the Mediterranean (Müller 1991: 559b–60a). In the Hebrew Bible (I Kings 10:1–13; II Chronicles 9:1–12) the story of the tenth-century BCE visit of the fabled Queen of Sheba to King Solomon is told, an incident that may have happened as part of a trade mission. For sure, the income capital from the caravan trade made investment in infrastructure projects possible, most importantly water engineering schemes. Ancient Mārib was renowned for the fertility and abundance of its irrigated farmland, the Mārib oasis.

Mārib is located on the eastern side of the Yemeni highlands, on the periphery of the great inner Arabian desert, and receives very little precipitation. Rain-fed farming is not an option to sustain the city. Agriculture is only possible by way of irrigation. The only source of water is the Wādī Dhana, on the bank of which Mārib is located, 8 km from the mouth of the gorge where the *wādī* debouches from the mountains. In accordance with the aforementioned biannual rainy seasons in spring and late summer, these are also the times of the year that are mentioned in the Old South Arabian inscriptions as irrigation seasons in Mārib.[2]

Over long periods of time, people constructed diversion barrages that originally must have been built of earth, in the same way that can still be observed today along the *wādīs* of Yemen (see Fig. 1). Because of the nature of the building material, though, they left no traces. With time, the barrages were moved further and further upstream, and the engineers began to cut stone blocks for bigger and more substantial diversion devices that date to the early first millennium BCE.[3]

The process culminated in the construction of a barrage across the mouth of the gorge, which happened most probably in the sixth century BCE (Gerlach 2012: 191, 196). In its final state that was recorded by the archaeologists, the so-called dam of Mārib was some 620 m long and 20 m high.[4] Its purpose was to block the spate and divert the water towards the fields, that is, like its more simple precursors it operated as a diversion barrage, not as a dam in the strict sense to store water in an artificial lake – even though in the literature the term 'dam' is used to refer to it. Two so-called sluices, massive cut-stone constructions at its northern and southern end, anchored it firmly on the bedrock on either side of the gorge. The northern sluice had two inlets that directed the water into a main canal; the southern sluice had only one. From a main division point

[1] Details of the irrigation methods and the archaeological remains they leave behind are discussed in Hehmeyer & Schmidt (1991: 40–46).

[2] E.g. Gl 1679 + Gl 1773 a+b, and Gl 1762 (Müller 1983: 270–71). Because of the variability and sometimes unreliability of the *sayl*, some inscriptions describe as well the desperate situation when the rains had failed, the fields were barren, the trees had died and the wells had dried up, e.g. Ja 735 (+ Ja 754) (Müller 1986: 10–11; Müller 1988: 450–52).

[3] These are the so-called structures A and B at Mārib that have previously caused much discussion about their age. The issue was most recently addressed by Iris Gerlach who comes to the convincing conclusion that they do not date before the early first millennium BCE (Gerlach 2012: 190–91, 195–96).

[4] The Mārib 'dam' has been described in numerous publications. A good general depiction including a schematic drawing can be found in Brunner (2000: 171–73). Since then, much work has been carried out on the barrage and the sluices by the German Archaeological Institute that has refined our understanding of some of the functional elements and in particular the dating (see Vogt 2004*a*, 2005 and – for the most recent account – 2007).

Fig. 1: Earth diversion barrage in the Wādī Zabīd (photo: Edward J. Keall).

Fig. 2: Field in the Wādī Zabīd, surrounded by earth bank (photo: Ingrid Hehmeyer).

at the end of the two primary canals the water was further distributed through a network of secondary and tertiary canals (for a description, see Schaloske 1995: 123–61).

The brilliance of the scheme is reflected in the fact that the centre part of the barrage was earthen and deliberately designed to be weak. It had the function of a fuse in an electric circuit: in case of an exceptional flood, the proverbial 'century flood,' the barrage would break, but the rest of the infrastructure – the sluices, the water distribution system and the fields – would remain intact. The earthworks of the barrage could be rebuilt in time for the next spate; the stone structures could not, and the water cutting deep erosion gullies through the oasis would lead to a disruption of the distribution system and destruction of the fields. However, repairing the barrage meant a huge communal effort, which is reflected in several inscriptions.

One of the most famous inscriptions from ancient South Arabia is CIH 541 that reports the breaking of the barrage in the year 548 CE and the ensuing construction work to rebuild it and repair the damage on the sluices.[5] The text describes the great efforts and the enormous expenses regarding building materials and provisions for the workers. Besides flour and dates as staples, 3,000 cattle and 207,000 small livestock were slaughtered to feed them. As for beverages, in addition to date wine 300 camel loads of grape wine were delivered to the construction site. After fifty-eight days the workers had completed the repairs and could finally return home. These figures underline the scale of the operation.

The limited duration of the *sayl* meant that the success of the irrigation system at Mārib depended on distribution of the water under gravity flow that had to be completed as quickly and efficiently as possible, so that the fullest possible extent of the oasis could be farmed. In order to accomplish this, the water was allocated according to the principle of upstream priority, implying that those areas further up in the network received water before the lower-lying ones. It leads to the lower-lying field systems not receiving any water during a weak *sayl*, or only receiving water during the normally stronger late summer *sayl*, that is, once a year instead of twice. The consequences are visible in the way the fields of the northern oasis are stepped down sequentially, starting from the main distribution point towards the fringes (Hehmeyer & Schmidt 1991: 80–82 and Tafel 12; Schaloske 1995: 138–39, see 148 for an exception).

The whole settlement, the city with its two oases on either side of the *wādī*, flourished until the first centuries of the Common Era when it became obvious that Mārib began to suffer from problems caused by political squabbles in South Arabia and, possibly even more importantly, by transfer of trade to the sea-route that led to a decline of caravan traffic and the income derived from it (Müller 1991: 561, 564). In addition, there were severe problems with the stability of the main irrigation structures. The average annual sediment build-up of the fields is currently estimated at approximately 1 cm per year (Brunner 2005: 4), at first sight not much at all, but it developed into a major problem because of the long-term overall success of the irrigation system at Mārib. Even though one should be careful not to apply the figure of 1 cm per year as a straight-forward tool by which to date sediment accumulation "by the yardstick" (Vogt 2004*b*: 70), 1000 years of irrigation translate into a considerable rise of the field level. As a consequence, the irrigation structures needed to be built higher and higher, and over time this led to a loss of stability. It is therefore not entirely surprising that the Old South Arabian inscriptions report five incidents of the barrage breaking between the beginning of the fourth century CE and the middle of the sixth century (Müller 1999: 563–64). A sixth breach in the late sixth century CE was postulated by Brunner based on differences in the cross-bedding of the sediment deposits behind the barrage, so-called discordances (Brunner 1983: 51–53, 118–19, 123).

Interestingly, at Mārib it was the problem of too much water – which can have as devastating an effect as lack of it – that led to the final catastrophe: a particularly strong flood towards the end of the sixth century caused the barrage to break. By this time "the system had reached its technical limits" (Vogt 2004*a*: 387). In the Koran (34:15–17a) the demise of Mārib and its fabled oasis is singled out as divine punishment of people who were disbelievers and as a warning against worldly pride:

> "For Sheba also there was a sign in their dwelling-place – two gardens, one on the right and one on the left: 'Eat of your Lord's provision, and give thanks to Him; a good land, and a Lord All-forgiving.' But they turned away; so We loosened on them the Flood of Arim, and We gave them, in exchange for their

[5] The inscription was most recently translated by Müller (1999); for the slightly revised date of the breaking of the barrage, see Nebes (2004: 229, n. 12).

Fig. 3: The ancient oasis of Mārib as seen in 1984 (photo: Ingrid Hehmeyer).

two gardens, two gardens bearing bitter produce and tamarisk-bushes, and here and there a few lote-trees. Thus We recompensed them for their unbelief."

Thus shortly before the coming of Islam the oasis of Mārib was destroyed and with it the most prominent example of large-scale *sayl* irrigation in the arid environment of ancient South Arabia. Without its intact irrigation infrastructure there was no life on the oasis, and the area was abandoned by the resident population – for archaeologists an ideal scenario because it resulted in a remarkable state of preservation of the archaeological record until the second half of the 1980s (Fig. 3) when recultivation of the ancient oasis started on a large scale.

SAYL IRRIGATION IN THE WĀDĪ ZABĪD DURING MEDIEVAL ISLAMIC TIMES[6]

After the rise of Islam in the seventh century CE, the ancient principle of *sayl* irrigation continued to be applied in Yemen. This comes as no surprise since for major parts of the country the *wādī* spate is the only source of water for anything but small-scale irrigation. The second case study of this chapter focusses on the city of Zabīd, located on the western side of the Yemeni highlands on the coastal plain called the Tihāma, about 25 km inland from the Red Sea.

As reported by the twelfth-century writer ʿUmāra al-Yamanī, Zabīd was founded in 820 CE by a certain Ibn Ziyād as a military camp that became the nucleus of a permanent settlement, the city of Zabīd (ʿUmāra 1968 [1892]: 3). The significant role of the *wādī* for providing the economic basis of the city is conveyed by the tenth-century scholar al-Hamdānī who points out that Zabīd was named after the *wādī* flowing by it (al-Hamdānī 1884–1891, vol. 1: 53/24–25, 119/17). Not long after its foundation, the city started to acquire an

[6] For a general description of *sayl* irrigation in Yemen during Islamic times, see Varisco (1983: 368–71).

'international' reputation as a centre of learning. The tenth-century geographer al-Muqaddasī, who travelled extensively in the Arabian Peninsula, describes Zabīd with the following words:

> "Zabīd, the capital of Tihāma, is one of its metropoles, this being the residence of the kings of al-Yaman. It is a splendid, well-built town, and popularly called 'the Baghdād of al-Yaman.' The inhabitants are reasonably polite, and among them are merchants, nobles, scholars, litterateurs. It is a profitable place for one who visits it, a blessed place for one who lives there. Their wells are sweet, their baths clean. [...] Around it are villages and cultivated fields. [...] Ibn Ziyād had a channel led to the town. It is an attractive town, without equal in al-Yaman." (Al-Muqaddasī 1994: 82)

Al-Muqaddasī's reference to Baghdad, the capital of the Islamic Empire during the so-called Golden Age, is clearly to be understood as an allusion to the level of scholarship that one would find in Zabīd,[7] and his description of the cultivated fields in the hinterland underlines that the Wādī Zabīd was controlled for irrigated agriculture at the time.

However, the reality of Zabīd's geographical location makes one wonder how the city could not only survive but thrive under the prevailing climatic conditions. The Red Sea coastal plain is one of the hottest areas of the Earth, and it receives an average of less than 150 mm of precipitation per year (Kopp 1981: 42 [tab. 2], 44 [figs. 5a and b]; Remmele 1989: 31 [fig. 4], 32 [fig. 5]). As with Mārib, the answer is skilful management of the *sayl* in the *wādī*. Other than the oasis of Mārib that lay abandoned from around 600 CE until the mid-1980s, the Wādī Zabīd has been farmed continuously until the present. Therefore it offers the unique opportunity of first-hand observation of the traditional irrigation and farming practices (Fig. 4), which can be of great help when it comes to piecing together archaeological remains. Working in the Islamic period also means that we have an enormous body of written sources at our disposal.

Zabīd's heyday was under the Rasulid dynasty (1229–1454), and the thirteenth and fourteenth centuries are a particular prosperous period in Yemen's history. The Rasulids made Zabīd their winter residence and they invested in a major way in infrastructure, including irrigation devices in the Wādī Zabīd (see below). The authority for the Rasulid era is a man by the name of al-Khazrajī, the official court historian of the Rasulids. He lived under four Rasulid sultans and died in 1410 at the age of over 70 (Bosworth 1978: 1188b). As a contemporary of many of the events that he reported, the information that we find in his main work poetically entitled *The Pearl-Strings* has a different quality than, for instance, ʿUmāra's references to occurrences that had happened up to more than 300 years before his time.

The Rasulid rulers' great personal interest in agriculture and horticulture is reflected in the fact that new plants were introduced into Yemen and cultivated in the royal gardens; among them were fragrant flowers such as jasmine and roses (al-Khazrajī 1906–1918, vol. 5: 139). The seventh Rasulid sultan, al-Ashraf Ismāʿīl (r. 1377–1400), grew exotic trees in his garden near Zabīd, and according to al-Khazrajī he was the first one to cultivate rice in the Wādī Zabīd, apparently with success (al-Khazrajī 1906–1918, vol. 5: 300, 318). A number of texts on various topics related to agriculture were written by the sultans themselves, or at least in the name of a sultan.[8]

The fourth Rasulid sultan, al-Muʾayyad Dāwūd (r. 1296–1321), has left us a tax register that was compiled during the first years of his reign, that is, right at the end of the thirteenth century (Vallet 2010: 74–75).[9] It is subdivided according to the administrative regions and includes a substantial section on Zabīd and its agricultural hinterland, with a priceless map of the irrigation system in the Wādī Zabīd (Fig. 5) (Jāzim 2008: 387). By comparison with Mārib, there is no barrage built across the *wādī*. Instead, the map shows a succession of main canals (sg. *sharīj*) along the central channel of the *wādī* that leads from the mountains in the east (at the top of Fig. 5) to the Red Sea in the west (at the bottom). The city of Zabīd is located on the northern bank. Five canals divert the *sayl* onto the southern bank, and twelve onto the northern bank of the *wādī*. Clearly, the irrigation system was firmly established at the end of the thirteenth century.

In local dialect, the term *sharīj* implies a primary canal that is connected to a diversion barrage at its head and that leads towards the fields lying above the banks of the *wādī*, as well as the system of contiguous fields

[7] For a different interpretation of al-Muqaddasī's remark on Zabīd being 'the Baghdād of Yemen,' see Keall (2012: 137–39).

[8] For an annotated bibliography of these medieval agricultural texts, see Varisco (1989).

[9] The manuscript was edited by Jāzim (2008).

Fig. 4: Farmer in the Wādī Zabīd building a diversion barrage in anticipation of the *sayl* (photo: Ingrid Hehmeyer).

that is irrigated by it. This linguistic detail shows beautifully that the land and the water form a natural unit. One without the other is worthless. In the manuscript, the term *maʿqam* (and *ʿaqm* as a synonym) is used for the diversion barrage at the head of a primary canal (*sharīj*) that diverts part of the *sayl* into it (Jāzim 2008: 10).

The tax register talks also about the Rasulids' investment in irrigation infrastructure in the Wādī Zabīd. For instance, as the highest-lying diversion barrage in the *wādī*, Maʿqam al-Bunay was particularly vulnerable to the force of the *sayl* and was regularly damaged or even washed away completely. Government administration paid for its reconstruction, the farmers were not expected to contribute to the costs (Jāzim 2008: 11). Clearly, everybody understood that having Maʿqam al-Bunay in place was essential for irrigation in Sharīj al-Bunay, but also to break the initial force of the *sayl* and thus protect the infrastructure further downstream.

By comparison with the ancient oasis of Mārib, the second major difference is the principle of water allocation in the Wādī Zabīd. In order to understand the implications, let us consider briefly water allocation rights in Islamic law, *Sharīʿa*. According to Muslim belief, the Koran is God's word as revealed to the Prophet Muḥammad and eventually compiled and written down in the form of a book. It constitutes the first source of the *Sharīʿa*. The Koran provides more general guidelines and does not give answers to all the specific questions and problems that kept emerging in day-to-day situations. Therefore the Prophet's sayings and exemplary way of acting, his *Sunna*, became the second source of the *Sharīʿa*. This is of particular significance in the context of Islamic water law: since specific legal provisions are absent in the Koran, the Prophet Muḥammad's *Sunna* provided the framework.

Following the eleventh-century legal scholar al-Māwardī (d. 1058), water is shared in accordance with upstream priority, that is, the higher-lying areas are irrigated first and then successively those further downstream (al-Māwardī 1996: 256–59). For spate irrigation this means that its overall reliability is "a function of proximity to the wadi, and distance downstream from it" (Tihama Development Authority n.d.: 31). Quite clearly, the land owners of the downstream areas are at a disadvantage, in particular in those years when the *sayl* is weak. Conflicts among the farmers are likely to happen.

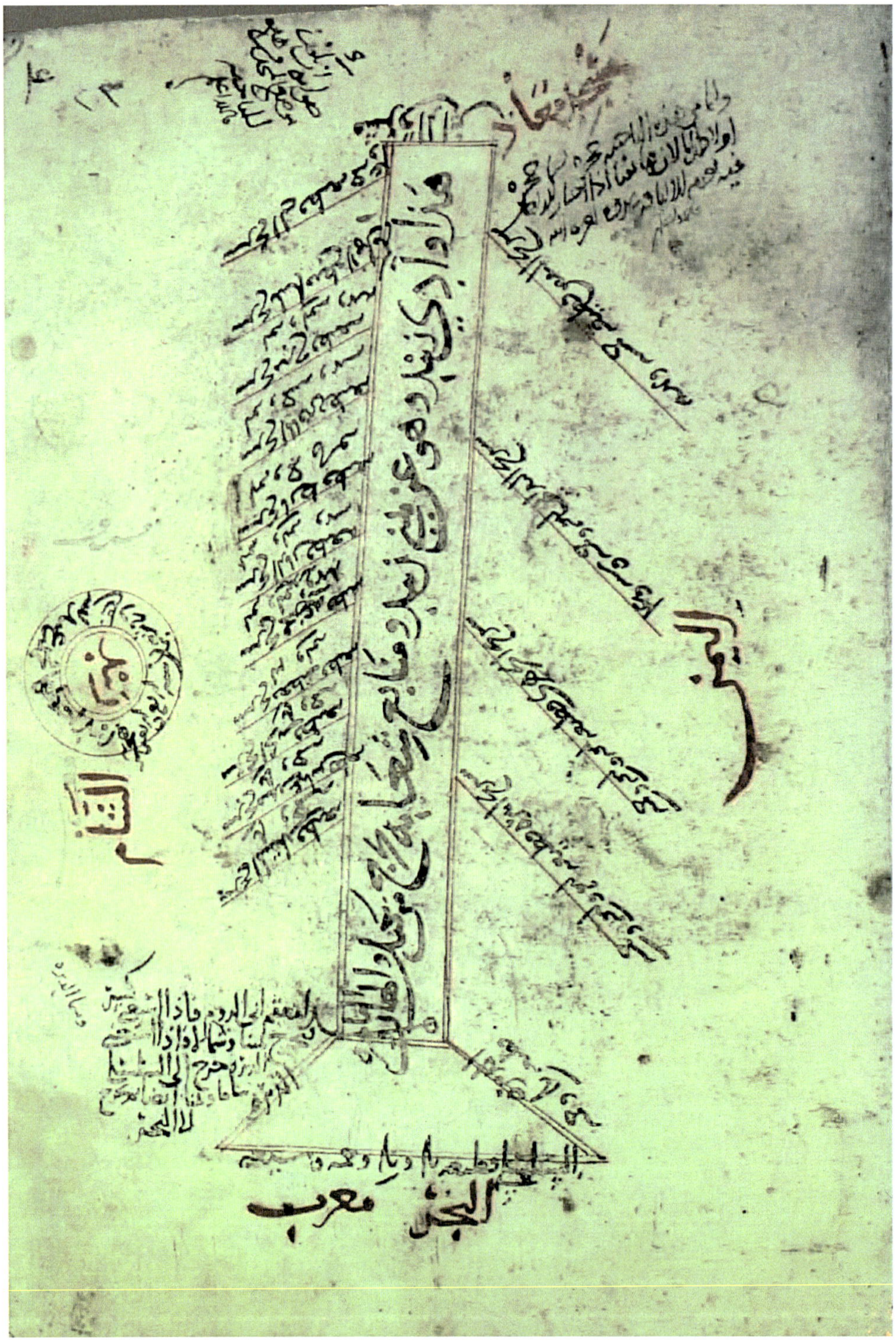

Fig. 5: Map of the Wādī Zabīd from the tax register of the fourth Rasulid sultan, al-Muʾayyad Dāwūd (r. 1296–1321) (from: Jāzim, Muḥammad ʿAbd al-Raḥīm (ed.). 2008. *Irtifāʿ al-dawla al-Muʾayyadiyya: Jibāyat bilād al-Yaman fī ʿahd al-sulṭān al-Malik al-Muʾayyad Dāwūd b. Yūsuf al-Rasūlī (al-mutawaffā sanat 721h/1321m)/Le Livre des Revenus du sultan rasûlide al-Malik al-Muʾayyad Dâwûd b. Yûsuf (m. 721/1321). (La bibliothèque yéménite/al-Maktaba al-Yamaniyya/Die Jemenitische Bibliothek, 2).* Ṣanʿāʾ: al-Maʿhad al-faransī li-l-āthār wa-l-ʿulūm al-ijtimāʿiyya bi-Ṣanʿāʾ, al-Maʿhad al-almānī li-l-āthār, Ṣanʿāʾ/Centre Français d'Archéologie et de Sciences Sociales, Deutsches Archäologisches Institut, Sanaa Branch, 387).

As reported in a manuscript, the water law of the Wādī Zabīd was codified in response to violent disputes among the farmers of the Wādī Zabīd over water towards the end of the fourteenth century. Clearly, they felt that the allocation of the *sayl* according to the principle of upstream priority was unfair. A certain Muwaffaq al-Dīn ʿAlī ibn Abī Bakr al-Nāshirī is credited with having drafted the new law. He held the position of judge, *qāḍī*, in Zabīd from 1391 to at least 1400, that is, under the reign of the seventh Rasulid sultan, al-Ashraf Ismāʿīl (r. 1377–1400) (Salameh 1995: "Vorwort," "Nachtrag September 1997," 41–42, 58–67; al-Khazrajī 1906–1918, vol. 5: 220, 316).

The new water law of the Wādī Zabīd deviates from the *Sharīʿa* principle of unrestricted upstream priority in so far as it allocates the *sayl* by combining upstream priority and prescribed calendar dates. For example, the highest-lying area would have the right to use the water starting on a specific day for the duration of several weeks, the next area further down the *wādī* during the following weeks and so forth. Apparently it was felt that in this way, with the relative unpredictability of the *sayl*, the risks as well as the bounty were spread more equitably across the system. Clearly, al-Nāshirī took the natural conditions and established practice among the farmers of the Wādī Zabīd into account when he formulated the new law, that is, he integrated local custom.

The important role of local custom can also be observed in field irrigation in the Wādī Zabīd and it involves a second deviation from the *Sharīʿa*. When water is the limiting factor, one of the fundamental questions concerns how much water the individual farmer is entitled to. According to a regulation that is attributed to the Prophet Muḥammad, his *Sunna*, a field should be submerged to the height of a man's ankle, and then the field bank should be breached to allow irrigation of the next plot in succession. The aforementioned eleventh-century legal authority al-Māwardī points out, however, that this practice is not necessarily binding for everybody at all times and everywhere, since crop requirements, soil, climate and the availability of water differ. He does not consider his cautionary remarks as implying rejection of an explicit rule given in the *Sunna*. Instead, he interprets the rule about ankle-deep irrigation as reflecting the custom of a location where the Prophet Muḥammad settled a conflict over irrigation practices (al-Māwardī 1996: 257). After all, irrigated agriculture did not start with the rise of Islam, but was well-established in pre-Islamic Arabia, for which the oasis of Mārib can serve as a prominent example. Al-Māwardī's remarks are a reflection of the fact that the legal authorities of early Islamic times encountered customary rules of conduct that had been shaped over long centuries in accordance with a specific location's natural conditions and in response to the requirements of a community. It is this situation that is clearly taken into consideration by jurists such as al-Māwardī, even though recognizing local custom as a source of law can be problematic for certain legal experts.[10] For the Wādī Zabīd, the archaeological remains of field banks indicate that knee-deep irrigation was practiced instead of ankle-deep. Figure 6 shows exposed in section a field bank at the side of the Wādī Zabīd that became eventually buried in the rising irrigation sediments. Its construction and function correspond to the field banks described for the ancient oasis of Mārib, whose purpose was also knee-deep submersion of the fields. Given the hot climate, lack of direct rainfall and short duration of the *sayl*, this was the only way of ensuring that sufficient moisture would be stored in the soil to allow a crop to grow to maturity from a single irrigation.

CONCLUSION

From legal documents we know that the new water allocation law in the Wādī Zabīd did not solve all the problems. It was challenged several times. As an example, in 1570 the scholar Kamāl al-Dīn Mūsā ibn Aḥmad al-Dijāʿī completed his work *The Clear Statements about the Infamous Actions Which Happened in the Wādī Zabīd* (Salameh 1999). The author lists twenty such infamous actions, unlawful because they circumvent the water law in place. For instance, case 1 deals with barrages that were extended and made more solid, i.e. more permanent, and would therefore allow to divert more water than a particular primary canal (*sharīj*) was entitled to. A similar kind of manipulation is described in case 2, where the small temporary earth dikes built across a canal to direct the water into a unit of fields were constructed with bricks and mortar, i.e. made

[10] For a detailed overview of the relationship between customary law and *Sharīʿa*, see Donaldson (2000: 42–51).

Fig. 6: Remains of a field bank in section in the Wādī Zabīd (photo: Ingrid Hehmeyer).

permanent and would not allow water to pass to the next unit of fields in succession. Al-Dijāʿī's text is a reminder for everybody involved that the existing water law is binding, and this law is customary law (*ʿurf*).

Each time it was challenged, the water law of the Wādī Zabīd was upheld and apart from minor modifications it has been in use until the present. In the 1970s continuous sedimentation had raised the field levels to a point that made irrigation from the *wādī* impossible. As part of the Tihāma Development Project (completed in 1979), the main irrigation structures were built higher, and this time the diversion barrages and primary canal intakes were made permanent by using concrete instead of earth and stones, while leaving the subsidiary irrigation works and the general layout of the irrigation system largely unchanged. In preparation of the Project, a *Survey of the Agricultural Potential of the Wadi Zabid, Yemen Arab Republic: Land Tenure and Water Rights* was commissioned (Tesco-Viziterv-Vituki 1971).[11] It documented in detail the cycle of traditional water allocation according to the integration of upstream priority and prescribed calendar dates that makes the Wādī Zabīd water law unique in all of Yemen. The work recommended leaving the existing water law unchanged (Tesco-Viziterv-Vituki 1971: vii, 16), and this is what happened to a large extent.

The reason for its overall and long-term success is closely linked to the fact that customary law is shaped by the farmers themselves – in fact, many generations of them – who are intimately familiar with the natural conditions of a site, in the case of the Wādī Zabīd most importantly the variability of the *sayl* with regard to time and volume, and not by a legal authority who is removed from the harsh day-to-day conditions of irrigated agriculture in an arid environment. Or, in the words of Walter Dostal, unlike *Sharīʿa*, customary law is tailored to the specific needs of a group of people (Dostal 1987: 345–46). Its strength is its adaptability "in a very flexible way to changing circumstances" and thus, strictly speaking, it "contrasts sharply with the ideological vision of Islamic law as absolute, trans-historical and immutable" (Dostal 2005: 2).

[11] The main points are summarized in Kopp (1981: 125–28).

REFERENCES

Bosworth, Clifford E. (1978). al-Khazradjī. In: *The Encyclopaedia of Islam (New Edition), 4* (1188b). Leiden: Brill.

Brunner, Ueli (1983). *Die Erforschung der antiken Oase von Mārib mit Hilfe geomorphologischer Untersuchungsmethoden. (Archäologische Berichte aus dem Yemen, 2).* Mainz: Zabern.

Brunner, Ueli (1999). *Jemen: Vom Weihrauch zum Erdöl.* Wien: Böhlau.

Brunner, Ueli (2000). The Great Dam and the Sabean Oasis of Maʾrib. *Irrigation and Drainage Systems, 14*, 167–82.

Brunner, Ueli (2005). The Geography and Economy of the Sabaean Homeland. *Archäologische Berichte aus dem Yemen, 10*, 1–7.

Donaldson, William J. (2000). *Sharecropping in the Yemen: A Study in Islamic Theory, Custom and Pragmatism. (Studies in Islamic Law and Society, 13).* Leiden: Brill.

Dostal, Walter (1987). Traditionelle Wirtschaft und Gesellschaft. In: Werner Daum (ed.), *Jemen: 3000 Jahre Kunst und Kultur des glücklichen Arabien* (331–64). Innsbruck: Pinguin and Frankfurt/Main: Umschau,.

Dostal, Walter (2005). Introduction. In: Walter Dostal & Wolfgang Krauss (eds.). *Shattering Tradition: Custom, Law and the Individual in the Muslim Mediterranean* (1–19). London and New York: Tauris.

Gerlach, Iris (2012). Vorislamische Bewässerungssysteme in der Oase von Mārib, Jemen. In: Florian Klimscha, Ricardo Eichmann, Christof Schuler & Henning Fahlbusch (eds.), *Wasserwirtschaftliche Innovationen im archäologischen Kontext. Von den prähistorischen Anfängen bis zu den Metropolen der Antike. (Menschen–Kulturen–Traditionen: Studien aus den Forschungsclustern des Deutschen Archäologischen Instituts, 5; Forschungscluster 2 – Innovationen: technisch, sozial)* (187–98). Rahden/Westfalen: Leidorf.

al-Hamdānī, al-Ḥasan ibn Aḥmad. *Al-Hamdânî's Geographie der arabischen Halbinsel nach den Handschriften von Berlin, Constantinopel, London, Paris und Strassburg.* 2 vols. (Ed. David Heinrich Müller, 1884–1891, Leiden: Brill).

Hehmeyer, Ingrid & Jürgen Schmidt (1991). *Antike Technologie - Die Sabäische Wasserwirtschaft von Mārib. (Archäologische Berichte aus dem Yemen, 5).* Mainz: Zabern.

Jāzim, Muḥammad ʿAbd al-Raḥīm (ed.). (2008). *Irtifāʿ al-dawla al-Muʾayyadiyya: Jibāyat bilād al-Yaman fī ʿahd al-sulṭān al-Malik al-Muʾayyad Dāwūd b. Yūsuf al-Rasūlī (al-mutawaffā sanat 721h/1321m)/Le Livre des Revenus du sultan rasûlide al-Malik al-Muʾayyad Dâwûd b. Yûsuf (m. 721/1321). (La bibliothèque yéménite/al-Maktaba al-Yamaniyya/Die Jemenitische Bibliothek, 2).* Ṣanʿāʾ: al-Maʿhad al-faransī li-l-āthār wa-l-ʿulūm al-ijtimāʿiyya bi-Ṣanʿāʾ, al-Maʿhad al-almānī li-l-āthār, Ṣanʿāʾ/Centre Français d'Archéologie et de Sciences Sociales, Deutsches Archäologisches Institut, Sanaa Branch.

Keall, Edward J. (2012). Getting to the Bottom of Zabīd: The Canadian Archaeological Mission in Yemen, 1982–2011. *Proceedings of the Seminar for Arabian Studies, 42*, 129–41.

al-Khazrajī, ʿAlī ibn al-Ḥasan. *The Pearl-Strings; A History of the Resúliyy Dynasty of Yemen, by ʿAliyyu ʾbnu ʾl-Ḥasan ʾel-Khazrejiyy.* 5 vols. (Trans. James W. Redhouse, ed. Muḥammad ʿAsal, 1906–1918, Leyden: Brill, London: Luzac).

Kopp, Horst (1981). *Agrargeographie der Arabischen Republik Jemen. (Erlanger Geographische Arbeiten, Sonderband 11).* Erlangen: Fränkische Geographische Gesellschaft.

Kopp, Horst (ed.). (2005). *Länderkunde Jemen.* Wiesbaden: Reichert.

al-Māwardī, ʿAlī ibn Muḥammad. *Al-Ahkam as-Sultaniyyah: The Laws of Islamic Governance.* (Trans. Asadullah Yate, 1996, London: Ta-Ha).

Müller, Walter W. (1983). Altsüdarabische Dokumente. In: Otto Kaiser (ed.), *Texte aus der Umwelt des Alten Testaments, I/3* (268–382). Gütersloh: Mohn.

Müller, Walter W. (1986). Eine Bitte um Regen bei Dürre aus sabäischer Zeit. *Jemen-Report, 17/1*, 10–11.

Müller, Walter W. (1988). Altsüdarabische Rituale und Beschwörungen. In: Otto Kaiser (ed.), *Texte aus der Umwelt des Alten Testaments, II/3* (438–52). Gütersloh: Mohn.

Müller, Walter W. (1991). Mārib. In: *The Encyclopaedia of Islam (New Edition), 6* (559a–67b). Leiden: Brill.

Müller, Walter W. (1999). Die Stele des ʾAbraha, des äthiopischen Königs im Jemen. In: Staatliches Museum für Völkerkunde München (ed.), *Im Land der Königin von Saba. Kunstschätze aus dem antiken Jemen. 7. Juli 1999 - 9. Januar 2000* (268–70). Germering/München: International Publishing.

al-Muqaddasī, Shams al-Dīn Muḥammad ibn Aḥmad. *The Best Divisions for Knowledge of the Regions: A Translation of* Ahsan al-Taqasim fi Maʿrifat al-Aqalim. (Trans. Basil Anthony Collins, 1994, Reading: Garnet).

Nebes, Norbert (2004). A New ʾAbraha Inscription from the Great Dam of Mārib. *Proceedings of the Seminar for Arabian Studies, 34*, 221–30.

Remmele, Gerhard (1989). Die Niederschlagsverhältnisse im Südwesten der arabischen Halbinsel. *Erdkunde, 43*, 27–36.

Salameh, Nadim H. (1995). *Šarīʿa und Gewohnheitsrecht in Zabīd: dargestellt an ausgewählten Fällen zum Wasserrecht aus der Lehrschrift des Muḥammad ibn Ziyād al-Waḍḍāḥī.* M.A. thesis. Johannes Gutenberg-Universität Mainz, Germany.

Salameh, Nadim H. (1999). Customary Water-Rights in Mediaeval Wādī Zabīd: Some Legal Cases on *al-ʿādil bi'l-qanāʿah*. *Proceedings of the Seminar for Arabian Studies, 29*, 137–42.

Schaloske, Michael (1995). *Antike Technologie - Die Sabäische Wasserwirtschaft von Mārib. Teil 3: Untersuchungen der Sabäischen Bewässerungsanlagen in Mārib. (Archäologische Berichte aus dem Yemen, 7).* Mainz: Zabern.

Seipel, Wilfried (ed.) (1998). *Jemen: Kunst und Archäologie im Land der Königin von Sabaʾ*. Vienna: Kunsthistorisches Museum, Milan: Skira.

Tesco-Viziterv-Vituki (1971). *Survey of the Agricultural Potential of the Wadi Zabid, Yemen Arab Republic: Land Tenure and Water Rights. Report prepared for the Food and Agriculture Organization of the United Nations acting as the executing agency for the United Nations Development Programme. (AGL: SF/YEM 1, Technical Report 9).* Budapest. [Unpublished].

Tihama Development Authority Yemen Arab Republic (no date). Wadi Development for Agriculture in Yemen Arab Republic. *Country Papers, 2*, 26–33. [Unpublished].

ʿUmāra al-Yamanī, Najm al-Dīn. *Yaman, its Early Mediaeval History, by Najm ad-Din ʿOmārah al-Ḥakami; also the abridged history of its dynasties by Ibn Khaldūn and an account of the Karmathians of Yaman by Abu ʿAbd Allah Baha ad-Din al-Janadi.* (Ed. and trans. Henry Cassels Kay, 1968 [1892], Farnborough/England: Gregg International [London: Arnold]).

Vallet, Éric (2010). *L'Arabie marchande : état et commerce sous les sultans rasūlides du Yémen (626–858/1229–1454).* Paris: Publications de la Sorbonne.

Varisco, Daniel M. (1983). *Sayl* and *Ghayl*: The Ecology of Water Allocation in Yemen. *Human Ecology, 11*, 365–83.

Varisco, Daniel M. (1989). Medieval Agricultural Texts from Rasulid Yemen. *Manuscripts of the Middle East, 4*, 150–54.

Vogt, Burkhard (2004*a*). Towards a New Dating of the Great Dam of Mārib: Preliminary Results of the 2002 Fieldwork of the German Institute of Archaeology. *Proceedings of the Seminar for Arabian Studies, 34*, 377–88.

Vogt, Burkhard (2004*b*). Grundzüge der antiken südarabischen Bewässerungslandwirtschaft. *Beiträge zur allgemeinen und vergleichenden Archäologie, 24*, 67–104.

Vogt, Burkhard (2005). The Great Dam, Eduardo Glaser and the Chronology of Ancient Irrigation in Maʾrib. In: Amida M. Sholan, Sabina Antonini & Mounir Arbach (eds.), *Sabaean Studies: Archaeological, Epigraphical and Historical Studies in Honour of Yūsuf M. ʿAbdallāh, Alessandro de Maigret and Christian J. Robin on the Occasion of their Sixtieth Birthdays* (501–20). Naples and Ṣanʿāʾ: University of Ṣanʿāʾ, Yemeni-Italian Centre for Archaeological Researches and Centre français d'archéologie et de sciences sociales de Ṣanʿāʾ.

Vogt, Burkhard (2007). Der aktuelle Forschungsstand zum Großen Damm von Marib, Jemen, nach der Winterkampagne 2005/2006. *Zeitschrift für Archäologie Außereuropäischer Kulturen, 2*, 121–42.

BIRKA AND BARAKA: CISTERN AND BLESSING

Notes on Custom and Islamic law regarding public cisterns in Northern Yemen

Eirik Hovden[1]

To collect rainwater during heavy rain and store it in tanks of various sizes for later use is an old traditional technology, which is highly widespread in most of Yemen. The common terms for these cisterns are *birka* (pl. *birak*)[2] and *mājil* (pl. *mawājil*). The water is usually collected during heavy rain by canals that lead it into an open tank dug into the ground. In rural areas these cisterns are a common and basic feature of everyday life yet they have hardly been written about.[3] Because they are so fundamental for domestic water supply in the rural areas in Hajja and elsewhere in Yemen they deserve more attention, both as a partial future solution to the water problems in Yemen and as a local technology and social institution from a historical and ethnographic perspective. The cisterns are connected to local ownership and management systems that are regulated by a mixture of state law, local customary law and Islamic law. In this chapter I will first explain how the cisterns are used and operated in practical terms and then move on to elaborate on how the cisterns are connected to the wider law of *waqf* and other related notions of public property.

The late Professor Walter Dostal was a central figure in the western academic ethnographic tradition on South Arabia. Dostal's works often had a strong material focus but he also looked at local systems of management of resources through institutions, rules and local custom. The present chapter is situated in that tradition of which he was a pioneer.

THE FIELDWORK AND DATA

The data for this chapter was collected during two separate projects. The first was the MA project of the author. Fieldwork was conducted for six months during 2005-2006 in the administrative districts (*mudīriyyāt*) immediately surrounding the city of Hajja (Hajja, Mabyan and Upper and Lower Shiris). The second fieldwork was conducted for the author's PhD project in the Sanaa area and focused more on the legal aspects and especially the institution of *waqf*, although several cisterns were also visited in the field. Most of the data is qualitative and obtained through observation, conversations and the readings of local legal texts together with informants. Most of the informants will remain anonymous here.

---

[1] This chapter is based on parts of the author's MA thesis at the University of Bergen (Norway) from 2006. The thesis was first made available online: https://bora.uib.no/handle/1956/2001 and in 2007 published in a thesis series called "The Lower Jordan River Basin Programme Publications" (Hovden 2007) The fieldwork for the MA was partly sponsored by BKK, Statens Lånekasse and the (now closed) Centre for the Study of the Environment and Resources (SMR). The thesis was supervised by Dr. Frode F. Jacobsen and Dr. Øystein LaBianca. Later fieldwork in the Sanaa area was undertaken as part of the author's PhD project by the support from the Faculty of Humanities, University of Bergen, in the form of a 3-year PhD fellowship and an additional travel grant from the Meltzer Foundation. The PhD thesis was supervised by Dr. Knut S. Vikør and Dr. Anne K. Bang. The support for writing this chapter on the basis of the aforementioned data is provided by the Viscom project (Austrian FWF, SFB) and the Institute for Social Anthropology (ISA), Austrian Academy of Sciences (OeAW). I am grateful for the help and cooperation from the many informants in the field, who cannot all be mentioned by name here. I also thank my collegues here at ISA who read and commented on the draft.

[2] The transliteration for this chapter follows the system of the International Journal of Middle East Studies (IJMES)

[3] Several historians and ethnographers mention the existence of cisterns, but few describe them in detail and usually only the spectacular ones. The first scientific descriptions are probably Rathjens and von Wissmann in the chapter "Die Vorislamischen Zisternen" (Rathjens & Wissmann 1932: 144-158; 1934, and photo no. 19). Eduard Glaser also mentioned and described certain special cisterns he observed during his travels, for example in Kawkaban and the fortress of Thula.(Dostal 1993: 96, 101, 104-5).

The geographical scope of this study is limited to data collected in parts of the governorates (*muḥāfaẓāt*) of Hajja and Sanaa. Since the geographical and cultural context is rather similar in several other governorates, however, these findings can also be relevant to, and with caution, even representative of other parts of highland Yemen. The legal data about *waqf* mainly comes from the Sanaa area, but the same applies there; the legal culture of Zaydi Islamic law has long been present in large parts of the highlands. Shorter trips to other parts of Yemen such as Haraz and Rayma were also undertaken and this complements the wider picture.[4]

THE PRACTICAL SIDE OF THESE CISTERNS

First, we shall have a look at how these cisterns are made and how they are used and function practically. However, before that, we must look closer at the basic geographic context to which these cisterns have been adapted and in which they are used.

The field area for this study includes two distinct geographical/ecological zones of Yemen: the western mountains and the highland plateau. The western mountain region drains westwards through deep wadis onto the coastal plain called Tihama and from there into the Red Sea. The rather flat coastal plain Tihama is distinct in many different ways and not part of the scope of this chapter. In the Western mountains, the relief in the landscape is high and most of the surfaces are steep mountainsides. In the Hajja region, which is a representative example of the Yemen's northern parts of these western mountains, the lowest part is located near the flood bed of Wadi Mawr at around 600 metres above sea level and the highest part is the mountain of Jabal Maswar at 3200 metres above sea level. In the east this zone is an escarpment line including the watershed east of which is the highland plateau zone where the water flows the long way eastward instead of westward, therefore not eroding the landscape in the same way. These highlands consist of plains between 2000 and 2500 metres above sea level with some surrounding mountains.

The western mountains receive most rains in the south around Ibb where irrigation is not necessary and where the average annual precipitation peaks at around 1000 millimetres per year. As one moves north and east the amount of rainfall decreases. It is not only the annual rainfall that is important, but also the timing and character of the rainfall. Most of the rain falls in two seasons - in March-April and in July-August - in the form of very heavy showers or thunderstorms. This means that even in areas where the annual rainfall is fairly low, rainwater will gather on the ground for a short time and totally change the landscape with flowing water and streams forming everywhere. It is these short intense periods, lasting a couple of hours at most, that the traditional water technology is made to harness and capture. The landscape is full of small canals and structures, ready made, leading the water from non-agricultural areas such as roads, barren lands and grazing lands onto agricultural fields and into cisterns where it can be stored. These canals are part of the local ownership system where each agricultural field and each cistern also has its own canals

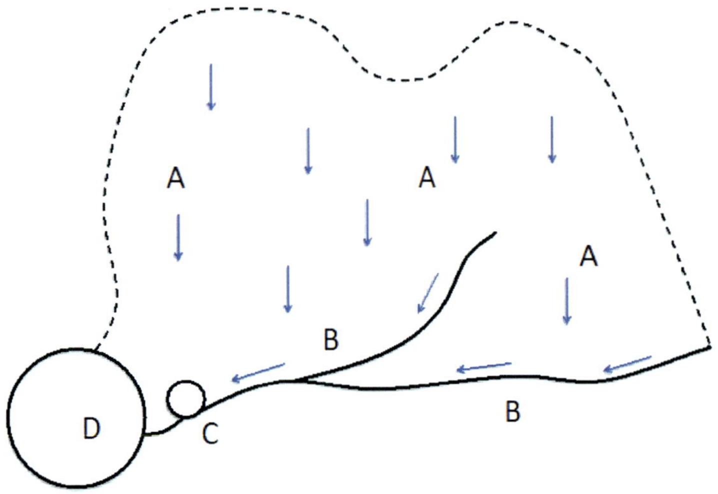

Figure 1: This figure shows the basic components of a cistern seen from above:
A: Catchment area, collection area or runoff area: *Rahaq* (pl. *marāhiq*)
B: Collection canal: *Misqā* (pl. *masāqī*), *Sāqiya*, (pl. *sawāqī*)
C: Settlement basin: *Mishanna*
D: Cistern: *Birka*, *barīk* (pl. *birak*, *buruk*, *barā'ik*), or *mājil*, *ma'jil* (pl. *mawājil*)

[4] Relevant to this study are several trips as a tourist in Yemen. As a researcher, I was also part of the yearly Joint Royal Ontario Museum-Ryerson University Yemen Project, in al-Jabin, in January 2010. Project Director is Dr. Ingrid Hehmeyer.

and its own rainwater harvesting areas (runoff area, collection area, catchment area). We shall return to this in more detail below.

In a narrow sense, a cistern is a tank for storing water. But a rainwater harvesting cistern is something more: it is a system designed also to fill the cistern during rain. Most cisterns described in this chapter are of the type that covers both functions: the collection of rainwater and storing it for later use.

The terminology is important. In local Arabic, the catchment area, the collection area or the runoff area is called *rahaq*[5], pl. *marāhiq*. The runoff itself - that is, the water that forms on the ground during heavy rain - is called *maṣabb* or simply *mā'* or *mayy* (water). The canal along the lower limit of the runoff area is called *misqā*[6] (pl. *masāqī*). This canal acts like a roof gutter where the roof is the collection area and the *misqā* collects the water along the lower edge. In many cases this canal really defines the physical extent of the whole runoff area and not only the lower limit because often there is another runoff area below it, belonging to another field or cistern located below. The *misqā* of the upper cistern marks the upper border of the runoff area of the lower cistern. In matters of border disputes or conflicts the *misqā* is an important defining physical structure; otherwise, the *rahaq* (collection area) is not always entirely delimited in absolute spatial terms. If there is no *misqā* above, the *rahaq* extends all the way up the mountain covering the natural watershed draining towards the *misqā*, as indicated in the figure above. Another name for the collection canal is *sāqiya* (pl. *sawāqī*), especially for a larger canal. Sometimes the water flows through a natural formation such as a gorge (*shuʿb*) rather than a man-made canal. The canal itself can have several additional functional details such as a *masqaṭ* or a *miʿqad,* which is a drop in the canal secured by rocks so that the water does not erode the canal. The inclination of the canal is usually carefully planned. It must not be so steep that the water erodes too much and not so flat that the canal silts up and fills with sand. Where the canal enters the cistern, one usually finds a small basin large enough for the water to slow down so that the sand sinks down and stops there before the water flows into the cistern. In technical English this structure would be called a "settlement basin"; in local language it is called a *mishanna*, a "sift".

The function of all these components and the balance between them was widespread common knowledge in the countryside. When asked, most men would know how all this worked. Clearly, many of the men who showed me around in their villages found these structures and their function and the maintenance of them so self-evident that this knowledge does not lend itself to strict ethnographic transcription or recording into text; it was not something that was readily available as textual knowledge, rather it was tacit, and it seemed to be embodied in practices and memories, and tied to specific localities and cisterns. In the cities and among the younger generation, however, hardly anyone had any knowledge about the topic. Needless to say, cisterns are by many seen as backward and undesirable as a water source compared to modern piped systems, and indeed its usage is mainly related to the poorer segments of the population. Biological contamination is a severe challenge, but we shall not focus on that here.

AGRICULTURAL AND DOMESTIC NEEDS

Both the western mountains and the highlands have been densely populated since ancient times due to the relatively favourable conditions for agriculture. In the western mountains most of the population live on the upper slopes and ridges of mountains. In terms of water technologies, the western mountains have the most spectacular man-made structures: the agricultural terraces. Sometimes they start all the way down in the wadi, continuing in series up to the highest mountains. These terraces are of fundamental importance: they prevent erosion and secure enough soil depth to store humidity for a sufficient time between sporadic rainfalls (Rappold 2004).[7] In some areas irrigation is added in the form of spring-fed systems (Varisco 1982, 1983) or some supplementary runoff/run-on systems where non-agricultural areas, such as mountain sides or grazing lands, are connected to the terraces with canals leading the rainwater runoff onto them (Eger 1984,

[5] This term was used in the Sanaa area and is well known in the highlands. In local Yemeni highland dialect the letter *qāf* is pronounced as a "g" in English "golf"; "*rahag*" and "*masgā*".

[6] Usually pronounced *masgā*

[7] See also the cross section of such terracing in Gingrich & Heiss (198: 44).

1986; Rappold 2004; Gingrich 1994). Down in the wadis, groundwater can easily be found in shallow wells in the flood bed, but transportation up the mountain is costly, be it in form of pipe systems or by the use of water trucks. It is important to point out that in the western mountains, little or no groundwater is found on the mountain-tops and ridges, where most of the population live. It is therefore in these settlements that the use of rainwater harvesting cisterns is still most commonly found.

In the highland plains, wells have always been more common than rainwater harvesting cisterns due to the relative ease of access to groundwater through wells[8]. Cisterns were rather used in more remote areas along the roads for travellers or livestock, or in places where the groundwater was too deep down. In this region, the use of deep groundwater wells has to a large extent replaced the use of runoff-based systems and old wells. (Al-Hamdi 2000; Lichtenthäler 2003). However, in the more marginal and hilly parts of the highlands the runoff/run-on systems are still used and the *masāqī* are still an important and defining feature, serving as border-markers. Eger provides a good description of such traditional systems in the ʿAmrān and Bawn areas, explaining how such a system worked both in the plains and in the more hilly parts (Eger 1984, 1986). For the Sa'da plain, a comprehensive analysis was made by Gerhard Lichtenthäler in which he described the shift from the traditional system of land and water use with runoff/run-on systems to the modern one based on deep drilled wells (Lichtenthäler 2003). For the western Khawlan al-Sham mountains, see also Gingrich (1994) for slope runoff and terrace irrigation.

In the western mountains the high cost and challenges related to transportation from the lower parts of the landscape to the upper parts makes the old technology still very much used, especially among the many poor. So far, we have talked mostly about water supply for agriculture, but the main use of cisterns has always been the supply of water for domestic use and for the animals in the village. Most cisterns are situated around the villages at the nearest, most practical distance, even if below the village. But some are also situated far away for the use for herders watering the livestock or along roads for travellers.[9] Before the advent of pipes and water trucks, the water would have to be carried from the cistern to the house and thus the walking distance would be part of the daily usage of the cistern. In the lower half of the landscape it is possible to make wells or use small springs; however, in the upper parts of the landscape, there is no groundwater and cisterns are often the only reliable, practical and affordable source of water. It is usually the women's responsibility to collect water from the cisterns and carry it home in containers. It is needless to say that the water consumption is minimal. Water is needed for drinking, cooking, washing and for the animals. Livestock can be herded to the water sources, but cows for milk are often kept inside the village. The whole matter of water usage inside the village very much belongs to the local culture of the women. The knowledge and attitudes toward water quality and quantity and the perceptions of problems and priorities is a highly important topic, but one that cannot be given place here.

In the Hajja area a rainwater harvesting cistern is called a *birka*, while in the Sanaa area it is called a *mājil* (classical Arabic: *ma'jil*, pl. *mawājil*). In Hajja a *mājil* is the special type of cistern which is not made to store rainwater, but rather to accumulate water coming from a spring and therefore it has no *misqā* or collection area attached to it.[10]

[8] For the functions of typical traditional wells see (Gingrich & Heiss 1986: 31-39) and (Lewcock 2013: 301-302)

[9] Cisterns along the old traditional roads are often found together with a shelter, a so-called *saqīf* (Höhfeld 1978). If the cistern is small, or simply a basin filled artificially by water-skins or the trickle from a spring they are rather called a *siqāya*. Typically, these would be closed structures with small openings or doors so that animals could not drink directly from them and thereby pollute the water. Such a public structure is also called a *sabīl* (pl. *asbila* or *subul*) or simply *qubba*, ("dome") from the domed roof often found in elaborate examples near the cities. A more abstract Islamic terminology is *maḥsana*, pl. *maḥāsin* and the term *manhal*, pl. *manāhil* is also frequently used in Zaydi Islamic legal texts. Walter Dostal made a comprehensive list over the *sabīls* in the market of Sanaa. (Dostal 1979: 114)

[10] Usually springs only give a tiny trickle of water and if it is led into traditional canals, the water would not reach far before it would seep into the ground. Therefore it is accumulated in a cistern (here: *mājil*) situated as near the spring as possible. When the cistern is full, say after a day, a hole near the bottom of the cistern is poked open by using a long stick and the water is led through canals to nearby fields. This system of spring water usage was the main topic of the PhD thesis of Daniel Varisco in which he described how this system worked in the valley of al-Ahjur, south of Hajja and west of Sanaa (Varisco 1982: 206-208). Today, the water in these cisterns is transported by pipes, thus making it possible to irrigate fields much farther away than in crude gravity-fed earth canals.

HOW THE CISTERNS ARE BUILT

The cisterns are usually situated in places that water can naturally reach by gravity. However, on steep mountainsides, the actual site of the cistern is often dug and hewn out of the bedrock and a supporting wall on the outer side is also common. Additional masonry is used to make the walls of the cistern as smooth as possible before plastering. Then the cistern is plastered with a thick layer of the traditional cement called *qaḍāḍ*.

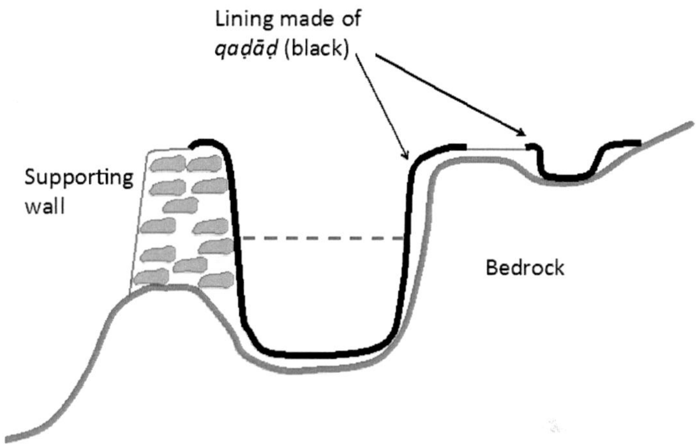

Figure 2: This figure shows the cross section of a cistern situated in steeply inclined terrain where the outer wall is supported by masonry. The watertight layer of plaster called *qaḍāḍ* is seen here in black. Under the plaster is a layer of smooth masonry made of small stones, not shown here, which the plaster adheres to.

Qaḍāḍ is made from nūra which is a powder-like substance made from limestone fired in kilns (*manwar*). In older times the *nūra* was made locally. Informants in Hajja showed me several such local kilns where the lime was burned in the past. In addition to the lime, aggregate in the form of crushed rock is added. In the Sanaa area, volcanic cinders are also used. The importance of this layer of watertight plaster cannot be overstated; without this layer, the water would seep into the ground and quickly disappear. The same is the case if cracks appear in the plastering. This could naturally occur over time with long term wear or slight settlements in the ground or the foundation of the cistern. The water itself also slowly dissolves the surface of the *qaḍāḍ*, especially in the lower part of the cistern that is in contact with water most of the time. If cracks occur, a new layer of *qaḍāḍ* is added. This is something easily visible in many old cisterns; over time they have been replastered several times. The work involved in preparing the *qaḍāḍ* and applying it is very laborious and takes a long time. Therefore this traditional material was no longer used after the introduction of modern cement after the civil war (from the early 1970s). Many informants commented that the old *qaḍāḍ* and the new type of cement did not adhere properly to each other, creating problems after a short time. However, few if any had seen the use of traditional *qaḍāḍ* in recent decades. Most older men still remembered how the *qaḍāḍ* was prepared and applied and all commented on the superior quality. Today, several restoration projects involving historical buildings elsewhere in Yemen have ensured the continued local knowledge of how to use the *qaḍāḍ* starting in the 1990s with the restoration of the Amiriyya in Radāʿ supervised by Selma al-Radi (Al-Radi 1997, 1994). Later, several other restoration projects have been undertaken using *qaḍāḍ*, including cisterns.[11] I interviewed one group who specialized in this work and saw how they used this material when making a new roof in Sanaa. According to them, cistern lining was made the same way, just with a thicker layer. It is also more demanding to work on a vertical surface than a horizontal one, since one must keep the *qaḍāḍ* just dry enough for it not to slip off the cistern wall while applying it. The work involves heavy mixing of *nūra* and aggregate for a long time and especially the application itself is very laborious since the *qaḍād* is beaten with a fist-size rock for several days until it hardens. This way more *qaḍāḍ* can be applied as the first layer hardens, thus merging the two, and it also ensures that the *qaḍāḍ* adheres properly to the underlying surface. *Qaḍāḍ* used for building details on houses and mosques is often polished several times and a layer of animal

[11] For example, the large cistern belonging to the mosque at Kawkabān. The Social Fund for Development has funded several such restorations, emphasizing the use of *qaḍāḍ* and local knowledge in the restoration. One such project is the one recently undertaken at al-Jabīn, Muḥāfaẓat Rayma under the leadership of Dr. Ingrid Hehmeyer (The joint Royal Ontario Museum-Ryerson University, Yemen Project in al-Jabin, Project Director Dr. Ingrid Hehmeyer.)

Figure 3: This is an old cistern where one can easily see how the *qaḍāḍ* has worn away near the bottom. The cistern was leaking and in need of re-plastering. (Photo: E. Hovden)

fat is added to make it waterproof.[12] Cisterns usually did not get this final polish, but in several places one can observe a thin layer of *nūra* added at the end with decorative continuous figure-8 shaped strokes.[13]

Since the 1970s new materials and technologies were introduced and these created a new pattern where old and new technologies are combined. Car roads and water trucks can transport water in the landscape over large distances; however, at relatively high cost. Pipes and plastic hoses can convey water for shorter distances and small portable pumps can decrease the need for gravity.

Most cisterns are open and without a roof and this seems to be the rule in the western mountains. One noticeable exception to this was seen in a visit to the area of Mudīriyyat Banī Ismāʿīl in Harāz, Governorate of Sanaa, where the majority of cisterns were covered with corbelled dome structures. These cisterns also tended to be privately owned and they had small wooden doors which could be easily locked (Hovden 2006: 142-145). The same is the case in nearby al-Maḥwīṭ, a short distance to the north (Tutwiler 1987).[14]

A series of agricultural terraces can use the same runoff area, but this is rarer for cisterns. However, once the cistern is full, the water might flow to a second cistern or a nearby field and in some cases they may share the same runoff area.

[12] This group was working on the roof the house of Mr. Sarbi Saleem and supervised by engineer al-Hadrami.

[13] For one such photo see (Hovden 2006: 75-86). See also page 11 in (Vision Hope International). Here one can see the same pattern for decorative purposes even in a cistern plastered with cement. For an article on the discovery and analysis of magic signs as rain invocations inscribed in a cistern wall, see (Hehmeyer 2008).

[14] Both these contradictory cases seem to have been in areas of lower altitude. Perhaps the functional need for a roof is greater in low-lying areas where the temperature is higher, the relative humidity is lower and evaporation rates are thus higher. Indeed the yearly evaporation from an open body of water can be significant in such small tanks.

THE MAINTENANCE OF CISTERNS

We can distinguish between three forms of maintenance. The first is the daily care when using the cistern and making sure that the canals leading to it are not damaged. If they are, they will not lead enough water to the cistern. For some, keeping the catchment area clean and tidy is important, and making sure that some cisterns are not used for swimming in, etc. This type of care and maintenance is just part of local village behaviour and morality and there is no occasion specially assigned for these practices. If the cistern has just filled, perhaps the settlement basin (*mishanna*) may need cleaning out.

The second "degree" of maintenance is the yearly maintenance related to cleaning out the cistern. Ideally, the cisterns should be emptied out completely and the clay that settles on the bottom should be removed. This normally occurs in wintertime when most or all of the water has been used up, just before the next year's rainy season. If the cistern is large, this work can be laborious and a communal work day (*jāyish*) is organized. How and to what extent this is done is very different from village to village. Some keep record of which family has contributed what, and allow those who are absent to pay for their missed share of the workload. If this yearly maintenance is carried out, then this is also a strong confirmation of the communal status of the cistern.

A third degree of maintenance is major repair of the structure of the cistern in the form of re-plastering or other significant repairs. This is a very expensive undertaking. It is easy not to see this when looking at a cistern in daily use, because since the cisterns are usually so sturdily built, they can easily last 100 years without needing repair or restoration. But eventually, a larger repair is necessary. If a crack develops, perhaps that crack can be repaired, but since the *qaḍāḍ* is exposed to water and slowly dissolves, eventually the whole cistern needs restoration, after which it can last for another long cycle of low maintenance use. The act of restoration is one where the ownership status of the cistern really comes to the foreground and is tested; the *waqf* documents I have seen (from the Sanaa area) relate to this stage in a cistern's life. Sometimes the restoration is so large that it is almost a rebuilding, and often new components are added. Either the village has to raise the funds necessary and share the costs, or one or more individuals pay for the restoration by emphasizing that the cistern remains public, but that the restoration is a charitable donation. In Islamic law, such a donation is rewarded by religious merit; from a social science perspective, the cultural and social capital involved in performing this act of charity towards the local community is significant. Almost as a side effect, this restoration or upgrading of the cistern also automatically becomes *waqf*, if the cistern originally is *waqf*. (Ibn Miftāḥ 2003, 8: 223-224; al-ʿAnsī, 3: 306; Qāsim b. Ibrāhīm, ʿAlī b. ʿAbd Allāh al-Ānisī, and ʿAbd Allāh b. Muḥammad al-Sarḥī 1986: 150) The question of whether or not a specific cistern is *waqf* does not always have a clear cut answer, something we shall try to elaborate below.

THE LEGAL FRAMEWORK AROUND A CISTERN

Who owns a cistern, and who manages it and repairs it? If we start with the basics, we must first think of cisterns as stationary objects very much like houses or agricultural fields. In Yemen there is a long tradition of ownership law consisting of a mix of customary and Islamic law that only recently has been codified into modern state law. It is important to point out that this mix is still used and can vary from place to place and even case to case, but at the same time it is not true that these are three separate, parallel legal systems which the actors can freely choose between. Brinkley Messick has written extensively about how Islamic law was used in ownership contracts and other sorts of transactions where rights and access to property changes hands between individual in sales, leases, *waqf*, and inheritance. The basic notion of property is called *milk* (Messick 1983, 1989, 1993, 1995, 2003). Although Messick describes the city of Ibb, which is located much further south, we can still expect the basics to be the same. The field study in Hajja did not include collection and analysis of ownership documents,[15] only structured conversations regarding the ownership of the cisterns. The fieldwork in Sanaa however, included the collection and analysis of *waqf* documents and cases (Hovden 2011).

The cisterns could thus have been private objects (*milk*) like the agricultural plots of land or houses. However, during the fieldwork in Hajja it became clear that most cisterns, and certainly the old, traditional

[15] For a study of older ownership documents from Hajja, see: (Volle 1984).

ones were public (ʾāmm, *mushtarak, mushāʿ*) to the village as a unit.[16] The fact that private ownership is a well-developed concept does not mean that all non-state property is privately owned. On the contrary, large parts of the landscape are "public", but not necessarily public as in "state owned". Actually, there is a basic assumption that unless stated, a thing or a plot of land is not "owned" and that it is only owned if it is in active use or claimed by someone. Most objects of value such as plots of land or houses are also represented by written ownership documents.

What is important to bear in mind is that the landscape is full of "owned" objects, i.e. private in our terms, but that the "base layer" is "unowned". This is not "public" in the sense that it is state property, but rather "*mushāʿ*" in the sense that it is communally owned and controlled. If someone wants to make a new cistern or agricultural field in communal grazing lands (*iḥyāʾ al-mawāt*: revival of barren lands, or *taḥjīr*: "demarcation"), then this is allowed and regulated in Islamic law as long as the plot is demarcated (*taḥjīr*) and the community is given three years to protest. If no one protests within three years, the unowned land (*mushāʿ*) becomes (private) property (*milk*).[17]

The communal level is often the level of the tribe or a sub-tribe when talking about grazing lands, but since the cisterns are usually clustered around villages, they are "*mushāʿ*" (communal) for the village as a unit, not for the tribe or other regional forms of communities. An exception here is certain cisterns located far away from a village, but even so, there is often one village or one family who has the responsibility for it (I will come back to this family responsibility for communal property below).

A recent change, as already mentioned, is the increase in the number of fully private cisterns in the western mountains. Many of these are new or newly restored old ones. These are privately owned just as private plots of agricultural land and are often owned together with the customary runoff rights. Often, these are used for qāt irrigation.

There are different words that can be used by informants to indicate that something is "public" or "common" or "communal". Some of them are referring to modern legal discourse, others to Islamic law, others to local custom. Many of these words are the same in all three discourses. Some words are less accurate and more general, such as the word "ʿāmm" meaning "public" or "general", in binary opposition to "*khāṣṣ*", meaning "private" or "special". The meaning of such words must in any case be related to the context and the specific strategies in which they are used and it is important to bear in mind that such terms are never fully neutral and objective. In one village, the inhabitants may be cautious in defining their communal cisterns as "public" because they might have had a legal conflict with the state. The same applies to the term "*waqf*", which in general Islamic terms only implies that the cistern is unowned and for public use; the inhabitants might fear that the Ministry of *Awqāf* would claim the right to administer them. Thus the word heard in a conversation in the field from one informant alone in the morning might be disputed or disagreed upon in a group discussion with the men of the village later during the same day. By keeping the status of the cistern ambiguous, the local inhabitants avoid limiting later opportunities to sell the plot or otherwise change its status. Often, there are ongoing conflicts, where some families claim that a certain cistern is actually theirs, but that they are just letting the poor in the village use it. If there are no documents, the legal status cannot be proved.

It is important to bear in mind that although a cistern in a narrow sense is only the tank where water is stored and perhaps the immediate structures surrounding it, such as a fence or a trough for watering animals, in a wider sense, however, a cistern also includes its collection canal and its runoff area, all belonging together as a system not only in practical terms but also legally. These units can of course be split up and separated from the cistern, but if so, the cistern would be cut off from its water supply and the original purpose of the cistern would cease to exist.

This is a complicated issue: every cistern needs a sufficient runoff area (*rahaq*) in order to function as a rainwater collecting cistern. Both agricultural lands and cisterns can have runoff areas attached to them, and especially in areas of low rainfall, where the size and quality of this area would have a lot to say for the value of the cistern/plot. Much of this runoff area is defined by the canal that leads the water in the lower

---

[16] But one noticeable exception was a visit to Banī Ismāʿīl in Haraz, where most cisterns were private. (Hovden 2006, 140-43) 140-43. The same was noted by Tutwiler in al-Mahwit in lower areas. (Tutwiler 1987: 87) and an example can also be seen in Gingrich (1994: 109)

[17] (Hovden 2011: 372; *Qānūn al-Madanī [2002]* 2008, article 1242-1253; Ibn Miftāḥ 2003, 7: 337-357)

end of the area into the cistern. Customary law stipulates that all the natural runoff that leads to a cistern is a "right" that belongs to it, so even if the actual runoff area to the cistern is located in communal (village or tribal) grazing lands, the right to fill the cistern with water from that area is still a legal right (usufruct, easement) belonging to the cistern, even if that grazing area is not owned by the cistern. The right is *rahaq*, the right to the runoff water from a certain area, but not to other usages of the land. This is not a problem as long as the grazing area is only used for grazing; however, if part of that area is sold to someone else for making an agricultural plot of land or building another private cistern inside it, then this would lead to less water reaching the first cistern. The owner of the first cistern, be it an individual or a community, can legally refuse this, or at least demand a compensation. Several informants claim that there are many conflicts over such issues because the ownership status of the various assets is not entirely defined, nor is the exact monetary value of these. According to the administrative leader of the appeal court of the governorate of Rayma, the disputes over runoff rights in relation to building new cisterns was one of the types of conflicts occurring most frequently in the appeal court there.[18]

The physical area that the cistern occupies represents much of the short-term monetary value of such a cistern and the water rights it has, especially if it is located in an area where agricultural intensification is possible, or in an area of urban growth where land value is high. If the village decides to sell the cistern to a private individual there are different models for how to share the communal value of the cistern and its water rights. It can, for example, be divided equally among the inhabitants in the village or among the households. If one village wants to sell some of its grazing lands located below the village, they might have to pay compensation to the village below since the village below probably has runoff rights to the land above their village.

HOW MANY CISTERNS ARE WAQF?

The history of the institution of *waqf* (pl. *awqāf*) is a long and rich one, both as a topic for Islamic jurisprudence and law and as a local way to manage public property. *Waqf* means that someone donates something he owns for the purpose of welfare or charity as a pious act. The control and management of that asset is then either given to public authority, or to a member of one's family. In practice the position as trustee is inherited, or at least follows the male line. Various Zaydi imams and other governments have throughout history sought to gather *waqf* assets and included them into their administrational system, appointing local *waqf* administrators to carry out the leases of *waqf* land and to make sure the assets are managed well. Most of the infrastructure was mosques, but water supply, schools, support for the poor and several other services were also provided through the institution of *waqf*, especially in urban areas. The bulk of income came from local holdings of land being leased to local farmers in long term sharecropping agreements. The distinction between private and public *waqf* is not a clear-cut one in Yemen and *waqf*s for a public purpose could also be privately administrated and held outside the governmental administration system, since this is legal according to Islamic law as long as the founders follow certain rules. In Yemen these tend to be called *waṣāyā* from the word for "testament" (in the singular form: *waṣīya*) (Hovden 2011; Mijallī 2002; Serjeant & al-ʿAmrī 1983: 151-154).

As already mentioned, there is a strong reluctance among people to use the term *waqf* when asking them about local legal issues in the village. Words can have implications, especially if found as text on paper. Quite a few cisterns are *waqf* if by *waqf* we mean those assets administered by the Ministry of *Awqāf* or its related local structures of administration. Certainly, all cisterns that are attached to mosques are *waqf*. But there are other types of *waqf* in Yemen that are not directly controlled by the Ministry of *Awqāf* and our knowledge about these is unfortunately still not sufficient. Because of the legal tensions over who should control these assets, we are most probably not going to see exact figures in the near future. Thus a very common reason for not upholding the *waqf* status of a cistern is that in such a case,[19] the *Ministry of Awqāf* would have rights and not only the inhabitants of the village itself.

If we look back to the more practical aspects of taking care of a cistern we remember that most cisterns do not need much maintenance for long periods at a time; however, major repairs are very costly even if they are seldom needed and rare. When some individuals donate plots of land for the upkeep of a specific cistern,

[18] Personal communication, al-Jabin, Rayma, January 2010

[19] For the complexities of one such case see (Hovden 2011: 422-343)

this act is *waqf* and in Yemen they are usually called *waṣāyā* just as most privately administered *waqf*s. In this case it is the land that has *waqf* status and not necessarily the cistern itself. These *waṣāyā* usually follow the line of the eldest son. That means that if he and his family take care of the cistern and occasionally repair it, he will be paid for that work from that special *waqf/waṣāyā*, or in more practical terms, he will be given the whole access to the agricultural land that was given as *waqf* to the cistern. If more land is given to a cistern than the actual expenses are over time, holding such a *waṣāyā* can be quite lucrative and it can be seen as a way to circumvent the ban on family *waqf* - a topic which has several times been raised in Zaydi Yemeni history. However, the manager of that *waṣīya* (*mutawallī*, trustee, guardian) would have to pay a quite large sum if he actually has to repair the cistern, although in reality the public control of such *waṣāyā* was often weak.[20] This type of *waqf* seems to have been common and this in-between status between family *waqf* and charitable *waqf* thus merges with the notion of communal ownership of the cistern and the private charity of taking care of it (Hovden 2011).

Despite new technologies and new technical solutions is it clear that rainwater harvesting will remain important in Yemen's future.[21] Cisterns are complex structures, not only technologically, but also in that they involve local custom and local forms of Islamic law. In this chapter I have given a very generalized overview, which undoubtedly should, and hopefully will, be more specified and contextualized by others. We need basic ethnography of local resources management, such as water management, both in the practical aspects and its normative sides in addition to the development of technical solutions to the water crisis. The study of custom and Islamic law in very local contexts poses great methodological challenges, which could not be fully discussed here, but the interdisciplinary perspective in these issues cannot be overemphasized, and ethnography must necessary have a strong role to play. There will be new management challenges and conflicts related to any new technological invention. Looking at the past and at local culture we can learn important lessons about how to adapt to a situation of marginal resources.

According to an ideal level of Islamic law, water cannot be owned by man; it is a blessing (*baraka*) from God which is public for everyone, be it water from a spring or rainwater. On a more pragmatic level though, Islamic law allows for the collection and containment of water by the use of private structures and containers in which the water becomes private, such as in a cistern (*birka*). However, by making the water available for those in need, the blessing (*baraka*) recurs.

REFERENCES

Dostal, Walter (1979). *Der Markt von Ṣanʿāʾ*. Vienna: Verlag der Österreichischen Akademie der Wissenschaften.

Dostal, Walter (1993). *Ethnographica Jemenica: Auszüge aus den Tagebüchern Eduard Glasers mit einem Kommentar versehen*. Wien: Verlag der Österreichischen Akademie der Wissenschaften.

Eger, Helmut (1984). Rainwater Harvesting in the Yemeni Highlands. *Jemen Studien: Entwicklungsprozesse in der Arabischen Republik Jemen, 1,* 147-194.

Eger, Helmut (1986). Runoff agriculture: A case study about the Yemeni highlands. PhD thesis, Eberhard-Karls-Universität Tübingen.

Gingrich, Andre (1994). *Südwestarabische Sternenkalender: Eine ethnologische Studie zu Struktur, Kontext und regionalem Vergleich des tribalen Agrarkalenders der Munebbih im Jemen. Wiener Beiträge zur Ethnologie und Anthropologie.* Wien: WUV-Universitätsverlag.

Gingrich, Andre & Heiss, Johann (1986). *Beiträge zur Ethnographie der Provinz Ṣaʿda (Nordjemen).* Wien: Verlag der Österreichischen Akademie der Wissenschaften.

Al-Hamdi, Mohamed I. (2000). *Competition for scarce groundwater in the Sanaʿa Plain, Yemen: a study on the incentive systems for urban and agricultural water use*. Rotterdam: A. A. Balkema.

Hehmeyer, Ingrid (2008). Water and sign magic in al-Jabin, Yemen. *The American Journal of Islamic Social Sciences, 25(3),* 82-96.

[20] This is one of the reasons why office of the "Inspector of the *waṣāyā*" was created roughly hundred years ago. (Hovden 2011: 173-74)

[21] The Social Fund for Development (SFD) invests heavily in cisterns: http://sfd.sfd-yemen.org/category/5

Hovden, Eirik (2006). *Rainwater harvesting cisterns and local water management: A qualitative geographical / socio-anthropological case study and ethnographic description from the districts of Hajja, Mabyan and Shiris*, MA in water resources and coastal management, Institutt for biologi, University of Bergen. [Online version: bora.uib.no/handle/1956/2001].

Hovden, Eirik (2007). *Rainwater harvesting and local water management. Vol. 15, The Lower Jordan River Basin Programme Publications*. Birzeit Univeristy – Bergen University.

Hovden, Eirik (2011). *Flowers in Fiqh and constructions of validity: Practices and norms in Yemeni foundations of forever flowing charity*, Unpublished PhD thesis, Institute for Archaeology, History, Cultural Studies and Religion (AHKR), Faculty of Humanities, University of Bergen.

Höhfeld, V. (1978). Saqīf. Ein Element der Jemenitischen Kulturlandschaft. In: H. Becker and H. Kopp (Eds.). *Resultate Aktueller Jemen-Forschung: Eine Zwischenbilanz*. Bamberg.

Ibn Miftāḥ, ʿAbd Allāh Abū al-Ḥasan (2003/1472). al-Muntaziʿ al-mukhtār min al-ghayth al-midrār al-maʿrūf bi Sharḥ al-azhār. Sanaa: Wizārat al-ʿAdl / Maktabat al-Turāth al-Islāmī.

Lewcock, Ronald (2013). Chapter 15: The Buildings of the Sūq/Market. In: R. B. Serjeant and R. Lewcock (Eds.). *Ṣanʿāʾ An Arabian Islamic City*. Mesliende. [First published as The World of Islamic Festival Trust, 1983].

Lichtenthäler, Gerhard (2003). *Political Ecology and the Role of Water: Environment, Society and Economy in Northern Yemen*. Aldershot: Ashgate.

Messick, Brinkley (1983). Prosecution in Yemen: The Introduction of the Niyaba. *International Journal of Middle East Studies, 15*, 507-518.

Messick, Brinkley (1989). Just Writing: Paradox and Political Economy in Yemeni Legal Documents. *Cultural Anthropology, 4(1)*, 26-50.

Messick, Brinkley (1993). *The Calligraphic State: Textual Domination and History in a Muslim Society*. Berkeley: University of California Press.

Messick, Brinkley (1995). Textual Properties: Writing and Wealth in a Shari'a Case. *Anthropological Quarterly, 68(3)*, 157-170.

Messick, Brinkley (2003). Property and the Private in a Sharia System. *Social Research, 70(3)*, 711-734.

Mijallī, Ḥasan ʿAlī. (2002). *al-Awqāf fī l-Yaman: al-Itār al-sharʿī wa-l-qānūnī li-l-waqf wa-maqāṣidihi al-ʿāmma wa-tārīkh al-waqf wa-dawrihi al-iqtiṣādī wa-l-ijtimāʿī*. Sanaa: Maktabat Khalid b. al-Walīd.

Qānūn al-Madanī (2008). 2. Edition. Ṣanʿāʾ: Wizārat al-Shuʾūn al-Qānūniyya.

Qāsim b. Ibrāhīm, ʿAlī b. ʿAbd Allāh al-Ānisī & ʿAbd Allāh b. Muḥammad al-Sarḥī. (1986). *Kitāb taysīr al-marām fī masāʾil al-aḥkām li-l-bāḥithīn wa-l-ḥukkām*. Manshūrāt al-Madīna.

Al-Radi, Selma (1994). Qudad, The Traditional Yemeni Plaster. *Yemen Update, 34*.

Al-Radi, Selma (1997). *The ‚Amiriya in Rada': The history and restoration of a sixteenth century madrasa in the Yemen*. Oxford: Oxford University Press.

Rappold, Gerhard D. (2004). *Hydrological Analysis for Agricultural Water Availability in a Semi-Arid Terraced Catchment. A Case Study from Ta'izz, Yemen, Geography*. Berlin: Die Freie Universität Berlin.

Rathjens, Carl & Wissmann, Hermann (1932). *Vorislamische Altertümer: Rathjens -v. Wissmannsche Südarabien-Reise 2. Abhandlungen aus dem Gebiet der Auslandskunde Band 38 - Reihe B. Völkerkunde, Kulturgeschichte und Sprachen Band 19*. Hamburg: Friederichsen, De Gruyter & Co. M. B. H.

Rathjens, Carl & Wissmann, Hermann (1934). *Landeskundliche Ergebnisse: Rathjens -v. Wissmannsche Südarabien-Reise 3. Vol. 3, Abhandlungen aus dem Gebiet der Auslandskunde Band 40 - Reihe B. Völkerkunde, Kulturgeschichte und Sprachen Band 20*. Hamburg.

Serjeant, R. B. & al-ʿAmrī, Ḥusayn (1983). Chapter 11: Administrative Organisation. In: R. B. Serjeant and R. Lewcock (Eds.). *Ṣanʿāʾ An Arabian Islamic City*. London: The World of Islamic Festival Trust.

Tutwiler, R. Richard Neel (1987). *Tribe, tribute, and trade: Social class formation in highland Yemen*. Unpublished PhD thesis, State University of New York, Binghamton.

Varisco, Daniel Martin (1982). *The adaptive dynamics of water allocation in Al-Ahjur, Yemen Arab Republic*. PhD thesis, University of Pennsylvania.

Varisco, Daniel Martin (1983). Sayl and Ghayl: The Ecology of Water Allocation in Yemen. *Human Ecology, 11(4)*.

Vision Hope International. Annual Report 2008. [http://vision-hope.org/annual-reports.html](Last accessed: June 2013).

Volle, Elena (1984). Ein Dokumentenfund aus Mabyan/ad-Danub. *Entwicklungsprozesse in der Arabischen Republik Jemen, 1*, 249-259.

al-ʿAnsī, Aḥmad b. Qāsim al-Yamānī al-Sanʿānī. *al-Tāj al-mudhhab li-aḥkām al-madhhab*. 4 Vols. Sanʿāʾ: Maktabat al-Yaman al-Kubrā.

CULTURAL HERITAGE AND IDENTITY POLITICS IN EARLY MEDIEVAL SOUTH ARABIA[1]

Daniel Mahoney

INTRODUCTION

Walter Dostal had an enduring commitment to the documentation of the cultural heritage of Arabia. This important part of his work developed out of a concern for its loss due to the rapid socio-economic developments in the regions of Ras al-Khaimah in the United Arab Emirates and Asir in Saudi Arabia (Dostal 1979, 1983, 1984, 2002). In order to promote the appreciation and further development of traditional culture across the peninsula, he aimed to create an ethnographic atlas that would map out various types of cultural phenomena such as domestic architecture, agricultural practices, and folk astronomy. These efforts demonstrate his strong belief in the importance and celebration of all types of heritage, and secure his contribution to the current movements dedicated to its preservation in Arabia today.

The safeguarding of cultural heritage has also been a prevalent activity within Yemen. Since the 1970s various international teams have sought to conserve the architecture of many cities, leading to the inscription of three cultural properties in Ṣan'ā', Shibām, and Zabīd onto the UNESCO World Heritage List as well as countless other preservation projects for domestic, public, and religious structures. Traditional construction practices also continue to be undertaken and cultivated for new building projects in revival styles, although those often have been criticized as superficial imitations (Lamprakos 2005, 2008). Additionally, the inventorying and conservation of manuscripts has been another major mission dedicated to cultural heritage in Yemen. Most recently, digitization of many of these documents has become a further important task for both ensuring the preservation of their contents and enabling them to be made available to a wider readership (Schmidtke & Thiele 2011).

Although these undertakings may be based on the intrinsic value of the cultural heritage itself, it is important to recognize and be aware of whose heritage is being celebrated. While UNESCO sites or Arabic manuscripts have been deemed to be of universal value for humankind, they also are linked to communities with strong national and local identities. For example, in the foreword of the edited volume *Yemen: 3000 Years of Art and Civilization in Arabia Felix* (Daum 1987), which accompanied an exhibition at the State Museum of Ethnology in Munich, Ali Abdallah Saleh, the president of the Yemen Arab Republic at the time, explicitly commemorates the twenty-fifth anniversary of the revolution from the Imamate. He views the cultural heritage celebrated in the volume and exhibition, ranging from ancient archaeological remains to contemporary popular songs, as an expression of Yemeni national identity. Furthermore, he acknowledges that both their pre-Islamic and Islamic past has shaped their current self-understanding, which enabled them to thrive throughout their struggle for independence. Thus, in this perspective, heritage becomes less about the inherent value of the sites, objects, or activities themselves, and more about how they aid in the formation and maintenance of political identities.

This approach to cultural heritage may be viewed in different ways. As a social process, the past is engaged through strategic acts of remembering in order for individuals and groups to understand and politically maneuver in the present (Harrison 2008; Smith 2006). In this way, places, objects, and practices, which are

[1] I would like to thank my colleagues at the Austrian Academy of Sciences (ÖAW) Institute for Social Anthropology (ISA) for the comments and advice I received in course of writing this chapter including Andre Gingrich, Johann Heiss, Eirik Hovden, and Magdalena Kloss. Financial support came from the Austrian Science Fund's (FWF) grant F4203 for the (SFB) "Visions of Community" (VISCOM) project. The transliteration in this text is based on the system of the *International Journal of Middle East Studies* (*IJMES*).

deemed to be of cultural value, are used to construct and maintain a range of identities, both personal and collective, for the legitimization of power. Through this process heritage aids in the production of feelings of belonging and community, but also because the past is remembered differently by various groups, it additionally may become a tool of governance or subversion to the established political order. Hence, commemoration is a socially constructed and politicized act that occurs continuously and diversely as the meaning of the past changes with the needs of the present. At the same time, cultural heritage may also be seen as a social action that a community undertakes in order to maintain its own cohesion through its connection to a particular place (Appadurai 2001; Byrne 2008). With local material remains and practices, a community is better able to assert and sustain its identity through the 'production of a locality,' especially in environments of increasing interaction and mobility. These physical and visible signatures provide durable and credible stakes for the community's sense of belonging to a place, and help create its collective memories. Thus, cultural heritage is also intimately linked to the anchoring and spatialization of identity politics. Although these concepts of heritage are commonly applied to the modern contexts of nationalism and globalization (Boynter, Swartz Dodd & Parker 2010; Goode 2007; Kohl & Fawcett 1995; Labadi & Long 2010; Meskell 1998), they also are a key component of a tenth century document from South Arabia.

SOUTH ARABIAN IDENTITY IN THE EARLY MEDIEVAL PERIOD

After their participation in the Islamic conquests of Mesopotamia, the Levant, and Egypt in the seventh century, many Yemenis settled with their families in the new garrison towns to the north. This emigration engendered an uncertain political situation in South Arabia, in which the local tribes undertook further consolidation of their territories and the emergent Islamic caliphate asserted its authority to varying degrees of success in the cities of Ṣanʿāʾ and al-Janad as well as in the Ḥaḍramawt region. Over the next few centuries the governors sent to South Arabia by the Rashidun Caliphate, the Umayyads, and the Abbasids faced increasing resistance to their rule, while representatives of minority religious groups, including the Kharijites, Isma'ilis, and Zaydis, entered the region and developed their own political bases (al-Mad'aj 1988). Concurrently during this period, a rivalry developed in the wider peninsula between the tribes of the northern Arabs and the tribes of the southern Arabs as both claimed legitimacy for political leadership of the Islamic community as whole (Crone 1994; Shaban 1971).

This competition between the Arabs of the north and south was reflected in various types of historiographic literature including the creation of ideologically driven genealogies. For example, *Jamharat al-nasab* (*Compendium of Genealogy*) (Caskel 1966), compiled by Hishām b. Muḥammad al-Kalbī (d. 204/819) of al-Kūfa, extensively documents the northern tribes beginning with the Quraysh, but offers less information about the southern tribes. The identity and pride of the northern Arabs was further established and expressed through the collection, transmission, and production of different genres of poetry as well as tales about pre-Islamic heroism and generosity known as the *ayyām al-ʿarab* (Agha & Khalidi 2002-3; Drory 1996). The southern Arabs, however, bolstered themselves by emphasizing reports of the glorious deeds and achievements of the pre-Islamic Himyarite kings, later termed the 'Qaḥṭān Saga[2]' (Pitrovsky 1986).

Early proponents of these South Arabian stories include ʿAbīd b. Sharya al-Jurhumī (d. 60/679), who wrote *Akhbār alYaman wa-ashʿārihā wa-ansābihā* (*Reports of the Yemen and its Poetry and Genealogy*) (Crosby 1985), and Wahb b. Munabbih (d. 110/728), who wrote *Kitāb al-mulūk al-mutawwaja min Ḥimyar wa-akhbārihim wa-qiṣaṣihim wa-qubūrihim wa-ashʿarihim* (*The Crowned Kings of Himyar, their Narratives, Stories, Tombs and Poems*)[3]. A later version is found in *al-Qaṣīda al-Ḥimyariyya* (*The Himyarite Qasida*) by Nashwān b. Saʿīd al-Ḥimyarī (d. ca. 573/1178) (Kremer 1865; Larcher 2003). These various manifestations of the Qaḥṭān Saga form a picture of the southern Arabs as superior in their monotheism, warfare, and language. But the historical value of their contents has been questioned and speculated to be little more than thinly

[2] Qaḥṭān was considered the genealogical forefather of South Arabia in contradistinction to ʿAdnan of North Arabia.

[3] This lost work is probably the basis for a later volume entitled *Kitāb al-tījān fī mulūk Ḥimyar wa-lYaman* (The Books of Crowns, concerning the Kings of Himyar and Yaman), which was transmitted by ʿAbd al-Malik b. Hishām and ascribed to Wahb b. Munnabih (Krenkow 1928). An edition of ʿAbīd b. Sharya al-Jurhumī's *Akhbār alYaman wa-ashʿārihā wa-ansābihā* is also included in Krenkow's book.

veiled folkloric propaganda with a minimal basis in actual events (Donner 1995: 196-197, 224; Duri 1983: 130-135). This skeptical assessment of these works is further buoyed by biographical evidence that the authors themselves were involved in politics in different ways. Although details on ʿAbīd b. Sharya al-Jurhumī's life are scarce, leading some modern scholars to believe him to be a fictitious figure, he is said to have been summoned to be the history tutor of the Umayyad Caliph al-Muʿāwiya (Crosby 1985: 3). Wahb b. Munnabih had been appointed as a judge in Ṣanʿāʾ, but later was put in jail and eventually flogged to death at the discretion of the Umayyad governor of Yemen (Khoury 2013). Finally, Nashwān b. Saʿīd al-Ḥimyarī attempted to be elected as the leader of the Zaydi community in Yemen with a platform that openly criticized the Quraysh, but did not gather enough support to win (al-Akwaʿ 1987: 216-228).

This type of politically engaged scholar is perhaps best epitomized in South Arabia by the most celebrated advocate of the Qaḥṭān Saga in the early medieval period. Nicknamed *Lisān alYaman* ("The Tongue of Yemen"), the polymath Abū Muḥammad al-Ḥasan b. Aḥmad b. Yaʿqūb b. Yūsuf al-Hamdānī (d. 334/945) belonged to the Bakīl section of the Hamdān confederation in the northern highlands (Löfgren 2013; Toll 2008). Born in Ṣanʿāʾ at the end of the ninth century to a family of traders and camel dealers, he journeyed extensively across the Arabian Peninsula to places such as Makka and al-Kūfa. These travels inspired him to write the geographic text *Ṣifat jazīrat al-ʿarab* (*The Description of the Peninsula of the Arabs*) (Müller 1884-91; al-Akwaʿ 1974) as well as other books on agriculture, astronomy, medicine, and metallurgy. In addition to this scientific writing, he also composed passionate political poetry supporting the South Arabian tribes and antagonizing those of the north including the Zaydi religious sect, whom he saw as interfering with local tribal affairs while he was living in the northern city of Ṣaʿda for twenty years (Gochenour 1984: 259-261; Hamdani 1986: 160-162; Heiss 1998: 18). These verbal attacks seemingly escalated to the extent that he was imprisoned in Ṣanʿāʾ for three years. Upon his release, he remained in the highland town of Rayda for the remainder of his life under the protection of a local shaykh where he wrote his most ambitious work, *al-Iklīl* (*The Crown*).

Although *al-Iklīl* is commonly considered a historical text, this classification may be inadequate due to its diverse content and clear political intent. Comprising ten volumes, it includes genealogies of the South Arabian tribes, an affirmation of their merits, a refutation of false statements and legends about them, records of their antiquities and ancient inscriptions, and finally an extended narrative covering the pre-Islamic history of South Arabia. Beyond a merely academic compendium of information compiled by al-Hamdānī about his pre-Islamic ancestors, altogether it represents a well-rounded celebratory work that establishes the identity and superiority of the South Arabian tribes in diverse ways. Not all tribesmen, however, seemed to have agreed with this presentation, and al-Qiftī reports that some had succeeded in destroying at least parts of it (1950: 283). As a result, only four of its volumes are known to have survived.

Three of the surviving volumes (1, 2, and 10) are the genealogical records of the beginning of humankind and the major South Arabian tribal confederations. In his first volume, al-Hamdānī openly criticizes the genealogies produced in the north and accuses their compilers to have minimized the presence of the tribes of South Arabia in order to demonstrate greater antiquity of the North Arabian tribes (Duri 1983: 17). In response, he compiled these volumes based on local written and oral sources including the records (*sijill*) of the Khawlān tribe in Ṣaʿda[4] and tribal experts such as Abū Naṣr Muḥammad ib.ʿAbdallāh b. Saʿīd al-Yaharī, Muḥammad b. ʿAbdallāh al-Awsānī, and Muḥammad b. Yūnis al-Abrahī, as well as the works of ʿAbīd b. Sharya al-Jurhumī and Wahb b. Munabbih (Heiss 1998: 24-26). Thus, through the use of this common historiographic genre, al-Hamdānī not only clearly delineates the internal cohesion and exclusionary boundaries of the South Arabian tribal community, but he also emphasizes their connections to the Arabs of antiquity and the biblical Old Testament. For the final surviving volume of *al-Iklīl* (8), however, he undertakes a less common approach to South Arabian identity explicitly focused on cultural heritage.

[4] The term *sijill* is first found in Arabic in the Quran (sura 21, verse 104) in reference to written documents or letters. But it may relate to the Byzantine Greek term *sigillion* or Roman term *sigillum*, whose meanings took on a more bureaucratic sense associated with imperial edicts, treaties, or the seals placed on them. For al-Hamdānī, *sijill* refers to written records of primarily genealogical content, but also contain information about historical events. They presumably originated in the pre-Islamic period, although some of them may have been fabricated at a later date (Heiss 1998: 48-56).

CULTURAL HERITAGE AND THE EIGHTH VOLUME OF *AL-IKLĪL*

The eighth volume of *al-Iklīl* contains three main sections including descriptions of monuments, reports on the uncovering of burials, and long elegiac poems, as well as two shorter entries on treasures and the Himyarite script. The volume has been fully edited three times (al-Akwaʿ 1979 [2004[5]]; al-Karmalī 1931; Faris 1940), partially translated into English (Faris 1938), and partially edited and translated into German (Müller 1879, 1880)[6]. Due to its unparalleled bounty of colorful information about early medieval South Arabia, many historians, philologists, and archaeologists often have mined this text for comparative place-names or graphic accounts of sites and structures found during their fieldwork (e.g., Müller 1986; Wade 1986). Nevertheless, this book has only been discussed or analyzed as an overall work when it is briefly cited together with the rest of the volumes of *al-Iklīl* as an example of political legitimation for the tribes of South Arabia. Subsequently, with a focus on the monuments section of the volume, the rest of this chapter examines more closely how al-Hamdānī undertakes this ideological task through the analytical lens of the modern conception of cultural heritage, although he does not use this terminology himself[7]. In this way, the eighth volume may be understood as a formulation and expression of the cultural and political identity of the South Arabian tribes not based on their genealogical ties, language, or origin story, but rather the landscape of monuments that surround them.

As a whole the structure of this volume appears disjointed, unorganized, and cobbled-together. Its usually brief entries, which are focused on a particular location with one or more monuments, do not seem to have clear continuity or connections among themselves. The phrase, "al-Hamdānī states," appears several times throughout the text in an irregular manner, emphasizing its compilatory nature and probably indicating its later editing. The recensions of this text come down through Nashwān b. Saʿīd al-Ḥimyarī whose influence on the text remains ambiguous albeit extant (Löfgren 2013; Heiss 1998: 25-26; Vida 1940: 162-164). The individual entries usually do not have a clear chain of transmission with the transmitters only haphazardly mentioned in the text itself. The main source al-Hamdānī seems to use for volume eight was the previously mentioned al-Yaharī, but the other sources utilized for the genealogical volumes were also likely consulted in addition to another work, entitled *Mafākhir Hamdān* (*The Glories of Hamdan*), by Ibn ʿAbbās al-Murhibī (Vida 1940: 164). Similarly, most entries do not follow a patterned structure, but rather veer off describing a monument in diverse ways for multiple periods from different perspectives with various types of evidence. Hence, this volume is not a historical document that reformulates the Qaḥṭān Saga in a direct narrative manner as presumably would have been found in volumes four through six, but rather it is a documentation of cultural heritage that uses scientific descriptions, historical reports, poetry, Quranic verses, astrological observations, and fantastical stories to support his larger political goal.

Despite this lack of an over-arching narrative structure and multiplicity of supporting evidence, a certain inner consistency does emerge in the eighth volume when approached as a work of historical geography[8]. As demonstrated by his travels and other geographic work, al-Hamdānī clearly had a broad knowledge of the diverse landscapes of Yemen, and specifically states his personal familiarity with its monuments in this volume[9]. Subsequently, it is not unexpected that he would choose to organize a text through a spatial lens.

---

5 For consistency and clarity the page numbers cited from *al-Iklīl* in this chapter come from the al-Akwaʿ edition reprint (2004).

6 These various editions are based on different manuscripts or fragments of manuscripts, but have sequentially built on one another for interpretation of unclear characters and words (Faris 1938: 4-6; Heiss 1998: 28-29; Löfgren 1939, 1942, 1943).

7 Despite the common practice by some Muslims of condemning or destroying antiquities from the pre-Islamic period or *al-Jahiliyya* (time of ignorance), there are also texts from the medieval period that discuss and celebrate them. These documents, including some early "excavation reports," describe the material record from Arabia, Iran, and Egypt (El Daly 2005; Khalidi 1994: 66; Milwright 2011: 1-2).

8 His use of evidence from the Greek geographer Claudius Ptolemy to give the latitude and longitude coordinates for the cities of Ẓafār, Māʾrib, and Ṣanʿāʾ shows direct influence from this scientific genre (al-Hamdānī 2004: 61).

9 Al-Hamdānī directly states in *Iklīl 8*: "I have seen all the ruins and the palaces of al-Yaman, except Ghumdān of which only a portion of the lower part of a wall is left" (al-Hamdānī 2004: 63). Near the end of the monuments section, however, he undercuts this statement by writing: "This was all we knew of the castles and public building of al-Yaman save a few of them which we could not locate" (al-Hamdānī 2004: 139). While the monuments he reports on in the volume are naturally not as comprehensive of a record as the archaeological remains known from modern research, they are distributed across a large part of what is now the Republic of Yemen. This distribution includes the Ḥaḍramawt region, but most of them are concentrated in the northern highlands and eastern desert.

Furthermore, the identity of the sedentary tribes of South Arabia was based on territory in addition to genealogy[10]. Various geographers over the course of the medieval period including al-Hamdānī documented these remarkably stable micro-regional divisions (Matsumoto 2003: 71-78). Hence, his approach to formulating a wider South Arabian identity through a precise sense of place based on its cultural heritage closely adhered to the already extant tribal world-view for group identity based on territory[11].

This writing strategy is seemingly in opposition to North Arabian nostalgia poetry, in which identity was expressed through a yearning for a (partly illusionary) homeland in the desert. While hundreds of place-names describing specific geographic localities were mentioned in the verses of this poetry, later on these names became more symbolic and in aggregate portrayed a more ambiguous or interchangeable sense of place that eventually came to be known simply as *Najd* (Agha & Khalidi 2002-3: 104-105). On the contrary, *al-Iklīl*'s monument descriptions *en masse* form a distinct spatialization of South Arabia that does not blend together into a more vague feeling of nostalgia. While much poetry is quoted in the descriptions, it is frequently juxtaposed with other types of evidence that contextualize it. Consequently, through this process of drawing on connections between the past and the present of specific places in order to define strategic collective memories, al-Hamdānī creates distinct localities for its inhabitants that anchor their overall regional identity. The remainder of this chapter gives a brief overview of the types of monuments that al-Hamdānī commemorates in this volume in order to express and produce feelings of community and pride in the southern Arabs. Additionally, it highlights the ways he connects these structures to various aspects of South Arabian identity including its architectural expertise, religious history, and agricultural practices.

SOUTH ARABIAN MONUMENTS AND THE FORMATION OF A REGIONAL POLITICAL IDENTITY

Palaces and other fortified architecture

Behold the great Ghumdān high and lofty
Pouring balsam on the aching heart;
Twenty stories, see it climbing
Up into heaven's utmost part;
A turban of clouds its head encircles
Its mantle is of marble made,
An alabaster girdle around it buckles,
And onyx stone, the brocade.
Made of copper on the roof you see
Flying eagles on diagonal corners standing,
Even so on the remaining two
Roaring lions the palace attending[12].
(al-Hamdānī 2004: 38)

The first and most often described type of monuments in the eighth volume of al-Iklīl are palaces (*quṣūr*, s. *qaṣr*), but in a similar style of architecture there are also forts (*ḥuṣūn*, s. *ḥiṣn*) and towers (*maḥāfid*, s. *maḥfid*[13]). Organized by place-name, al-Hamdānī usually begins these entries with a technical appraisal of the structures. Although many of the monuments are described to be at least partially destroyed, the great-

[10] This concept of tribal identity in South Arabia has been examined in medieval and modern contexts (Brandt 2012; Dresch 1991; Wilson 1989).

[11] Political unity of South Arabia as a whole, however, did not occur until briefly in the seventeenth century under the Qasimi dynasty (Klaric 2008), and then in 1990 with the formation of the Republic of Yemen.

[12] This translation comes from Faris (1938: 15).

[13] This translation of the term *maḥfid* comes from al-Selwi's specialized dictionary of words found in the works of al-Hamdani and Nashwan b. Sa'id al-Himyari (1987: 71). But reviewing the way it is used throughout this volume in different contexts, it also may be interpreted more broadly as 'monument' or 'stronghold.'

ness of their unique technological construction is commonly expounded upon in both prose and poetry. Some examples include the giant square towers of Nāʿit that are climbed using inset iron nails in order to signal a warning to the surrounding mountains by burning wax (al-Hamdānī 2004: 64), and the marble slab floor in a palace of Ḍahr on which the king would beat victims with a wooden rod (al-Hamdānī 2004: 96). But the most celebrated structure is the twenty story Ghumdān palace of Ṣanʿāʾ, which has been argued to be the inspiration for the architectural style of the Dome of the Rock built by the Umayyad caliph ʿAbd al-Malik in the seventh century in al-Quds/Jerusalem (Khoury 1993). As specified in the panegyric verses above, beyond its exceptional height, it was significant for the various precious materials used in its construction such as alabaster, onyx stone, and marble[14]. Nonetheless, its penthouse, topped with a transparent marble ceiling and surrounded by four copper lion statues that would roar when the wind blew, was its most impressive feature with descriptions cited from both Wahb b. Munabbih and ʿAbīd b. Sharyah al-Jurhumī (al-Hamdānī 2004: 44-45).

In addition to the exceptional quality of the palaces' construction, the identity of their builders is another major topic repeatedly addressed throughout the volume. Answers put forward range from more fantastical speculation based on religious texts to specific historical figures based on documentary evidence. From a religious perspective, *jinn* sent by Solomon are attributed to have helped Bilqīs, queen of Sabāʾ, build several palaces across the region, including the Ghumdān in Ṣanʿāʾ and Salhīn in Māʾrib (al-Hamdānī 2004: 51-52, 79-81). But al-Hamdānī aggressively denies this claim, and points out that the probable reason for the continuation of this story is based on the Quranic verse that describes the *jinn*'s servitude for Solomon[15]. Thus, al-Hamdānī's decision to include this perspective in the volume, despite doubts in its veracity, reveals his desire to exploit its still potent ideological power. While it may undercut the achievements of the actual local builders, it also profitably connects South Arabia to important historical and religious figures of the pre-Islamic period. Moreover, for many other structures, al-Hamdānī counteractively references inscriptions of the names of the original Himyarite builders, which are found on stone blocks at the sites themselves such as at Shiḥrār (al-Hamdānī 2004: 84) or Ḥadaqān (al-Hamdānī 2004: 117). Some palaces, such as one at Rawthān (al-Hamdānī 2004: 123-124), are stated to have been passed down to its contemporary occupants indicating a stable continuity between the past and present. At other sites, such as Bayt Maḥfid (al-Hamdānī 2004: 87), the tribal groups currently living there do not have a direct relationship to the original builders. Nonetheless, the memory of the ones who laid the first foundations persists as a reminder of the exceptional accomplishments of the Himyarite past and by implication their political glory.

Beyond these descriptions of the architecture and records of their first builders, al-Hamdānī also cites events from the deep and recent past that occurred at these sites in order to further anchor their locality in collective memory and evoke feelings of community. Many of these events emphasize the political struggle of the southern Arabs through description of the, at least, partial destruction of these structures by enemies from outside South Arabia. For example, the Aksumite invasion of the region is commemorated through a reference of their destruction of the Dāmigh palaces[16] (al-Hamdānī 2004: 91), and the Fatimid military campaigns are remembered through an account of the burning down of the palace of Bayt Ḥanbaṣ by Barāʾ b. Abī al-Mulāḥif and the subsequent fleeing of its owner Abū Naṣr to Ṣaʿḍa in 295 A.H./907 A.D. (al-Hamdānī 2004: 83). Other entries contain legendary stories from the pre-Islamic period that connect a site to the wider historical processes of South Arabia. For example, at the end of the entry for the palace of Ghaymān, there is a long anecdote about the local royal families' difficulties with succession and problems with rulership due to the intense and bloody political competition of the time (al-Hamdānī 2004: 104-107). While al-Hamdānī ties this story to a particular ruler in order to establish it as an actual historical event, it may also be interpreted more generally as an allegory for the nature of political survival during the pre-Islamic period and the gradual decline of the Himyarite kingdom. Thus, these events from all periods induce collective memories

[14] There is a different short entry in the volume that focused on the various sources for precious minerals in South Arabia (al-Hamdani 2004: 58-59).

[15] Sura 34, verse 13: They made for him what he willed of elevated chambers, statues, bowls like reservoirs, and stationary kettles.

[16] In reaction to the massacre of the Christian community at Najrān by the last Himyarite king Yūsuf Asʿar Yathʿar, commonly known as Dhū-Nuwās, the Aksumites invaded and controlled South Arabia from 525 A.D. until the arrival of the Persians in 570 A.D. under the command of Wahriz in response to a Yemeni plea for help to the Sassanid court.

of not only the struggles, but also, by implication, the recovery and continuing perseverance of the southern Arabs throughout their history.

This approach to non-sequential historical writing that layers multiple periods and emphasizes geography for the sake of utilizing its cultural heritage to produce feelings of pride, solidarity, and endurance is best exemplified in al-Hamdānī's long entry on the city of Ṣanʿāʾ and its palace of Ghumdān. Intertwined in this description he switches between ancient history, modern history, and contemporary events, but here I will put the different periods back into chronological order to more easily demonstrate how they relate to each other. The first period of distant antiquity instills the Ghumdān with importance through its connection to the Arabs' eponymous ancestor Sām (Shem), son of Nūh (Noah). Al-Hamdānī states that he surveyed this location, measured its foundations, and dug its well (al-Hamdānī 2004: 27-28). The second period refers to the powerful Himyarite empire focusing on the construction of the Ghumdān by the possibly mythical Ilā Sharaḥ Yaḥḍib (al-Hamdānī 2004: 45). The third period al-Hamdānī chooses to commemorate is the very emergence of Islam. Yet, instead of a religious story of the acceptance of Islam by the local inhabitants, he unequivocally emphasizes the non-subservience of South Arabia to the newly empowered northern Arabs. First, he quotes a Quranic verse implying the questionable nature of the Ghumdān palace[17], before then giving a brief account of Muḥammad's command to Farwa b. Musayk to undertake an ultimately unsuccessful mission to destroy it (al-Hamdānī 2004: 48). Elsewhere, however, al-Hamdānī quickly reveals in passing that the palace was demolished in the time of Muḥammad's successor ʿUthmān b. ʿAffān (al-Hamdānī 2004: 40). Finally, the fourth period of remembrance for Ṣanʿāʾ belongs to the tumultuous period of history during al-Hamdānī's childhood and adolescence, in which the local dynasty of the Yuʿfirids were in continual conflict with both the Zaydis and Fatimids for political dominance of the northern highlands. A reference to the effects of the Zaydi occupation of Ṣanʿāʾ briefly appears in the middle of a section of astrological analysis of the planets correlations to events in the city[18]. Presumably assuming the contemporary readers' knowledge of what would have been regarded as a current event, he does not focus on or even mention the Zaydi invaders in the text. Instead, al-Hamdānī explicitly concentrates on the consequences of their presence in the region for the local population by describing a massacre on a Friday in 288 A.H./901 A.D., in which five hundred people of Ṣanʿāʾ were killed at the nearby village of Bayt Baws[19] (2004: 34). Remembrance of the Fatimid occupation of Ṣanʿāʾ, however, is more explicit as their destruction of the city a few years later is alluded to twice in the text. The first reference to this event appears in a short statement noting the almost complete restoration of the city after its demolition a few years after 290 A.H./903 A.D. (al-Hamdānī 2004: 28-29). The second more informative description of this event appears in a passage mentioning the houses near the ruins of Ghumdān. Al-Hamdānī notes that one of them was utilized by the Fatimid leader "Ibn Faḍl al-Qarmatī" on the day he besieged Ṣanʿāʾ, stormed its congregational mosque, and subjugated its ruler and his people[20] (al-Hamdānī 2004: 37). Overall, although these events are spaced out throughout the entry in non-sequential order, they are contextualized to make a political statement rather than simply narrate a chronological history. Through the layering of these multiple periods, he parallels the prophetic, ancient, historical, and recent importance of the city of Ṣanʿāʾ, and promotes the consolidation of a South Arabian identity in the face of contemporary intruding political forces.

[17] Sura 9, verse 110: The building which they built will not cease to be a misgiving in their hearts.

[18] Imam al-Ḥādī ilā al-Ḥaqq, the leader of the Zaydis, first took control of Ṣanʿāʾ in 22 Muḥarram 288 A.H./16 January 901 A.D., but continued to battle with the Yuʿfirids until evacuating the city in Jumādā II 289/June 902 (al-Ḥusayn 1968: 176-187).

[19] The specific event does not seem to be directly recounted in the biography of al-Ḥādī, but during the second half of that year the village of Bayt Baws, located just south of Sanaa, is named several times as a main military station for the local groups that were fighting against him (al-ʿAlawī 1971: 227-229).

[20] Ibn al-Faḍl arrived to Yemen in 268 A.H./881 A.D. with his colleague Abū al-Qāsim in order to establish a base for the Fatimids. After taking control of southern Yemen, Ibn al-Faḍl made his way northward and conquered Ṣanʿāʾ in 293 A.H./905 A.D. (al-Ḥusayn 1968: 196-198).

PRE-ISLAMIC AND ISLAMIC RELIGIOUS BUILDINGS

> There are columns in the mosque of Madar that were taken from these palaces. There are nothing like them in *al-Masjid al-Haram*. The columns at Madar are longer, thicker, and better hewn as if they were cast in a mold (al-Hamdānī 2004: 128-129).

Religious monuments make up the second major type of structure described in the eighth volume of *al-Iklīl*. The fact that al-Hamdānī chose to discuss pre-Islamic and Islamic buildings insinuates the significance of both periods for the history and identity of the inhabitants of South Arabia, as well as reveals a more relaxed attitude toward the pre-Islamic period than is found in the polemics of many other Muslim scholars. This perspective is similar to that expressed by former President Saleh in the previously mentioned museum exhibition volume. As the remains of the Himyarite fortified architecture were still ubiquitous in the landscape of al-Hamdānī's Yemen, so were their earlier temples. Instead of ignoring them or sharply criticizing their previous purpose, al-Hamdānī addresses them succinctly in mainly a single entry entitled, "Riʾām and the source of fire in al-Yaman" (al-Hamdānī 2004: 99-101). In this passage, he describes in a mostly objective manner a place of pilgrimage where an ascetic hermit lived on a mountain summit in the territory of the Hamdān tribal confederation. Additionally, he mentions a nearby palace where a former king of Riʾām would perform a ritual genuflection outside its gate in front of a wall containing a stone carved with the pictures of a sun and crescent moon. These icons are the only direct, albeit ambiguous, indications and acknowledgement of the polytheism of their past. Nevertheless, after referencing a few other places of pilgrimage in South Arabia, al-Hamdānī finishes the entry by mentioning the destruction of the site of Ghaṭfān by the Yemeni Zuhayr b. Junāb during the pre-Islamic period, thereby emphasizing not only South Arabia's transition to monotheism but also their denigration of un-Islamic practices even before the time of the prophet Muḥammad.

The main entry on Islamic religious monuments entitled, "The Holy Mosques of al-Yaman," is located, probably not unintentionally, directly next in the volume (al-Hamdānī 2004: 102-103). This section, however, is even shorter than the previous, and consists of little more than a list of mosques. This brevity may be due to the lack of interest or futility in using Islamic architecture as a basis for demonstrating superiority over the northern Arabs, although an attempt at this type of claim is described below. Nonetheless, the most important of the mosques, designated by him specifically as the "Islamic mosques," were those of Ṣanʿāʾ, al-Janad, and Ṣaʿḍa. At these cities al-Hamdānī metaphorically states the Prophet's she-camel knelt down. By utilizing this manner of description that mimics the way the prophet's mosque was chosen in al-Madīna, he possibly insinuates them to be the first locations of Islam in Yemen. Normally, however, only the first two are identified in the historical record as the places where the first Muslim missionaries established their bases with a third one set up at an unidentified site in the Ḥaḍramawt region.

A final important detail about the interface between pre-Islamic and Islamic buildings as reflective of attitudes toward the past is found in the entry on the monuments of Madar[21] (al-Hamdānī 2004: 128-129). As quoted above, the columns of the mosque of Madar were extracted from the ruins of its former Himyarite palaces, demonstrating there was no problem or shame for the southern Arabs to use pre-Islamic architecture to create their sacred buildings. This practice was common for the construction of mosques in Yemen with art historical research indicating that many of their decorated columns and capitals were taken from pre-Islamic secular or religious buildings (Finster 1992). Fieldwork at the site of Madar, however, indicates its current mosque does not reflect al-Hamdānī's description (al-Akwaʿ 1995-1996: 1995). Nevertheless, by emphasizing the better aesthetics of the ancient columns over those used to construct the Sacred Mosque of Makka (*al-Masjid al-Harām*), al-Hamdānī points out once again the predominance of the technical proficiency of the inhabitants of South Arabia over even those that constructed the sacred area around the Kaʿba.

[21] At the end of this entry, al-Hamdānī also gives a description of a stone across from the palace bearing a picture of a sun and crescent moon that the king faces whenever he leaves the palace. This statement is very similar to that found in the Riʾām chapter, indicating either misplaced editing or another rare description of the pre-Islamic temples, albeit the same type of one.

Dams and other water management structures

All hopes of succor from distress are gone,
The Mā'rib Dam by the flood was burst;
Of marble stone Ḥimyar this dam had built
To store the water for the time of thirst.
Thence to every field and every vineyard,
At fixed hours, the water they disperst[22].
(al-Hamdānī 2004: 146)

Dams and other water management structures are the third major type of monument written about by al-Hamdānī in *al-Iklīl*. As the tribes of South Arabia were mostly sedentary, structures for the collection and distribution of water were necessary for maintaining the cultivation of crops. Dams, terraces, cisterns, and wells are mentioned numerous times throughout the eighth volume, demonstrating the large role irrigation played in the everyday lives of the southern Arabs[23]and its subsequent importance for their cultural heritage. In his entry on Ḍahr, al-Hamdānī describes the wide variety of fruits found in its gardens, and precisely details the irrigation practices used to maintain them (2004: 92-93). In a similar manner, he also boasts of the Himyarite well of Tulfum built into what he claims is the spring with the best quality water in all of South Arabia (al-Hamdānī 2004: 129). Finally, as they are the most prominent monuments dedicated to water management, al-Hamdānī dedicates an entry specifically to list the Himyarite dams across the entire region (2004: 146-149).

By far the most famous and celebrated structure discussed by al-Hamdānī is the Mā'rib dam (al-Hamdānī 2004: 72-76). Like other architectural entries he marvels at its construction including the quality of its massive masonry and its current preservation, as well as provides various options for whom the original builders may be. But the main framing of the entry hangs on the dam's story from the Quran. Al-Hamdānī begins the entry with a verse describing the fecundity of the two gardens provisioned by God on both sides of the dam[24], and then a few lines down he follows with a second verse describing the great flood sent by God that broke the dam and left the gardens bearing only bitter fruit[25]. After these verses, instead of dwelling on the meaning of this divine act of retribution, he moves on to speculate on the tree from which the bitter fruit comes. Hence, he seems to reference this story only to acknowledge the supreme significance of the dam in ancient Arab history, but does not want to dwell on its later destruction and the subsequent socio-political repercussions, e.g. the supposed mass emigration of many South Arabian tribes to the north. In this way, the passage's limitations suggest al-Hamdānī 's desire to celebrate it mainly as an exceptional feat of pre-Islamic architecture, and mostly ignore its deeper and more complicated significance for early Islamic history at a point when the dominance of South Arabia in the wider peninsula is perceived to have declined.

CONCLUSION

In the eighth volume of *al-Iklīl*, al-Hamdānī succeeds in promoting and legitimizing the cultural, regional, and political identity of the inhabitants of South Arabia by intertwining its different aspects with various types of monuments distributed throughout their landscape. It most explicitly inspires pride and feelings of superiority over northern Arabs through the continual enumeration of exceptional secular and religious structures distributed across the region, directly harkening back to the prosperity of the pre-Islamic Himyarite kingdom. It is most powerful, however, when it connects certain monuments to specific events or periods in their collective memory that resulted in negative consequences for the local population. The reason

[22] This translation comes from Faris (1938: 68).

[23] Water management and irrigation structures from as early as the third millennium B.C. have been well-documented by archaeologists all over Yemen (Wilkinson 2006).

[24] Sura 34, verse 15: There was for Sabā' in their dwelling place a sign: two gardens on the right and on the left. Eat from the provisions of your Lord and be grateful to Him. A good land and a forgiving lord.

[25] Sura 34, verse 16: But they turned away, so We sent upon them the flood of the dam, and We replaced their two gardens with gardens of bitter fruit, tamarisks, and something of sparse lote trees.

al-Hamdānī chose to commemorate these darker aspects of their past seems to be an attempt to engender specific motivation for the contemporary population of his time to act against their current invaders in the form of the Zaydis and Fatimids.

REFERENCES

Agha, Saleh Said & Khalidi, Tarif (2002–3). Poetry and Identity in the Umayyad Age, *al-Abhath* 50–51, 55–120.

al-Akwaʿ, Ismāʿīl b. ʿAlī (1987). Nashwān Ibn Saʿīd al-Ḥimyarī and the Spiritual, Religious and Political Conflicts of his Era. In: Werner Daum (Ed.), *Yemen: 3000 Years of Art and Civilisation in Arabia Felix* (212–231). Innsbruck: Pinguin-Verlag.

al-Akwaʿ, Ismāʿīl b. ʿAlī (1995–1996). *Ḥijar al-ʿilm wa-maʿāqiluhu fī al-yaman*, 4 Vols., Bayrūt: Dār al-fikr li-l-ṭibāʿa wa-l-nashr wa-l-tawzīʿ.

al-ʿAlawī (ʿAlī b. Muḥammad) *Sīrat al-Hādī ilā al-Ḥaqq Yaḥyā b. al-Ḥusayn b. al-Qāsim* (Ed. Suhayl Zakār, 1981, 2nd ed., Bayrūt: Dār al-fikr li-l-ṭibāʿa wa-l-nashr wa-l-tawzīʿ).

Appadurai, Arjun (2001). The globalization of archaeology and heritage: A discussion with Arjun Appadurai. *Social Archaeology, 1*, 35–49.

Boynter, Ran, Swartz Dodd, Lynn & Parker, Bradley (Eds.) (2010). *Controlling the Past, Owning the Future: The Political Uses of Archaeology in the Middle East*. Tucson: The University of Arizona Press.

Brandt, Marieke (2012). Some remarks on tribal structures among Khawlān and Jumāʿah of Khawlān b. ʿĀmir confederation in Ṣaʿdah region, Yemen, and their historical formation according to al-Hamdānī (10 ctr. AD). *Anthropology of the Middle East, 8(2)*.

Byrne, Denis (2008). Heritage as social action. In: Fairclough *et al.* (Eds.), *The Heritage Reader* (149–173). Abingdon and New York: Routledge.

Crone, Patricia (1994). Were the Qays and Yemen of the Umayyad Period Political Parties?. *Der Islam, 71*, 1–57.

Crosby, Elise Werner (1985). *Akhbār alYaman wa-ashʿāruhā wa-ansābuhā, the history, poetry, and genealogy of the Yemen ʿAbīd b. Sharya al-Jurhumī*, PhD thesis. Yale University.

Daum, Werner (Ed.) (1987). *Yemen: 3000 Years of Art and Civilisation in Arabia Felix*. Innsbruck: Pinguin-Verlag.

Donner, Fred (1998). *Narratives of Islamic Origins: The Beginnings of Islamic Historical Writings*. Princeton: Darwin Press.

Dostal, Walter (1979). Towards an ethnographic atlas of Arabia. *Proceedings of the Seminar for Arabian Studies, 9*, 45–52.

Dostal, Walter (1983). *The traditional architecture of Ras al-Khaimah (North)*. Wiesbaden: Reichert.

Dostal, Walter (1984). Toward Ethnographic Cartography: A Case Study. *Current Anthropology, 25*, 340–344.

Dostal, Walter (2002).The Austrian-Saudi collaborative project in the south-western region of the Kingdom of Saudi Arabia: a preliminary report. *Proceedings of the Seminar for Arabian Studies, 32*, 225–232.

Dresch, Paul (1991). The Tribes of Ḥāshid wa-Bakīl as Historical and Geographic Entities. In: A. Jones (Ed.), *Arabicus Felix: Liminosus Britannicus Essays in Honor of A.F.L. Beeston on his Eightieth Birthday* (8–24). Reading: Ithaca Press.

Drory, Rina (1996). The Abbasid Construction of the Jahiliyya: Cultural Authority in the Making. *Studia Islamica, 83*, 33–49.

Duri, Abd al-Aziz (1983). *The rise of historical writing among the Arabs*, (Ed. and transl. L. Conrad). Princeton: Princeton University Press.

El Daly, Okasha (2005). *Egyptology: The Missing Millennium. Ancient Egypt in Medieval Arabic Writing*. Portland: Cavendish Publishing.

Finster, Barbara (1992). An Outline of the History of Islamic Religious Architecture in Yemen. *Muqarnas, 9*, 124–147.

Gochenour, David (1984). *The Penetration of Zaydi Islam into Early Medieval Yemen*, PhD thesis. Harvard University.

Goode, James (2007). *Negotiating for the Past: Archaeology, Nationalism, and Diplomacy in the Middle East, 1919–1941*. Austin: University of Texas Press.

Hamdani, Abbas (1986). Al-Hamdānī, the outset of the domination of the Hamdān over Yaman. In: Yūsuf Muḥammad ʿAbdallāh (Ed.). *al-Hamdānī, lisān alYaman* (159–167). Ṣanʿāʾ: Dār al-tanwīr li-l-ṭibāʿat wa-l-nashr.

al-Hamdānī (Abū Muḥammad al-Ḥasan b. Aḥmad b. Yaʿqūb) *al-Iklīl: al-juzʿ al-thāmin* (Ed. and transl. D. H. Müller, Die Burgen und Schlösser Südarabiens nach dem Iklīl des Hamdānī. In: *Sitzungsberichte der Kaiserlichen Akademie der Wissenschaften, Philosophisch-Historische Klasse* 94/1879: 335–423, 97/1880: 955–10510; Ed. A. M. al-Karmalī, 1931, Baghdad; Transl. N. A. Faris, 1938, *The Antiquities of South Arabia. A translation from the Arabic with linguistic, geographic, and historic notes of the eighth book of al-Hamdānī's al-Iklil,* Princeton: Princeton University Press; Ed. N. A. Faris, 1940, Princeton: Princeton Oriental Texts 7; Ed. M. A. al-Akwaʿ, 1979, Damascus, reprinted 2004, Ṣanʿāʾ: Ministry of Culture and Tourism)

al-Hamdānī (Abū Muḥammad al-Ḥasan b. Aḥmad b. Yaʿqūb) *Ṣifat jazīrat al-ʿarab* (Ed. D. H. Müller 1884–91, *Geographie der arabischen Halbinsel: nach den Handschriften von Berlin, Constantinopol, London, Paris und Strassburg*, Leiden: Brill; Ed. M. A. al-Akwaʿ, 1974, Riyadh)

Harrison, Rodney (2008). The Politics of the Past: Conflict in the use of heritage in the modern world. In: G. J. Fairclough *et al.* (Eds.).*The Heritage Reader* (177–190). London: Routledge.

Heiss, Johann (1998). Tribale Selbstorganisation und Konfliktregelung: Der Norden des Jemen zur Zeit des ertes Imams (10. Jahrhundert). PhD thesis. University of Vienna.

al-Ḥusayn (Yaḥyā b.) *Ghāyat al-amānī fī akhbār al-quṭr al-yamānī* (Ed. S. al-ʿĀshūr, 1968, al-Qahīra: Dār al-kātib al-ʿārabī).

Ibn Hishām (ʿAbd al-Mālik) *Kitāb al-tījān fī mulūk Ḥimyar wa-lYaman*, (Ed. F. Krenkow, 1928, Haydarābād al-Dakkan: Maṭbaʿat majlis dāʾirat al-maʿārif al-ʿuthmāniyya).

al-Kalbī (Hishām b. Muḥammad) *Jamharat al-nasab* (Ed. W. Caskel, 1966, Leiden: Brill)

Khalidi, Tarif (1994). *Arabic historical thought in the classical period.* Cambridge: Cambridge University Press.

Khoury, R. G. (2013). Wahb b. Munabbih. In: P. Bearman *et al.* (Eds.). *Encyclopedia of Islam*, Second edition. Brill Online.

Khoury, Nuha (1993). The Dome of the Rock, the Kaʿba, and Ghumdān: Arab Myths and Umayyad Monuments, *Muqarnas, 10*, 57–65.

Klaric, Tomislav (2008). Le Yémen au XVIIe siècle: territoire et identités. *Revue des mondes musulmans et de la Méditerranée, 121–122*, 69–78.

Kohl, Phillip & Clare Fawcett (Eds.) (1995). *Nationalism, Politics, and the Practice of Archaeology*. Cambridge: Cambridge University Press.

Kremer, Alfred von (1865). *Die Himjarische Kasideh*. Leipzig: F. A. Brockhaus.

Krenkow, F. (1928). *Kitāb al-tījān fī mulūk Ḥimyar*, Haydarābād al-Dakkan: Maṭbaʿat majlis dāʾirat al-maʿārif al-ʿuthmāniyya.

Labadi, Sophia & Long, Colin (Eds.) (2010). *Heritage and Globalization*. London: Routledge.

Lamprakos, Michele (2005). Rethinking Cultural Heritage: Lessons from Sana'a, Yemen.*Traditional Dwellings and Settlement Review, 16,* 17–37.

Lamprakos, Michele (2008). Old Heritage, New Heritage: Building in Sana'a, Yemen. *The Middle East Institute Viewpoints: Architecture and Urbanism in the Middle East* (33–36). Washington, D.C.: Middle East Institute.

Larcher, Peter (2003). *L'Ode à Himyar*: Traduction de la *qaṣīda ḥimyariyya de Našwān b. Saʿīd,* avec une introduction et des notes, *Middle Eastern Literatures, 6*, 159–175.

Löfgren, Oscar (1939). Review of The Antiquities of South Arabia. *The Moslem World, 29*, 295–297.

Löfgren, Oscar (1942). Review of *Al-Iklīl (al-Juz' al-thāmin).The Moslem World, 32*, 92–94.

Löfgren, Oscar (1943). Über eine neuentdeckte besser Textüberlieferung von al-Hamdānī's Iklīl VIII. *Orientalia NS 12*, 135–145.

Löfgren, Oscar (2013). al-Hamdānī. In: P. Bearman *et al.* (Eds). *Encyclopedia of Islam*, Second edition. Brill Online.

al-Mad'aj, Abd al-Muhsin (1988). *The Yemen in early Islam (9–233/630–847): a political history*. London: Ithaca Press.

Matsumoto, Hiroshi (2003). *The tribes and regional divisions in northern Yemen*. Tokyo: Fujiwara Printing.

Meskell, Lynn (Ed.) (1998). *Archaeology under Fire: Nationalism, Politics and Heritage in the Eastern Mediterranean and Middle East*. London: Routledge.

Milwright, Marcus (2010). *An introduction to Islamic archaeology*. Edinburgh: Edinburgh University Press.

Müller, Walter W. (1986). Ancient castles mentioned in the eighth volume of al-Hamdānī's Iklīl and evidence of them in pre-Islamic inscription. In: Yūsuf Muḥammad ʿAbdallāh (Ed.). *al-Hamdānī, lisān alYaman* (139–157). Ṣanʿāʾ: Dār al-tanwīr li-l-ṭibāʿat wa-l-nashr.

Pitrovsky, Michael (1986). Al-Hamdānī and Qahtanide epos. In: Yūsuf Muḥammad ʿAbdallāh (Ed.). *al-Hamdānī, lisān alYaman* (17–25). Ṣanʿāʾ: Dār al-tanwīr li-l-ṭibāʿat wa al-nashr.

al-Qifṭī (ʿAlī b. Yūsuf) *Inbāh al-ruwāt ʿalā anbāh al-nuḥāt.* (Ed. M. A. Ibrahīm, 1950, al-Qāhira: Dār al-kutub al-miṣriyya, 1, 279–84).

Schmidtke, Sabine & Thiele, Jan (2001). *Preserving Yemen's Cultural Heritage: The Yemen Manuscript Digitalization Project, Hefte zur Kulturgeschichte des Jemen 5.* Ṣanʿāʾ: Embassy of the Federal Republic of Germany in Ṣanʿāʾ and the German Archaeological Institute.

al-Selwi, Ibrahim (1987). *Jemenitische Wörter in den Werken von al-Hamdānī und Našwān und ihre Parallelen in den semitische Sprachen*. Berlin: Dietrich Reimer.

Shaban, M. A. (1971). *Islamic history, a new interpretation*. Cambridge: Cambridge University Press.

Smith, Laurajane (2006). *Uses of heritage*. London: Routledge.

Toll, Christopher (2008). Al-Hamdānī. In: *Encyclopaedia of the History of Science, Technology, and Medicine in Non-Western Cultures* (120–127). Berlin: Springer-Verlag.

Vida, G. Levi della (1940). Review of *The Antiquities of South Arabia. Orientalia NS 9*, 160–173.

Wade, Rosalind (1986). Some of the archaeological sites mentioned by Hamdani. In: Yūsuf Muḥammad ʿAbdallāh (Ed.). *al-Hamdānī, lisān alYaman* (169–172). Ṣanʿāʾ: Dār al-tanwīr li-l-ṭibāʿat wa-l-nashr.

Wilkinson, Tony (2006). From highlands to desert: the organization of landscape and irrigation in Southern Arabia. In: J. Marcus & C. Stanish (Eds.). *Agricultural Strategies* (38–70). Los Angeles: Costen Institute of Archaeology, University of California.

Wilson, Robert (1989). *Gazetteer of Historical North-West Yemen*. Hildesheim – Zurich – New York: Georg Olms.

ṢA'DA REVISITED

JOHANN HEISS

Colonial and orientalist tainted visions of an "islamic" or a "muslim" city (singular intended), a view which flourished from roughly the thirties to the seventies of the last century, are to a large part obsolete (cf. Raymond 2008[1]). This leaves room for glances in directions that only rarely would have been possible for minds confined by an idea of one essential prototype of the islamic city. The short-lived invention of the Muslim city is over, and we can now direct our – at least in that instance – impartial eyes to cities without having to form our thoughts along the ever so labyrinthic/chaotic or rectangular/orderly/modern grid. We therefore can take into account differences and similarities in town-planning and in the organization of urban life without paying undue heed to religion, since this is what that invention was aiming at. This is not to deny that religion can certainly have influence on town-planning and the organization of urban life, but it is by far not the only influence, and in some cases it even is of minor importance.

In the course of his "Anthropologische Untersuchungen zur sozialen Evolution" (so the subtitle of his "Egalität und Klassengesellschaft in Südarabien") Walter Dostal incorporated two south Arabian towns into the concluding presentation of his model of social evolution in southern Arabia, Ṣan'ā' and Tarīm. By means of these two towns he referred to two "Grundmuster" (basic patterns):

"In Ṣan'ā' wird das Grundmuster durch die ausgebildete tribale Klassengesellschaft mit vollzogener gesellschaftlicher Arbeitsteilung bestimmt; Tarīm ist durch ein Grundmuster geprägt, in welchem sich das tribale Element lediglich auf die Schutzgewährung beschränkt." (Dostal 1985: 363)[2]

In the following chapter Ṣa'da, the capital town of the northernmost province of Yemen and for a long period of time capital of the Yemeni Zaydi Imams, will again be at the center of my considerations.[3] I want to show that Ṣa'da corresponded originally to the model of Ṣan'ā' as presented by Dostal. Yet through the arrival of the first imam and through the second foundation of the town in the wake of the imam's arrival it evolved to something else, situated between the models of Ṣan'ā' and Tarīm: through the presence of the members of the Prophet's family (originally the Imams and their entourage) the town matched the role of Tarīm, whereas the presence of tribal inhabitants gave the town a certain similarity to Ṣan'ā'.

This second visit to Ṣa'da is caused by some additional texts that were edited or came to my knowledge since my first article was published. The new material permits to tell more about the old, in essence pre-islamic and pre-imamic town Ṣa'da which lay at the foot of Jabal Tulummuṣ, not far away of the modern and now sadly destroyed town (see fig. 4).

Before that, an additional consideration of materials concerning towns in Ḥaḍramawt might be helpful. In her book "On the Edge of Empire" Linda Boxberger describes the organization of some towns there. Boxberger, dealing with "urban and rural life in the interior" (Boxberger 2002: 67 – 95), describes among others Say'ūn between ca. 1880 and 1930, where she speaks of "two true quarters, al-Suhayl in the densely populated eastern third of the town and al-Hawta in the west." (Boxberger 2002: 72). She continues: "Say'un had perhaps the greatest rivalry between the quarters of any town in Hadhramawt. At times of celebrations, the two quarters competed formally in extemporaneous poetry composition and in dancing" (ibid.). The rivalry

[1] "There is no great difficulty in defining the principles underlying the Orientalist approach vis-à-vis the Mediterranean Arab cities. Chief among these is the assumption that in a globalizing civilization like the Muslim one every phenomenon must be regarded as specifically Muslim." (Raymond 2008: 49)

[2] „In Ṣan'ā' the basic pattern is determined through a developed tribal class society with an effective social division of labor; Tarīm is characterized by a basic pattern where the tribal element is limited to the provision of protection."

[3] after a first article (1987) in Proceedings of the Seminar for Arabian Studies 17: 63-80, called "Historical and Social Aspects of Ṣa'da, a Yemeni Town", pitifully marred by many printing errors

between the quarters (or rather halves) manifested itself also in everyday-situations, "when members of one quarter were considered by the other to have 'crossed the line' into their territory and thus merited attack by fists, clubs, or even knives. The rivalry was so severe that the only time that al-huwik[4] from al-Suhayl could enter Say'un as a group through the town's main gate in al-Hawta quarter was during the ceremonial return from the ziyara, ritual visit, to the tomb of Prophet Hud" (Boxberger 2002: 72 – 73). The dividing line between the halves could be crossed for e.g. Friday prayers and for visits of relatives. At special occasions, "emergencies or celebrations" (Boxberger 2002: 73) for instance, the people of the other half "could not appear there without risk", and there were only few exceptions. Relatives of one half attending e.g. a wedding in the other half were closely watched. "He or she could not even sing or dance at a wedding of a relative in the other quarter." Service men from one half were not allowed to work in the other half; even the sultans were "subject to the system of service providers" (Boxberger 2002: 73). This enforced partition of the town was bound to lead to conflicts: "The sultans … mediated in disputes between the quarters that their leaders were unable to resolve" (Boxberger 2002: 73). Boxberger relates a case where a funeral procession had to lead from one half to the other. The service-providers or ḥuwīk bearing the bier had to hand over the corpse at the dividing line to the service-providers of the other half.

Competition and frequent disputes between residential quarters, however, existed not only in inland Ḥaḍramawt. As Boxberger relates, in the coastal town al-Šiḥr "service providers, tradesmen, and workers of the quarters … were almost as competitive as those of Say'un" (Boxberger 2002: 105). She continues: "Late in the nineteenth century, a rivalry between two quarters led to a fracas with knives in which seven people died."

There obviously existed dividing lines between ḥārāt or quarters of towns in Wādī Ḥaḍramawt and on the coast that were intensively maintained and much more emphasized than usual. For many persons and/or on many occasions it was not possible to cross this line without incurring difficulties and provoking disputes. Other towns seem to lack such clear and controversial demarcations: at least Boxberger does not mention a sharp division between quarters in Mukallā or Tarīm, and for Šibām she explicitly states: "There was no system of quarters with corresponding organization of providers of social services as found in other towns" (Boxberger 2002: 81).

It would be not only presumptuous but certainly wrong to directly transfer data from the turn of the 19th to the 20th century's Ḥaḍramawt to Ṣa'da in the north of Yemen in an even more distant time around the end of the 9th/beginning of the 10th century CE. Yet the examples from Ḥaḍramawt show at least that there are differing possibilities of regulations for living together in south Arabian towns, among them one where explicit borders between living quarters (and inhabitants of towns) are effectively kept up, and where this sharply drawn line can cause disputes and even violent conflicts thus necessitating occasional mediation which optimally is provided by somebody from outside and/or high up like the sultans in the case of Ḥaḍramawt. A comparison between towns in Ḥaḍramawt and in the north of Yemen makes sense insofar as it shows diverse possibilities of developments but certainly not any historical continuity or a diffusion between Ṣa'da and the towns in Ḥaḍramawt in much later times.

THE OLD TOWN AND ITS INHABITANTS

The old town of Ṣa'da, which obviously was not or only partly destroyed when the dam of al-Ḫāniq (now Wādī al-'Abdīn or al-'Abdīyīn) was demolished in the year 815/16 (Heiss 1987: 66; Heiss 1998: 182f), was still in use for a considerable time. This old town, the organization of the townspeople and the end of the use of the old town will be the main subjects of my contribution. From the biography of the first imam, the sīrat al-Hādī,[5] we learn of the existence of two halves of the old town which were separated from each other, the

---

[4] The word "ḥuwīk" is a plural in Ḥaḍramī dialect of "ḥā'ik", the weaver (Boxberger 2002: 32). The word is used as a generic name for service-providers of non-elite, non-tribal origin (like ahl al-ṯulṯ or muzayyinīn in the north). They comprised certain craftsmen, drummers and singers. The women of this group assisted at births and marriages.

[5] The sīrat al-Hādī ilā al-Ḥaqq Yaḥyā b. al-Ḥusayn is (at least to a greater part) written by 'Alī b. Muḥammad b. 'Ubaydallāh al-'Abbāsī al-'Alawī, a combatant and younger contemporary of the first imam al-Hādī ilā al-Ḥaqq (cf. Arendonk 1960; Heiss 1998, esp. 1-16)

šiqq[6] Ukayl and the šiqq Yursam. The two halves or sides of the town obviously had separate entrances: it was possible to enter the town on the Ukaylī side (al-'Abbāsī al-'Alawī 1981/1401: 410, 411, 413) or on the Yursamī side (al-'Abbāsī al-'Alawī 1981/1401: 413, 414). The Ukaylī half was inhabited also by merchants (tujjār) from Ṣan'ā' (al-'Abbāsī al-'Alawī 1401/1981: 412), who had lived in this half of Ṣa'da apparently for quite some time and who at least partly bore weapons. At another, earlier instance we are told by the author of the sīra that there existed a "sāḥat al-Yursamīyīn" (a gathering place of Yursam) at one side of the town (fī jānib al-qarya; al-'Abbāsī al-'Alawī 1981/1401: 156) possibly on its outside. It can be conjectured that there was also a similar sāḥa outside the (old) town belonging to Ukayl. At least those persons who entered the šiqq Ukayl had to pay, because when the Ukayl tried to draw one of the tribal leaders of their time, Ibn al-Ḍaḥḥāk to their side, they "offered their obedience and asked him to levy taxes for the town and to take the maks[7] from those who entered the half of Ukayl" (al-'Abbāsī al-'Alawī 1981/1401: 413). The situation in the old town was perhaps similar to the situation in Say'ūn as described by Linda Boxberger, certainly with one difference: there is no mentioning of any obligation to pay if someone wanted to enter a half of Say'ūn.

In a schematic way, the old town can be imagined like that:

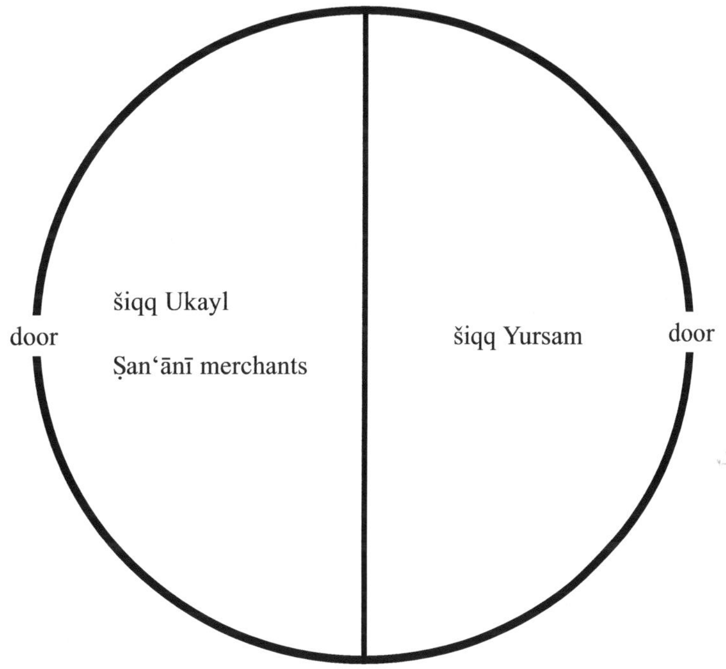

Figure 1: The halves of old Ṣa'da according to al-'Abbāsī al-'Alawī

We can render this information by 'Alī b. Muḥammad b. 'Ubaydallāh al-'Abbāsī al-'Alawī even somewhat more precise if data are included with which al-Hamdānī[8] provides us in his "Description of the Arab Peninsula", where he describes the "miḫlāf [district] Ṣa'da" (al-Hamdānī 1984/1394: 248-250, esp. 249):

6 šiqq is "The half … of a thing … or the half of a thing when it is cloven, or split" (Lane 1984: 1577 b) and "the side, or lateral part". Consequently, one could translate "the Ukayl half" or "the Ukayl side" of the town Ṣa'da.

7 maks is a word designing non-canonical taxes, and "passage, droit pour passer" (Dozy 1968 [1881]: 614)

8 Abū Muḥammad al-Ḥasan b. Aḥmad b. Ya'qūb al-Hamdānī was born (possibly 893) around the time when the later imam Yaḥyā b. al-Ḥusayn reached the Yemen (which was in 897). He belonged to the tribal stratum of Yemeni inhabitants and was an important polymath; he lived in Ṣa'da for twenty years, and some leading persons of Ukayl were among his friends there. He wrote among other themes on genealogy (al-Iklīl or "The Diadem", originally 10 volumes) and geography in a wider sense (ṣifat jazīrat al-'Arab or "Description of the Arabic Peninsula"). For him cf. Heiss 1998: 17-60.

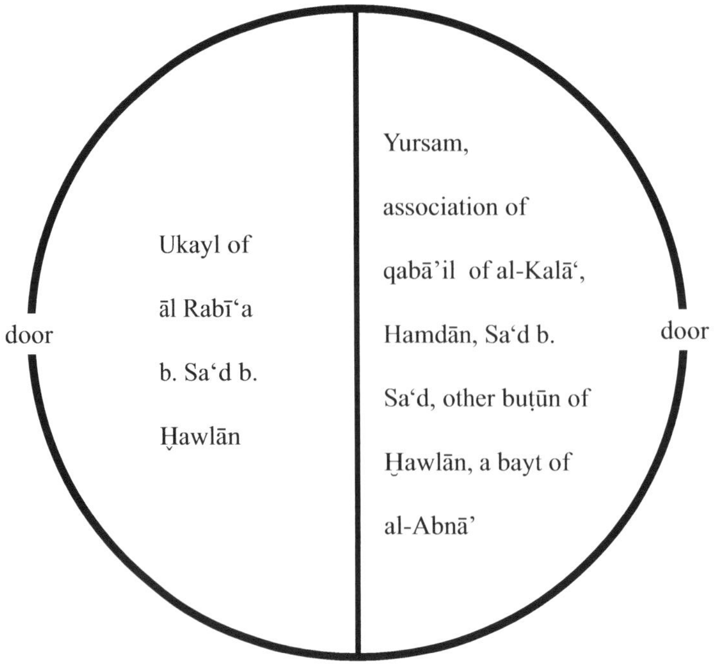

Figure 2: The halves of old Ṣa'da according to al-Hamdānī

In al-Hamdānī's presentation, one half of the town was inhabited by the Ukayl, a group with a thorough tribal pedigree, whereas the other half was inhabited by a mixture of members of many, genealogically very different groups who nevertheless had a certain feeling of belonging together, if one can interpret the existence of a common name in that way. There is a certain possibility that this presentation is biased, because al-Hamdānī preferred the political and religious views of the Ukayl and was friends with some of them. Consequently he could have been motivated to denigrate their opponents.

THE CONFLICT IN ṢA'DA AND ITS ENVIRONMENTS

The halves of the town with their respective inhabitants precisely reflect the conflict of the time when the later imam Yaḥyā b. al-Ḥusayn arrived in the region. The conflict is presented by al-Hamdānī in genealogical terms as one between brothers, whose relatives and allies involved in the conflict lived in and to a greater part around the town of Ṣa'da:[9]

The two principal parties of conflict, imagined as brothers in the genealogy of the Ḫawlān-federation, were al-Rabī'a b. Sa'd with the banū Kulayb, the Ukayl and their leading family, the āl 'Abbād, on one side, and Sa'd b. Sa'd together with Sa'd b. Ḥāḏir with their leading family, the āl Abī Fuṭayma on the other. On the side of Ukayl were as allies banū 'Uwayr, al-Muhāḏir, banū Šihāb and groups of Ḥimyar who inhabited Ṣa'da. On the side of Sa'd b. Ḥāḏir and Sa'd b. Sa'd stood Yursam, Sufyān of Arḥab (Hamdān), Wādi'a of Ḥāšid (Hamdān) and again groups of Ḥimyar. As usual, one has to keep in mind that not all persons of the mentioned groups took part in the conflict.

With these arrangements concerning the old town of Ṣa'da in mind it is quite instructive to read about the arrival of the later imam Yaḥyā b. al-Ḥusayn, as his biographer al-'Abbāsī al-'Alawī relates it:

> "Arrival of al-Hādī ilā al-Ḥaqq (ṣalawāt Allāh 'alayhi) in Ṣa'da: Muḥammad b. 'Ubaydallāh[10] said: We arrived in Ṣa'da when six days had passed of Ṣafar of the year 284.[11] We came to Ḫawlān, among whom

[9] for the conflict see Heiss 1998: 176-185
[10] The father of the author and his main source before he himself arrived in Yemen
[11] corresponds to 16 March 897

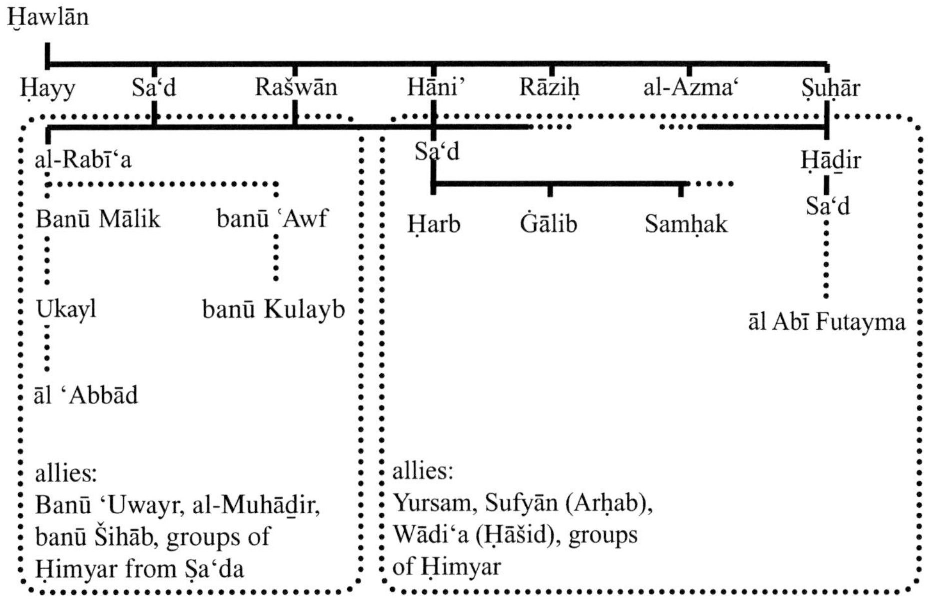

Figure 3: The parties of the conflict in and around the old town of Ṣa'da in the year 897, when Yaḥyā b. al-Ḥusayn, the later al-Hādī ilā al-Ḥaqq, arrived (cf. Heiss 1998: 184)

there was a severe fitna[12], in the course of which men perished and possessions dwindled away. The town was without rain, the earth had become dry. This was the time of the fruits, and I saw the crops partly dried out because of water shortness, and I saw the animals famished to death.

When Yaḥyā b. al-Ḥusayn came close to the town, he pitched his tents near to it and gave us the order to camp in them, so we camped. The people came out to him voluntarily; he did not force a single one of them to come out to him, and he had sent to no one of them to exempt him. So the inhabitants of Ṣa'da, among whom the fitna was, came out to him; they were Sa'd and al-Rabī'a. All of them came to meet him, and they greeted him. So he greeted them and gave them the order to greet one another.
Then he began and made a speech, a powerful and eloquent one. He praised God (ta'ālā) and extolled him, and he prayed for the prophet (ṣallā Allāh 'alayhi wa-sallam). He reminded them of God and exhorted them with many exhortations. I saw the people, and they were shocked and cried because of his words and his exhortations which they heard. They were noisy, like the pilgrims are noisy at the house of God, the ḥarām" (al-'Abbāsī al-'Alawī 1981/1401: 41).

The imam did not enter the town – in that case, the old town – of Ṣa'da. He stayed at the outside near the town and waited until the inhabitants came out to him.[13] The two groups of inhabitants are called with the names of their forefathers, Sa'd and al-Rabī'a, giving once more the impression that whole groups participated in the events, and thus keeping up the ideology of tribal solidarity. If the imam would have entered the town, he would at the same time have to enter one of the halves and would have stayed with one of the two groups of inhabitants and opponents, which would have meant in the eyes of the other group that he was not impartial in their conflict. Mediation in the conflict would then have been a difficult if not impossible endeavor. To enter the town (and one šiqq) would have endangered his whole mission, but Yaḥyā b. al-Ḥusayn was prepared by the group of people he had sent to Ṣa'da already months before to explore the situation and to prepare his arrival. The imam was invited by members of the āl Abī Futayma (cf. al-Hamdānī 1954/65: 133;

[12] fitna denotes originally a "burning with fire", or, among others, in the Coran, a "trial", "whereby the condition of a man is evinced, in respect of good and of evil", and "civil war, or conflict occurring among people" (Lane 1984 [1863/93]: 2335c)

[13] The use of neutral places for gatherings, often uninhabited and sometimes called ḥaram, hijra or ḥawṭa in Yemen, is also attested by Dresch 1993: 147 -149; it would be tempting to compare saints in Morocco who by living on the seams of tribal borders preserve their impartiality, cf. Gellner 1969: 10.

Figure 4: Ṣaʻda in the background, seen from the foot of Jabal Tulummuṣ (Johann Heiss, 1983)

al-ʻAbbāsī al-ʻAlawī 1981/1401: 17), representatives of one side of the conflict: so already on these grounds he could have been accused of being biased for one side.

ṢAʻDA AND AL-ĠAYL

After the imam's successful mediation in the conflict – if he was ever successful in the long run, as will be seen – the āl Abī Fuṭayma lived in al-Ġayl, and al-Ġayl belonged to Saʻd b. Saʻd (al-Hamdānī 1984/1394: 249), with whom the āl Abī Fuṭayma were allied through intermarriage (Heiss 1987: 67; Heiss 1998: 181).

The fact that the first imam built his mosque not inside the old town may have partly had the reason that he did not want to appear too partial in the local conflict: if there was a place for a mosque it would have to be in one of the halves of the town, and that would entail resentment in the other half. So al-Ġayl with its relatively new population, the āl Abī Fuṭayma who were his foremost friends (al-Hamdānī 1954/65: 133) clearly was the best choice to build a mosque and living quarters for the imam. Additionally, when al-Hādī ilā al-Ḥaqq founded his new mosque, he had to choose a place where water was available for ablutions. As the name al-Ġayl indicates, there was water, because the name means "the water which flows from springs on the surface of the earth." (al-Ḥimyarī 1999/1420: 8, 5038 sv)

For the imam, the situation in al-Ġayl was propitious, whereas in (old) Ṣaʻda hostility against him prevailed. This emerges from an event of the year 286/899 (al-ʻAbbāsī al-ʻAlawī 1981/1401: 133) when the first imam had taken some prisoners in Najrān, brought them to Ṣaʻda and imprisoned them in al-Ġayl; for that choice of place the author of the biography gives the following explanation:

"He detained them in a nearby [i.e. near Ṣaʻda] village [qarya] called al-Ġayl; between it and Ṣaʻda lies roughly half a mile. It is a qarya which belongs to the banū Ḥamza [read Ḥamra or Ḥumra] and the banū Saʻd, and there are the Fuṭaymīyūn, who were his trustworthy ones and his friends. He detained them [i.e. the prisoners from Najrān] in al-Ġayl, because Muḥammad b. ʻUbaydallāh had taken captive a man from

Duhma of Hamdān whose name was Ḥusayn b. Ḥabaš, who was an evil one. He had him detained in the jail in Ṣa'da, but persons of Ukayl were busy because of him until they got him out [of jail]. So he did not detain these [persons from Najrān] in Ṣa'da because of that reason, rather he detained them in al-Ġayl."

al-Ġayl belonged not only to Sa'd b. Sa'd, the allies of the first imam, it was the dwelling place of āl Abī Fuṭayma, who had sent a delegation to Yaḥyā b. al-Ḥusayn to bring him to the region as mediator. It is therefore understandable that the imam and his family and sons preferred to live there. It seems quite logical that he also built his mosque there and choose the area adjacent to the mosque as his burial place. If the market of Ṣa'da was not already there, the relocation of the market to the place in front of the mosque brought further importance to the location, and it seems quite probable that out of al-Ġayl, which may originally have been a small village, developed what we know today as Ṣa'da. Old Ṣa'da was situated at the foot of Jabal Tulummuṣ, as Ibn al-Mujāwir[14] was told: "It is said that old Ṣa'da (Ṣa'da al-qadīma) was in the beginning near the ḥiṣn [fortress] Tulummuṣ. After the ruin of Ṣa'da and its high places, al-Hādī Yaḥyā b. al-Ḥusayn rebuilt it" (Ibn al-Mujāwir 1986/1407: 204; Ibn al-Mujāwir & Smith 2008: 212, translation slightly changed). If we take Ibn al-Mujāwir or his informant by the word, the old town was a few kilometers south of the modern town or the former village al-Ġayl (see figure 4; cf. Gingrich & Heiss 1986: 15 and 87, figure 9).

"OLD ṢA'DA"

Ḥumayd b. Aḥmad al-Muḥallī (killed in battle 652/1254), the author of "al-ḥadā'iq al-wardīyya" ("Gardens of Roses"), a collection of biographies of Zaydī imams, included a biography of the son of the first imam and his second successor, Aḥmad b. Yaḥyā or al-Imām al-Nāṣir li-Dīn Allāh. There he presents the scene when the people paid homage to Aḥmad as imām[15] on a Friday in Ṣafar 301/September 913, which took place in the mosque of his father al-Hādī, who was already buried there. This shows that during that ritual procedure Aḥmad was at the location of al-Ġayl or perhaps new Ṣa'da. After the oath or bay'a (presumably after the Friday-prayer) he left the place and rode to "old Ṣa'da" or "Ṣa'da qadīma" (al-Muḥallī n. d.: 2, 48) on the same day (which hints at the proximity of the two sites), and many people gathered around him. They were mostly Ḫawlān, as Yaḥyā b. al-Ḥusayn b. Hārūn al-Hārūnī al-Ḥasanī, the author of an older collection of biographies relates (al-Hārūnī al-Ḥasanī 1996/1417: 172). Others maintain, we are told, that the gathering of people occurred between Ṣa'da and al-Ġayl. This location indicates a point between Ṣa'da (meaning the old town) and the village (qarya) al-Ġayl which presumably denotes the location of what today is Ṣa'da, the new town. According to al-Hamdānī in his "ṣifat jazīrat al-'Arab" "the qaryat [village] al-Ġayl was founded near Ṣa'da." (al-Hamdānī 1984/1394: 249) With Ṣa'da al-Hamdānī designated "old Ṣa'da", and the foundation of the qaryat al-Ġayl possibly happened not so long before he wrote his description.

The author al-Muḥallī apparently knew the scene cited above from the biography of the mentioned imam Aḥmad written by the imam's intimate 'Abdallāh b. 'Umar al-Hamdānī (d. ca. 315/927). This biography is not preserved, but Musallam al-Laḥjī (d. 545/1150) included it in a probably shortened version in the second volume of his "aḫbār al-Zaydīya bi al-Yaman". From this version, Wilferd Madelung edited the biography of Aḥmad b. Yaḥyā in the year 1990. There, the people present at the gathering are designated as "Ḫawlān and others of unknown descent" (Madelung 1990: 11) and what is important, the biographer does not speak of Ṣa'da qadīma but only of Ṣa'da. The house of the imam Aḥmad b. Yaḥyā, as his biographer repeatedly mentions (Madelung 1990: 24, 28, 57), was in the village al-Ġayl.

In the fourth volume of his "aḫbār al-Zaydīya bi al-Yaman" Musallam al-Laḥjī adds biographies of people of his own generation and two or three generations before that. The first of these biographies concerns a certain Muḥammad b. Aḥmad b. 'Alī b. Ibrāhīm b. al-Muḥsin al-'Alawī who is described as a qāḍī, a learned man and a collector and heir of partly precious books. By the son of the collector, the author Musallam

[14] Ibn al-Mujāwir is given as the author of a travelogue; obviously he came from the east of the islamic regions. During the second quarter of the 13th century he traveled repeatedly presumably as merchant in the Yemen but never reached Ṣa'da, at least he gives no dates for this region. He traveled in the time of the imam 'Abdallāh b. Ḥamza, when the importance of the new town of Ṣa'da had already surpassed that of the old town.

[15] the bay'a, or "A striking together of the hands of two contracting parties in token of the ratification of a sale" or "The act of … promising, or swearing allegiance and obedience" (Lane 1984: 285b)

al-Laḥjī is told: "In the bookshelves of my father (raḥimahu Allāh) were 600 volumes, among them valuable books of members of the family of Muḥammad (ṣallā Allāhu ʿalayhi), important ones and rare ones which were lost [otherwise]. Among them were some which he had inherited from the books of his grandfather Ibrāhīm b. al-Muḥsin (raḥimahu Allāh), some of which in the handwriting of al-Murtaḍā Muḥammad b. Yaḥyā (ʿalayhumā al-salām), which he wrote in the hijra of al-Hādī ilā al-Ḥaqq (ʿalayhi al-salām) in al-Ġayl of Ṣaʿda, and among them some which were written in the darb al-Nāṣir li-Dīn Allāh (ʿalayhumā al-salām), which is well known in the space between al-Ġayl of Ṣaʿda and darb Yursam." al-Ġayl of Ṣaʿda again is cited here, and the author (or the narrator) combines with it the word "hijra". The meaning of this word is a multiple one, among others "emigration from an unbelieving society to a place held by Believers." (Donner 2012: 203, cf. 85f, 118, 134; for its contemporary usage cf. Dresch 1993: 145 - 149) al-Hādī Yaḥyā's son al-Murtaḍā Muḥammad, who as successor of his father reigned as imam for only a relatively short time, abdicated in favor of his brother al-Nāṣir Aḥmad but remained an important and famous learned man until his death in May 922. He obviously lived in al-Ġayl, in this place held by believers, among them his father al-Hādī ilā al-Ḥaqq. Of the old town of Ṣaʿda, the author just mentions the darb Yursam. darb obviously is used here with a similar meaning as Ibn al-Mujāwir's usage, as a quarter of a town (or a town, or a group of houses) surrounded by a wall:[16] It seems relatively clear that with this half of the imam's old friends, the Yursam, the old town of Ṣaʿda is intended. Between the two, al-Ġayl and Ṣaʿda, the "darb al-Nāṣir li-Dīn Allāh" was situated, a fortified cluster of houses which possibly corresponds with the western, now destroyed imam's quarter which at a later point of time was incorporated into the town (cf. Niewöhner-Eberhard 1985: fig. 4). In any case, if we remember the scene of al-Nāṣir Aḥmad's oath of allegiance or bayʿa, the following gathering of people occurred between Ṣaʿda and al-Ġayl. Maybe this was the place where Aḥmad built his dwelling houses (see figure 5).

WHEN DID AL-ĠAYL BECOME ṢAʿDA?

How long the old town named Ṣaʿda was in use, and at what time the qaryat al-Ġayl was renamed to Ṣaʿda cannot be stated exactly. But it seems logical that al-Ġayl was renamed only when old Ṣaʿda had lost its importance at least to a great extent. In any case, this process must have taken place after the death of ʿAbdallāh b. ʿUmar al-Hamdānī (d. ca. 315/927), the author of the biography of imam Aḥmad, or after the death of Musallam al-Laḥjī (d. 545/1150): in their texts, the old town is just called Ṣaʿda, and there was no necessity to specify further which one was meant, the old or the new one: al-Ġayl still was al-Ġayl. But when al-Muḥallī takes up the same narrative, he has to specify that he means old Ṣaʿda. Consequently there must have been a possibility of ambivalence in his time: it was not clear whether Ṣaʿda designated the old or the new town. Obviously, the old town was still functioning at al-Muḥallī's time, but the new town (the former al-Ġayl) could already also be called Ṣaʿda. We can sum up and maintain that somewhere during the hundred years between 1150 and 1250 the new town had gained enough importance to be called with the name of the old town.

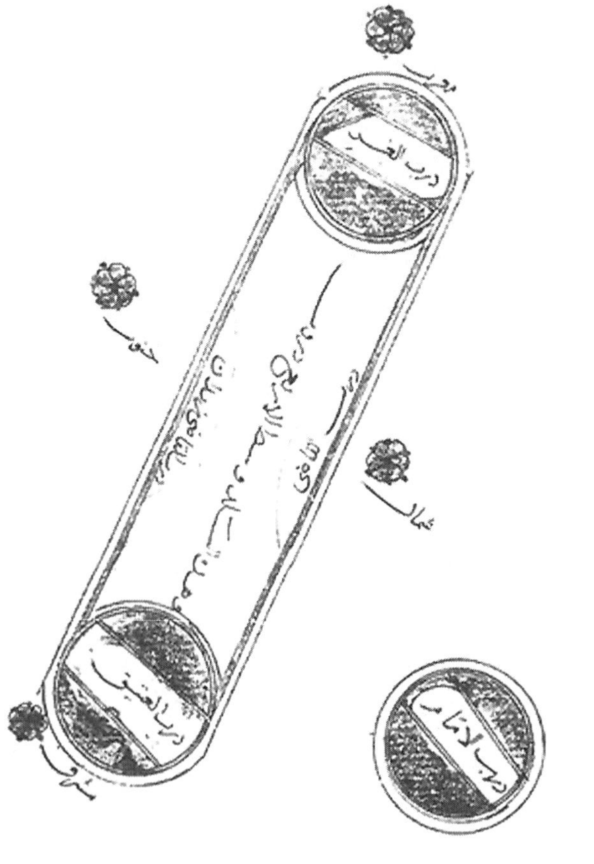

Figure 5: Ibn al-Mujāwir's map of Ṣaʿda (from the Istanbul manuscript): north is shown on the right side, the circle to the right is called "darb al-imām", the imam's quarter

[16] Ibn al-Mujāwir 1986/1407: 204-206, describing Ṣaʿda, cf. Ibn al-Mujāwir & Smith 2008: 213-214

CONFLICT AGAIN

In a text towards the end of the biography of al-Hādī ilā al-Ḥaqq (at least in the form as it came down to us), in a part which possibly was not written by al-'Abbāsī al-'Alawī, a fitna brakes out again in (old) Ṣa'da (al-'Abbāsī al-'Alawī 1981/1401: 406) between Ukayl (with Ṣan'ānī merchants on their side) and Yursam. Like in former times, each side had their allies, and their areas of retreat. This happened at the beginning of the year 322, corresponding to December 22nd, 933, when the imam al-Naṣir Aḥmad b. Yaḥyā was still alive. But he died in the following year, on June 6th, 934. Immediately after his death two of his sons, al-Qāsim b. Aḥmad and al-Ḥasan b. Aḥmad, began to quarrel about the succession.

One of the brothers, al-Ḥasan b. Aḥmad, cooperated with Ukayl and the Ṣan'ānis in (old) Ṣa'da, and with banū Baḥr[17], banū Kulayb and banū Jumā'a (al-'Abbāsī al-'Alawī 1981/1401: 411) from the surroundings of the town. One of the strongholds of that party was Wādī 'Alāf which according to al-Hamdānī (al-Hamdānī 1984/1394: 249) was "the best wādī of Ḫawlān" and which "belonged to the banū Kulayb and to inhabitants of Ṣa'da". Since banū Kulayb were allies of Ukayl, their fertile valley becomes a safe haven for Ukayl. We can now specify al-Hamdānī's "inhabitants of Ṣa'da": clearly he intends the Ukayl.

The other one of the sons of imam al-Nāṣir Aḥmad, al-Qāsim b. Aḥmad was allied with banū Ḥamra or Ḥumra[18] (who stayed in al-Ġayl), banū Sa'd and Yursam (al-'Abbāsī al-'Alawī 1981/1401: 410). Besides al-Ġayl, one of his strongholds was al-'Aššā, a wādī not far from the town, which again according to al-Hamdānī belonged to the banū Sa'd b. Sa'd together with al-Ġayl and another wādī named al-Baṭina (or al-Buṭna). If one tries to integrate the parties of this conflict of the years 326/7 or 938/9 into a schematic sketch, it would be the following:

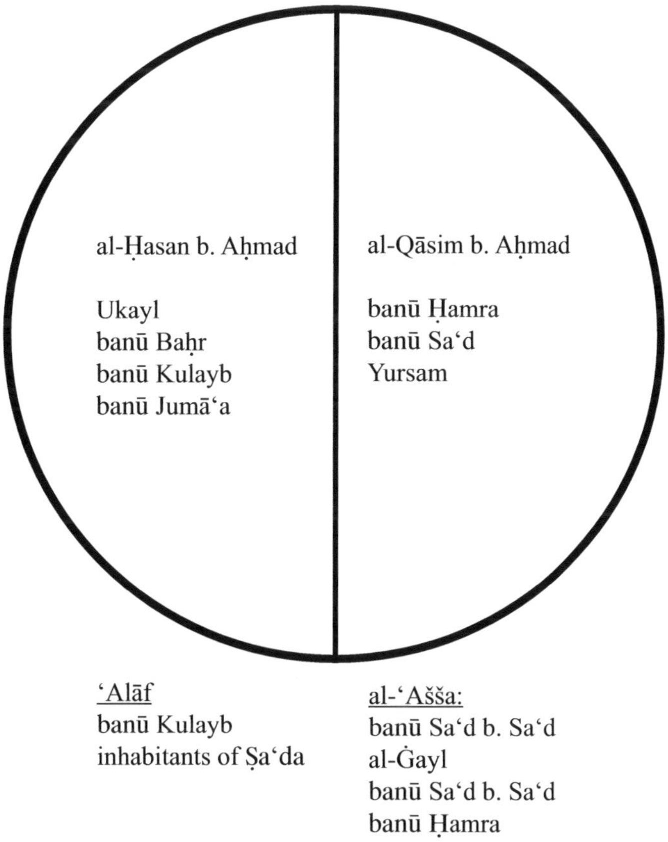

Figure 6: The conflict in Ṣa'da between 322/934 and 327/939

---

17 in Suhayl Zakkār's edition "banū Naḥr", which should be corrected.

18 the editor Suhayl Zakkār writes „banū Ḥamza" which should be corrected.

If one compares the figures 1, 2, 3 and 6 it becomes immediately clear that there are important similarities between the conflict parties, with only few differences: on figure 6 banū Baḥr and banū Jumā'a appear for the first time on the Ukaylī side, and banū Ḥamra or Ḥumra on the Yursamī side. But banū Baḥr, a group of mixed origin, are originally built into the genealogy of al-Rabī'a b. Sa'd like Ukayl (cf. Heiss 1998: 126-130, 245). The banū Ḥamra or Ḥumra, like banū Baḥr a group of mixed origin, consisted partly of groups reckoned to be the offspring of Sa'd b. Sa'd (cf. Heiss 1998: 131-137). It comes as no surprise that in a variant of their genealogy banū Ḥamra or Ḥumra appear as sons of Sa'd b. Sa'd (cf. Heiss 1998: 136; al-Hamdānī 1954/65: 146). In a loose way these groups genealogically belonged to their respective sides and possibly were not mentioned before – partly because greater units were given by the authors, e.g. Sa'd b. Sa'd, comprising the bigger part of banū Ḥamra or Ḥumra, or al-Rabī'a b. Sa'd including banū Baḥr. It is remarkable that two groups show up here with no fixed or with mixed descents. This fact alone shows that there existed conflicts which necessitated a flexible and changeable genealogy, particularly when old commitments were dissolving and new ones were not quite formed. Only the mention of banū Jumā'a constitutes something new which could point to a change in intratribal relations in the Ḫawlān-federation.

A comparison of the figures furthermore shows that nothing much changed in the conflict in and around Ṣa'da between at least the time of the arrival of Yaḥyā b. al-Ḥusayn in the year 897 (and presumably earlier) and the conflict between his grandchildren, the sons of al-Nāṣir Aḥmad, which ended with the death of one of them, al-Ḥasan b. Aḥmad, on 13th of ḏū al-Qa'da 327/August 31st, 939. The conflict which supposedly was settled by al-Hādī ilā al-Ḥaqq in reality had lingered on for the next forty years, possibly in a rather suppressed state for some years. Judging from the final outcome, the first imam was not able to end the conflict successfully. But it is revealing and in a way trendsetting how the two quarreling brothers, al-Ḥasan b. Aḥmad and al-Qāsim b. Aḥmad, intervened in that conflict and used the parties as allies for their purposes. Or was it the other way around: Did the conflict parties use the two quarreling brothers for their respective purposes?

The answer would be that both, the sons of the imam and the conflict parties hoped to gain from their alliances. With this alliance of religious and tribal players in a conflict at that time (and presumably already before that time) the actors introduced a kind of cooperation which was perpetuated for many years after, and possibly such alliances disclose a political/religious interconnectedness and (hopes for) mutual gain which are typical for the relations between the tribal society like the one prevailing in southern Arabia, and religiously legitimated elites. The result was a kind of unstable or uneasy equilibrium which could easily be disturbed and was disturbed again and again, granting the imams new instances of mediation.

CONCLUSION

Like similar instances in the Ḥaḍramawt, the old town of Ṣa'da with its two groups of inhabitants represented a conflict-prone model of living together, in the northern case resulting in two separated halves which had to be entered through different gates. The separation of the halves did not prevent the development of a major conflict between the groups of the inhabitants and their allies. As a mediator in this conflict, the first imam was invited to come to Yemen, but in the long run he was not successful: the conflict lingered on and broke out again after forty years. Yet the situation had changed: the first imam and his two successors and sons could use their tribal allies in their wars against their adversaries who in most of the cases were also groups of tribal origin. The grandsons had to proceed differently: they had to use the tribal conflict for their purposes: in their quarrel for succession they had to decide between one of the two parties of the conflict as allies: one side had to build an alliance with the former adversaries and had to justify this change of opinion.

The town (or the towns) of Ṣa'da are examples for different kinds of towns, of which the younger one shows clear influences of religion regarding its foundation and its center consisting of the mosque of al-Hādī with his tomb and those of his sons. The sūq in the neighborhood cannot be counted as primarily influenced by religious concerns. Regarding the first version of Ṣa'da we simply do not know if there was a mosque in the center with a sūq near to it. But the variants of these two cities alone and the differences between the towns of Ḥaḍramawt as described by Linda Boxberger indicate the validity of a sentence like the following:

"Viewed from such a religious standpoint, sub specie aeternitatis, urban phenomena appear as constants within a historical continuum stretching over some thirteen centuries, and within a Muslim world covering three continents, as far as distant China" (Raymond 2008: 49).

There certainly are no constants concerning urban organization. Urban phenomena are bound to change from time to time, and they can have a deceptively stable outlook if seen only from the reduced perspective of religion, economics, ideologies etc. alone. To modify Raymond's formulation: urban phenomena have to be looked at with a whole complex of determinants in mind.

REFERENCES

al-'Abbāsī al-'Alawī, 'Alī b. Muḥammad b. 'Ubayd Allāh (1981/1401). *Sīrat al-Hādī ilā al-Ḥaqq Yaḥyā b. al-Ḥusayn b. al-Qāsim* (Ed. Suhayl Zakār, 1981, 2nd ed., Bayrūt: Dār al-fikr li-l-ṭibā'a wa-l-nashr wa-l-tawzī').

van Arendonk, C. (1960). *Les debuts de l'imāmat Zaidite au Yemen.* (Transl. Jacques Ryckmans). Leyde: Brill.

Boxberger, Linda (2002). *On the Edge of Empire. Hadhramawt, Emigration, and the Indian Ocean, 1880s-1930s.* Albany: State University of New York Press.

Donner, Fred M. (2012). *Muhammad and the Believers. At the Origins of Islam.* Cambridge: The Belknap Press of Harvard University Press.

Dostal, Walter (1985). *Egalität und Klassengesellschaft in Südarabien. Anthropologische Untersuchungen zur sozialen Evolution (Wiener Beiträge zur Kulturgeschichte und Linguistik 20).* Horn-Wien: Berger Verlag.

Dozy, Reinhart (1968). *Supplément aux Dictionnaires Arabes* (Reprint of edition from 1881). Beyrouth: Librairie du Liban.

Dresch, Paul (1993). *Tribes, Government, and History in Yemen.* Oxford: Clarendon Press.

Forrer, Ludwig (1966). Südarabien nach al-Hamdānī's „Beschreinung der arabischen Halbinsel". *Abhandlungen für die Kunde des Morgenlandes, 27*(3). (Reprint of edition from 1942, Nendeln: Kraus).

Gellner, Ernest (1969). *Saints of the Atlas.* Londen: Weidenfeld & Nicolson.

Gingrich, Andre & Heiss, Johann (1986). *Beiträge zur Ethnographie der Provinz Sa'da (Nordjemen). Aspekte der traditionellen materiellen Kultur in bäuerlichen Stammesgesellschaften.* Wien: Verlag der Österreichischen Akademie der Wissenschaften

al-Hamdānī, Abū Muḥammad al-Ḥasan b. Aḥmad b. Ya'qūb. *Kitāb al-iklīl al-juz' al-awwal.* (Ed. Oskar Löfgren, 1954/65, Uppsala, Wiesbaden, Haag, Genève: Almqvist & Wiksell).

al-Hamdānī (1974). Ṣifat Jazīrat al-'Arab. (Ed. Muḥammad b. 'Alī al-Akwa' al-Ḥiwālī. al-Riyāḍ: Manšūrāt Dār al-Yamāma li-al-Baḥt wa-al-Tarjama wa-al-Našr).

al-Hārūnī al-Ḥasanī, Yaḥyā b. al-Ḥusayn b. Hārūn (1996/1417). *al-ifāda fī tārīḫ a'immat al-Zaydīya (Original Title: al-ifāda fī tārīḫ a'immat al-sāda)* (Ed. Muḥammad Yaḥyā Sālim 'Izzān). Ṣan'ā': dār al-ḥikma al-Yamānīya.

Heiss, Johann (1987). Historical Aspects of Ṣa'da, a Yemeni Town. *Proceedings of the Seminar of Arabian Studies, 17*, 63-80.

Heiss, Johann (1998). *Tribale Selbstorganisation und Konfliktregelung. Der Norden des Jemen zur Zeit des ersten Imams (10. Jahrhundert).* PhD thesis. University of Vienna.

Ḥumayd b. Aḥmad al-Muḥallī (1982/1402). *Kitāb al-ḥadā'iq al-wardīya fī manāqib a'immat al-Zaydīya. s.l.* (Copy of a manuscript from the year 1938/1357).

Lane, Edward William (1984). *Madd al-Qāmūs. An Arabic English Lexicon.* (Reprint of edition from 1863/93). Cambridge: Islamic Texts Society.

Ibn al-Mujāwir (1986/1407). *ṣifat bilād al-Yaman wa-Makka wa-ba'ḍ al-Ḥijāz al-musammā ta'rīḫ al-mustabṣir.* (Ed. Oskar Löfgren. Bayrut: dār al-tanwīr li-l-ṭibā'a wa-al-našr. Reprint of edition from 1951/54).

Ibn al-Mujāwir. *A Traveller in Thirteenth-Century Arabia: Ibn al-Mujāwir's Tārīkh al-Mustabṣir.* (Ed. G. Rex Smith, 2008, London: Hakluyt Society).

Madelung, Wilferd (1990). *The Sīra of Imām Aḥmad b. Yaḥyā Al-Nāṣir li-Dīn Allāh from Musallam al-Laḥjī's Kitāb Akhbār Al-Zaydiyya bi al-Yaman.* Exeter: Ithaca Press.

Našwān b. Sa'īd al-Ḥimyarī (1999/1420). *Šams al-'ulūm wa-dawā' kalām al-'Arab min al-kulūm.* 12 Vols. (Ed. Ḥusayn b. 'Abdallāh al-'Amrī, Muṭahhar b. 'Alī al-Iryānī, Yūsuf Muḥammad 'Abdallāh. Beirut/Damaskus: Dār al-fikr/Dār al-fikr al-mu'āṣir).

Niewöhner-Eberhard, Elke (1985). *Ṣa'da. Bauten und Bewohner in einer traditionellen islamischen Stadt. (Beihefte zum Tübinger Atlas des Vorderen Orients. Reihe B, Nr. 64).* Wiesbaden.

Raymond, André (2008). The Spatial Organization of the City. In: Salma K. Jayyusi, Renata Holod, Attilio Petruccioli & André Raymond (Eds.). *The City in the Islamic World, Vol. 1* (47–70). Leiden: Brill.

INHABITING TRIBAL STRUCTURES: LEADERSHIP HIERARCHIES IN TRIBAL UPPER YEMEN (HAMDĀN & KHAWLĀN B. ʿĀMIR)

Marieke Brandt

INTRODUCTION

During his fieldwork in Yemen in the early 1970s, Walter Dostal had the opportunity to make observations of the social and economic organization of the Banī Ḥushaysh, a member tribe of the Bakīl confederation. These observations were incorporated into his article *Sozio-ökonomische Aspekte der Stammesdemokratie in Nordost-Jemen* (1974) and were later elaborated in his monograph *Egalität und Klassengesellschaft in Südarabien: Anthopologische Untersuchungen zur sozialen Evolution* (1983). *Egalität und Klassengesellschaft* includes a detailed exploration of the genealogy, religion, social stratification, kinship system, and political and economic organization of the Banī Ḥushaysh and compares it with the tribal societies of the Shiḥūḥ and the Banī Shumaylī of Rās al-Khaymah (UAE). It reflects Dostal's comprehensive approach to the study of local societies; in other words, his conviction that no understanding of a society is complete without the study of a broad range of its aspects and features. Yet the neo-evolutionist assumptions Dostal uses in *Egalität und Klassengesellschaft* may now seem exotic to those not immersed in the debates of that time.

The period of his stay with the Banī Ḥushaysh was characterized by the aftershocks of the 1962 revolution and the subsequent eight-year civil war that led to the overthrow of the imāmate and the establishment of the Yemen Arab Republic (YAR). The profound changes in the political landscape throughout Upper Yemen had direct repercussions on the tribal society of the Banī Ḥushaysh. The incipient realignment of political positions and alliances in the early YAR triggered reshuffles in tribal power relations among the Banī Ḥushaysh; it is therefore not surprising that one of Dostal's key observations was related to the rapid changes of tribal leaders and their empowerment and disempowerment through their tribal groups. The frequent changes in the office of the tribal leaders and the absence of a fixed duration of their tenure led Dostal to the formulation of his theory of "uninheritability of political offices" (Unvererbbarkeit der politischen Ämter). Dostal also observed that the higher a tribal leader's rank in the hierarchy of the tribe, the more obvious the "fluid nature" and "instability" of his position and authority became. With these observations, Dostal covers central points of the complex organization of tribal leadership in Upper Yemen, namely the question of the connection between tribal structure, leadership hierarchies, and fluidity and stability of authority.

This chapter is dedicated to an investigation of these connections. In comparison to the beginning of the 1970s, and due to profound ethnological and social anthropological research in that area since then, we today have a far greater knowledge available of the tribal societies of Upper Yemen. This makes it possible not only to focus on a single tribe (e.g. the Banī Ḥushaysh), but to evaluate tribes and even tribal confederations in a comparative perspective. For this reason, I have chosen two tribal confederations of Upper Yemen as subjects of this investigation: the large confederation of Hamdān (which consists of the two independent confederations Ḥāshid and Bakīl) and the confederation of Khawlān b. ʿĀmir. Using the empirical example of these confederations, this chapter aims at answering the following research questions: How do tribal structures and leadership hierarchies of tribes and confederations relate to each other? How are power and authority conceptualized and distributed among the tribal leaders? And what are the differences between these confederations with regard to the concept of tribal leadership?

Both confederations are made up of similar constituent elements and are structured in a similar hierarchical way. Tribal leaders, entitled *shaykh*, administer the tribal groups of both confederations. Yet the investigation of two central tasks of these shaykhs, namely representation and jurisprudence (arbitration), reveals that both confederations have developed slightly different models of tribal leadership. Whereas among Hamdān the concept of leadership is reflected in the term *shaykh mashāyikh*, the specific conceptualization of tribal leadership among Khawlān b. ʿĀmir manifests itself in the leadership model of the *shaykh al-shaml*. In other words, both confederations have developed different modes to organize and to "inhabit" actually homologous tribal structures. Hence, the structures of tribes and of confederations and the features, which make up their socio-political organization, need to be distinguished.

The entities, called tribes and tribal confederations, found throughout rural North Africa and the Middle East are diverse polities and the differences between them are worth further investigation. In the recent past, several ambitious studies have been published which proposed a new reading of "the Arab tribe", by emphasizing hierarchical status differences.[1] The tribes inhabiting Upper Yemen are in many respects also very different, while academic awareness of the differences between them is underdeveloped. The following investigation shows that they must not be "lumped together" but rather considered differently, in all their aspects, and that we should indeed talk about the "tribal societies" of Upper Yemen, in the plural.

THE CONFEDERATIONS OF HAMDĀN AND KHAWLĀN B. ʿĀMIR

Upper Yemen (*al-Yaman al-Aʿlā*) is a landscape dominated by mountains and plateaus, which extends from some 100 km south of Ṣanʿāʾ to the Saudi border in the north, and from the steppe and desert areas of the large Empty Quarter (*Al-Rubʿ al-Khālī* and its southern extension, the *Arḍ al-Jannatayn*) in the northeast and east to the escarpment to the Tihāmah coastal plain in the West. South of Ṣanʿāʾ, approximately at the Sumārah pass, Upper Yemen changes into Lower Yemen (*al-Yaman al-Asfal*). Upper and Lower Yemen are not only geographically diverse regions, but also vary in sociological and denominational terms. A relatively large proportion of rural Upper Yemen's inhabitants are tribally organized and followers of the Zaydī-Shiite school of thought and jurisprudence. In Lower Yemen, by contrast, tribal norms are less pronounced and a majority of its inhabitants follows the Sunni-Shāfiʿī school of thought and jurisprudence.[2]

The tribes (sing. *qabīlah*, pl. *qabāʾil* or *qubul*)[3] of Upper Yemen have organized themselves into confederations: associations of independent tribal units, which occasionally act together outwardly, but retain their sovereignty. The main confederations of Upper Yemen are the large Hamdān[4] confederation (which consists of the two separate smaller confederations of Ḥāshid and Bakīl, also referred to as the "two wings" of Hamdān) and the confederation of Khawlān b. ʿĀmir. The Hamdān (Ḥāshid and Bakīl) make up the largest tribal confederation of Upper Yemen. It consists of politically important tribes, which occupy strategically significant territory from around Yemen's present-day capital Ṣanʿāʾ to the Saudi Arabian border in Yemen's Northeast. A large part of the area around and north of Ṣanʿāʾ and east of the western mountain chain (*Sarawāt*) is called the land or territory of Ḥāshid and Bakīl (*bilād Ḥāshid wa Bakīl*).

Note on transliteration: For transcribing Arabic, I have used the system of the *International Journal of Middle Eastern Studies* (IJMES) for both written and spoken words. Common words, such as Yemen and Saudi Arabia, are given in an Anglicized version. Many Arabic words I have treated as English words (e.g., *shaykhs, marāghahs, naqībs, Ḥūthīs*) instead of using their Arabic plural form (*shuyūkh/mashāyikh, marāghāt, nuqabāʾ, Ḥūthiyyūn*). The Arabic *bin* or *ibn* ("son of"), where it comes between two names, has been given as simply *b.* throughout. Initial *hamzah* is unmarked.

[1] See, for example, Bonte et al. 2001.

[2] Although tribalism is particularly pronounced in Upper Yemen, areas in the south and east of Yemen are also influenced by tribal norms, such as Shabwah, al-Mahrah, Yāfiʿ, Abyān, etc.

[3] The use of the term "tribe" is contentious, including among anthropologists. With regard to the Province of Ṣaʿdah, Weir (2007: 1-5) describes tribes as political-territorial (rather than descent-based) units. Because rural Upper Yemen is divided into territorially contiguous tribes, everyone unavoidably lives in a tribe. For a critique of the term "tribe" cf. Mundy (1995), Wedeen (2008: 170-176) and Blumi (2010: 19-34). For an overall discussion of the term cf. Gingrich (2001b: 15906-15909).

[4] The large Hamdān confederation (consisting of the sub-confederations of Ḥāshid and Bakīl), also called Hamdān b. Zayd, must be distinguished from the homonymous member tribe Hamdān of the Ḥāshid confederation (for a better distinction usually called Hamdān Ṣanʿāʾ) and Hamdān al-Jawf, a Hamdānid tribe which neither belongs to Ḥāshid nor to Bakīl. Furthermore, among the Shākir, Wāʾilah and some segments of Dahm together are referred to as Hamdān al-Shām ("northern Hamdān") or Hamdān Ṣaʿdah (Lichtenthäler 2003: 44).

Parts of the northwest quadrant of Upper Yemen and the adjacent areas of Saudi Arabia are inhabited by the tribes of the confederation of Khawlān b. ʿĀmir.[5] The settlement area of the Yemeni tribes of the Khawlān b. ʿĀmir confederation reaches from a few miles east of the provincial capital, Ṣaʿdah, extending over the town in the west to the border of the Saudi Arabian Jīzān province. In the south, the territory of the confederation begins about ten or fifteen miles from Ṣaʿdah and extends to the north and northwest to the Saudi provinces of ʿAsīr and Najrān.

The names Ḥāshid and Bakīl as well as Khawlān b. ʿĀmir are pre-Islamic.[6] Ḥāshid and Bakīl see themselves as genealogically linked with each other; their genealogy perceives them as descendants from a common ancestor named Jusham b. Ḥubrān b. Nawf b. Hamdān (Al-Jirāfī 1951: 19; Dresch 1989: 5, 1991a). By contrast, the tribes of Khawlān b. ʿĀmir trace their origin back to an ancestor called Quḍāʿah (Caskel 1966 (II): 56-57; Robin 1982a: 35-36; Bāfaqīh 1990: 99-103; Brandt i.pr.). These genealogical descent lines are largely constructs and results of manifold processes of tribal fusion and fission; the perception of a shared "ancestry" is to a greater or a lesser extent a statement of identification following the general Middle Eastern practice in conceptualizing groups as kin. Such statements of identity are, however, seldom understood by the tribesmen themselves in actual genealogical terms (Dresch 1989: 78-79, Weir 2007: 121, Brandt i. pr.). The perceived common ancestry corresponds to the common visual representation of tribes as "segmentary groups": tree-like structures, which divide and subdivide in the manner of the branches of a tree, though there is no central and pre-eminent trunk, all branches being equal (fig. 1 and 2).[7]

The confederations of Ḥāshid and Bakīl subdivide into a number of member tribes. The constituent tribes of Ḥāshid are al-ʿUṣaymāt, ʿIdhar, Khārif, Banī Ṣuraym, Sanḥān, Bilād al-Rūs, and Hamdān Ṣanʿāʾ; the member tribes of Bakīl are Sufyān, Arḥab, Nihm, ʿIyāl Yazīd, ʿIyāl Surayḥ, al-Ahnūm, Murhibah, Banī Maṭar, Banī Ḥushaysh, Khawlān al-Ṭiyāl, and the Shākir tribes which consist of Dahm and Wāʾilah (Dresch 1989: 24). All member tribes further subdivide extensively. In spatial respect, the tribes of Ḥāshid and Bakīl do not form territorially contiguous blocks, but rather resemble a chessboard pattern with the eastern part of Upper Yemen, especially the Northeast, dominated by Bakīl.

The territory of the confederation of Khawlān b. ʿĀmir in the north-western part of Upper Yemen is bisected through the international boundary between Yemen and Saudi Arabia into a Saudi and a (territorially and demographically) larger Yemeni part.[8] The so called Ṭāʾif line of 1934, which was confirmed by the Treaty of Jeddah in 2000, places five out of eight member tribes of Khawlān b. ʿĀmir on Yemeni territory (Jumāʿah, Saḥār, Rāziḥ, Munabbih and the homonymous member tribe Khawlān) and three on Saudi territory (Fayfāʾ, Banī Mālik, and Balghāzī). The Yemeni Khawlān b. ʿĀmir tribes Saḥār, Jumāʿah and Khawlān dwell on the high plateau of Upper Yemen above the rift valley-edge to the Red Sea, with which also the Jabal Rāziḥ is still connected by the elevated basin of Ghamr. Munabbih is located below this edge of the rift valley on an isolated mountain massif. The tribal neighbours of Khawlān b. ʿĀmir are Hamdān (Bakīlī Shākir tribes and Sufyān) to the east and south, the Tihāma to the west and tribes of the Saudi ʿAsīr confederation to the north.

---

[5] The confederation is sometimes also called Khawlān b. ʿAmrū, Khawlān Quḍāʿah or Khawlān al-Shām, see Gingrich & Heiss 1986: 16-20; Gingrich 1989a: 145-158, 1994: 11; Heiss 1997: 53; Weir 2007: 121-123.

[6] Serjeant 1982: 16-18. The confederation of Khawlān b. ʿĀmir must be distinguished from Khawlān al-Ṭiyāl, a Bakīl member tribe dwelling east of Ṣanʿāʾ.

[7] The segmentary model was introduced by Evans-Pritchard (1940) with regard to the Cyrenaican Bedouins and further elaborated by Gellner (1969: 41-44; 1981: 117; 1991: 109) for the Berber of the High Atlas. According to this theory, these tree-like structures are essentially homologous, and each comprises more or less egalitarian kin groups, which replicate in all but size those of which they are part. According to segmentary theory, neither within segments nor between them are there any specialized political institutions or groups, and the fundamental concept of segmentarism as theory of politico-legal action is that of "balanced opposition": no segment has specialized or permanent political functions, and there is no "crucial level of social organization" (Gellner 1981:117; 1991: 109). In the absence of effective leaders, order and the balance of power are maintained by collective action, mainly in response to external threats. The segmentary model has been challenged by several anthropologists and is now regarded defunct (Dresch 1986: 321; Caton 1987, 1991; Weir 2007: 3-4 with regard to Yemen). It is useful, however, for illustrating the tree-like pattern of structural organization of a tribe, and in this chapter the term *segmentary* denotes solely structural (rather than socio-political) phenomena.

[8] For the Yemeni-Saudi boundary dispute, see Schofield 1999, 2000; al-Enazy 2005; Heinze 2010.

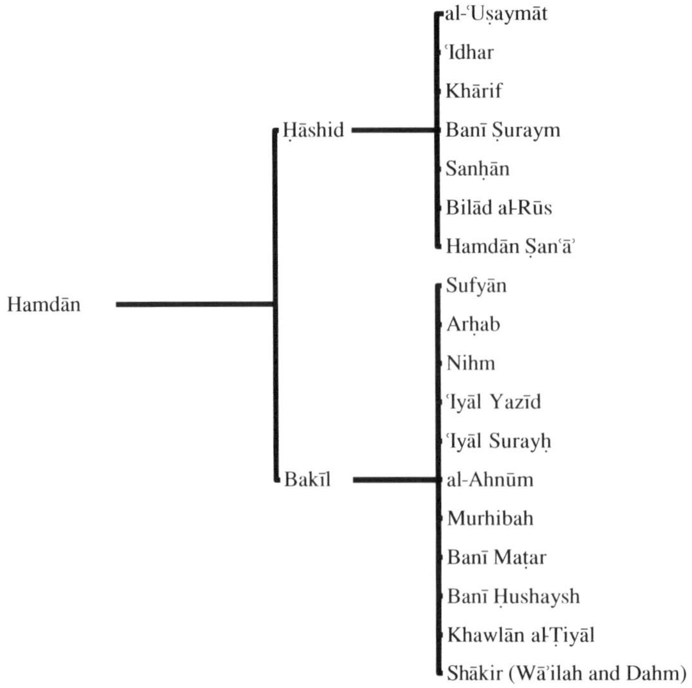

Figure 1: The confederation of Hamdān b. Zayd

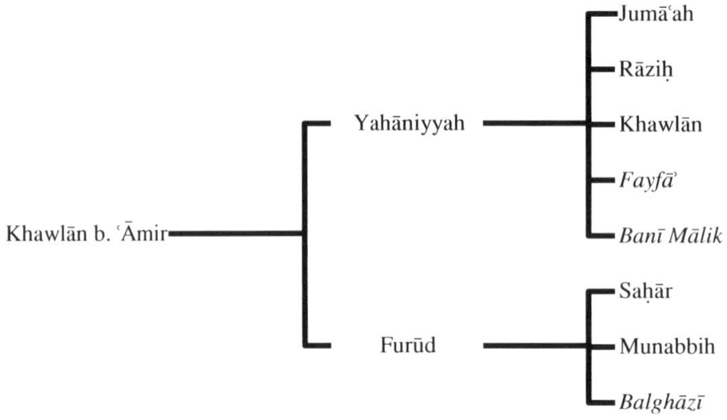

Figure 2: The confederation of Khawlān b. ʿĀmir (italics: Saudi tribes)

The confederation of Khawlān b. ʿĀmir is segregated into the territorially interspersed moieties of Furūd and Yahāniyyah (Philby 1952: 486, 488-506; Gingrich 1989a: 158-166; 1994: 21-22, Brandt i. pr.). The moieties of Khawlān b. ʿĀmir are genealogical constructs, which do not denote independent confederations, as do Ḥāshid and Bakīl of Hamdān (Brandt i. pr.). The tribes of the Yahāniyyah moiety include Rāziḥ, Khawlān, Jumāʿah, Fayfāʾ, and Banī Mālik. The tribes of the Furūd moiety include the tribes Saḥār, Munabbih, and Balghāzī. Each of these eight member tribes is subdivided into tribal moieties, and the tribal moieties further subdivide into numerous sections, segments, and clans.

To a certain extent, the terminology used in Yemen to designate tribal divisions is inconsistent and ambiguous.[9] The conventional academic terminology in describing a tribe – for instance, *baṭn* (pl. *buṭūn*), *fakhdh*

[9] Among the Hamdān confederation there seems to be no privileged level of organization that stands out in all circumstances, nor any standard distinction of terminology between one level and the next, and the vocabulary denoting sections and sub-sections varies

(pl. *afkhādh*), and *ḥabl* (pl. *ḥibāl*), referring to divisions and sub-divisions of confederations and of tribes – is rarely applied consistently within the tribes of Upper Yemen.[10] The tribes of Upper Yemen use the term *qabīlah* (tribe) to describe Ḥāshid, Bakīl or the Khawlān b. ʿĀmir federation as a whole, but they also refer to the constituent tribes of these confederations, such as al-ʿUṣaymāt or Sufyān, and sometimes even to smaller units, such as "the tribes of Rāziḥ" (Weir 2007), as *qabīlah*. Most tribal sub-divisions are referred to as *farʿ* (branch, section) or *ʿasharīyyah* (pl. *ʿashāʾir*), meaning tenths, which can of course also be thirds (*thulth*, pl. *athlāth*), quarters (*rubʿ*, pl. *arbāʿ*), etc., rather than in generic terms, such as *fakhdh*, or *ḥabl*. To all tribal divisions applies the term *qism* (pl. *aqsām*), meaning, division, part, which is therefore commonly used by local sources to describe tribal affiliations. In the following, in order to harmonize the terminology, the term *confederation* will be used to describe the overall communities of Ḥāshid, Bakīl and Khawlān b. ʿĀmir, the term *tribe* will be used to describe the constituent tribes of these confederations, and the terms *section* or *segment, sub-division* and *clan* will describe the divisions of those tribes in descending order.

Although they make up the majority of the population of Upper Yemen, the tribespeople are not the only social category in Yemen. The stratification system of Upper Yemen comprises three principal status categories:[11] the religious aristocracy (*sādah*, sing. *sayyid*), the tribespeople (*qabāʾil*, sing. *qabīlī*), and a third diverse low status occupational category known as "weak" people (*ḍuʿafāʾ*, sing. *ḍāʿif*). Both *sādah* and *ḍuʿafāʾ* are under the "protection" of the tribes, with *ḍuʿafāʾ* being considered "below" them and the *sādah* being considered "above" them. The religious aristocracy of the *sādah* exercises important religious and legal functions; until 1962 the imāms and the administrative elite of the imāmic state emerged from this stratum. Another once politically important status category, which stands apart from this tripartite formulation, is that of the hereditary jurist-administrators (*quḍāʾ*, sing. *qāḍī*), who are considered of *qabīlī* stock, but were formerly ranked above other *qabīlīs* because of their education (the study of Islamic law), and their role in the imāmic state (Dresch 1989: 136-140).

Basic principles of tribal leadership: As a general feature of the tribal societies of North Africa, the Near and the Middle East, tribal groups (except the smallest units on clan level) are usually represented by chieftains or "headmen", as translated by Serjeant from the Arabic term *shaykh* (pl. *mashāyikh* or *shuyūkh*).[12] Given the number of tribal units, the number of shaykhs is therefore almost indeterminately large. It does, however, happen that tribal sections have no shaykh or numerous shaykhs without clear affiliations to certain tribal divisions (we shall touch on such examples later).

The shaykhs perform important tasks for the benefit of the community. These include the administration of their tribal units and the promotion of its welfare through representation of tribal interests, both internally and externally, i.e., towards other tribal groups as well as towards state institutions. Another key task of the shaykhs is problem solving, and mediation and arbitration in tribal conflict in accordance with the tribal customary law. In times of conflict and crisis, the military mobilization of their tribal units according to tribal norms and traditions is incumbent upon the shaykhs.[13] During the imāmate, the shaykhly duties also comprised the collection of the *zakāt* tax (together with the local *sādah*), a task that is now often performed by the Local Authorities (*al-sulṭah al-maḥalliyyah*) of the republican Yemeni state.

The shaykhs administer their tribal groups through a second tier of tribal officials, called the "notables" or "elders". These elders have regionally different names, such as *aʿyān* (sing. *ʿayn)* or *kibār* (sing. *kabīr*), and are chosen from other leading clans. These elders represent and administer their clans and assist and deputize

from place to place, see Dresch 1989: 78. The same applies to Khawlān b. ʿĀmir terminology describing tribal structures, see Brandt (i. pr.). However, this ambiguity of local nomenclature seems to be highly unusual in all but few areas of Southwest Arabia.

[10] For the generic terminology describing tribal structures, see Dostal 1974: 3.

[11] On Yemeni status categories, see Gerholm 1977: 109-138; Adra 1982; Meissner 1987; Dresch 1989: 117-157; Gingrich 1989a: 137-144, 1989b; Weir 2007: 51-52. In addition, on Ṣanʿāʾ, see Dostal 1979; Mermier 1985, 1993.

[12] Serjeant 1977: 228. The role of shaykhs in Yemeni tribal society is well documented, see for example Serjeant 1977: 228-230; Dresch 1984a; 1989: 97-106; Weir 2007: 95-120, Adra 1982, Gingrich 1989a: 105-136, 1989b.
The term can denote both a tribal or a religious leadership position, as expressed in the terms *shaykh al-qabīlah* (tribal leader) and *shaykh al-dīn* (Islamic scholar). Whereas in the extreme Northwestern parts of Yemen the common plural of *shaykh* is *shuyūkh*, in central Yemen the plural is *mashāyikh* (Gingrich 1989a: 572 n. 66). Also a shaykh's close agnates may be called shaykh.

[13] In some tribal areas, e.g., Munabbih of Khawlān b. ʿĀmir, shaykhs themselves rarely participate in armed conflict as this is usually left to minor local shaykhs (Gingrich 1989a: 123, 1989b: 77, 1993: 26; Brandt 2012).

for the shaykh (Weir 2007: 68). Below them is a third tier of head men (*umanā*, sing. *amīn*) or *ʿuqqāl* (pl. of *ʿāqil*), a kind of "village mayor", who represent and administer hamlets (Weir 2007: 68; Dresch 1984a: 36; Dupret 2000b). Shaykhs are therefore part of a governing team, a practice which helps the institution of shaykhdom (*mashīkh*) survive the inadequacies of individual shaykhs (Weir 2007: 102).

Group cohesion is created through the principles of solidarity and collective responsibility, which are a legal extension of the basic values of "tribalism" (*qabyalah*), and upheld by the rules of tribal law (Adra 1982). The shaykhs do not have supreme and/or coercive power over their tribal groups; they do not "govern" them (Dresch 1984a: 41; Weir 2007: 79). Shaykhly rule is not equivalent to forms of coercive leadership, such as royal leadership, which requires the leader to exercise a restraining influence by force. Terms such as "shaykhly rule" or "shaykhly power" are therefore to some extent inappropriate and ambiguous because the concept of "power" is linked with the ability to achieve desired goals, if necessary, without the consent of all persons affected. The position of a shaykh in his tribal constituency can be better denoted as a position of "authority" because the principle of authority refers to the capacity of individuals to influence events as a result of widely recognized knowledge, prestige, or position. The shaykh is therefore forced to avoid antagonising the members of his group; otherwise his leadership will not last. Only in certain situations, i.e., during the process of arbitration and legal appeal, a temporary binding, coercive relationship between the concerned tribesmen and the involved shaykh is established (we will return to this point below). It is up to every member of the tribe not to agree with the opinion and actions of his shaykh and in particularly severe cases of disagreement, tribal members may also leave a tribe and entrust themselves to the representation and jurisdiction of another shaykh (Weir 2007: 112-120).

The absence of formal power and command implies that the concept of shaykhly authority should be understood essentially in symbolic terms. Shaykhs normally have no coercive power. Depending on their personal reputation and abilities they can, however, exert enormous influence on the members of their tribal constituencies. Caton has demonstrated that power, such as it exists in this system, must be achieved through persuasion, and a shaykh's ability to verbal suasion is one of the most important prerequisites for the successful tenure of a shaykh's office (Caton 1987, 1990). Burckhardt, the Swiss traveller in Arabia, noted the following (for southern Ḥijāz): "a shaikh, however renowned he may be for bravery, or skill in war, can never expect to possess great influence over his Arabs without the talent for oratory. A Bedouin will not submit to any command, but readily yields to persuasion" (Burckhard 1831: 250). Only through personal influence, not by coercive powers, can shaykhs mobilise large numbers of men in tribal affairs and national politics alike.

Shaykhs are not socially superior to their tribesmen as they are – usually, but not always – basically of the same stock (Serjeant 1977: 236). The shaykhs are elected by their tribal constituency from families in whom the office of the shaykh is hereditary; shaykhly succession is therefore both hereditary and elective. The shaykh is a "primus inter pares" (Gingrich & Heiss 1986: 19) whose investiture and performance must be in accordance with the members of his tribal constituency. The elective element of shaykhly succession and the absence of a strict and exclusive pattern of succession, such as primogeniture, mean that succession in shaykhdom is not passed on from the father to one of his male offspring, but can be transferred to any eligible, prominent and able person of the chief's clan.

The absence of primogeniture can cause intense competition for office within shaykhly clans because ancestry alone (without conjunction with primogeniture or some other form of restrictive rule) normally over-produces leadership.[14] Ideally, superior attributes and abilities decide whether a candidate can prevail against his rivals for the office of the shaykh. The age is not decisive, what matters is "superiority of abilities" (Niebuhr 1792: 18). These superior abilities include the aspirant having demonstrated that he is capable of administering a tribe or tribal unit and dealing with other tribes and officials; before his election he has usually been for a time part of the "escort" of its predecessor (Gingrich 2011: 40-44). He should be familiar with the tribe's rules and customs in mediation and arbitration. In addition, by referring to the famous phrase of Dresch, "his 'belly' should be 'full of politics'" (Dresch 1989: 100), he should be able to assert the interests of his tribe not only against other tribes, but also against the government. To a certain degree, the status of

[14] This is a common feature of tribal societies in the Near and Middle East, see Gellner 1981: 210. It also applies to imāmic rule in Yemen; as pointed out by Madelung (1987: 176), the disapproval of hereditary succession in the Zaydī doctrine created dynastic problems and Zaydī history witnessed bitter struggles among brothers, relatives and other sāda lines for succession.

the shaykh is not only inherited, but also "earned" through continuous and honourable performance of his intra-and intertribal duties and tasks before and after his investiture (Gingrich 1989a: 131). Dostal described the complex election processes of shaykhs, which consist partly in direct, partly in indirect elections, through electoral committees (Dostal 1985: 230). The investiture of a new shaykh is confirmed within a tribal document, which all who have elected him sign.

Ideally, the most capable successor is selected, and both the preferences of the old shaykhs as well as public opinion play a crucial role in the nomination of a successor. In practice, however, it often happens that not the "superiority of abilities", but the influence of groups from within and outside the tribe controls the selection of the shaykh. For example, the incumbent shaykh can prefer a certain son or relative and introduce him preferentially in the practice of leadership and its privileged knowledge (Gingrich 1989a: 129, 131-132; Abū Ghānim 1985: 251-298). Some candidates may have large support groups within the tribe which compete with other groups and both will try to impose their candidates in the election by asserting that only their branch of sub-clans is entitled to office (Weir 2007: 989). Moreover, particularly influential and/or strategically important tribes often attract external attempts to influence the shaykhly succession and to control the investiture of the shaykhs. Such interference is reported from the time of the Ḥamīd al-Dīn imāms, when imāms – notably Imām Aḥmad – tried to influence the succession of certain (often from the imām's point of view "recalcitrant") shaykhly lines and in some cases attempted to depose entire shaykhly lines and replace them with more "suitable" ones (Wenner 1967: 65; O'Ballance 1971: 27-28). Since the end of the 1960s civil war, the patronage politics of the Yemeni government has achieved similar effects. Governmental influence in areas with strong tribal traditions relies mainly on the political and financial co-optation of local shaykhs. In addition, the "superiority of abilities" (Niebuhr) is a relatively ambiguous category because, depending on local conditions, different character traits and skills can qualify a potential successor to the shaykhly office, and these preferences can, just as political situations and other external circumstances, be subject to rapid changes.

By way of example, at the time when the shaykh of a minor, but strategically and politically important tribal segment of a Khawlān b. ʿĀmir member tribe died in 1997, this tribe was facing a menacing environment characterized by the looming Ḥūthī conflict. One could say that the interests of the Ḥūthīs were diametrically opposed to the interests of that particular shaykhly line. After the death of the old shaykh his second born son was elected his successor because he had a reputation of boldness and recklessness and the courage to face armed conflict; character traits which at that time were considered being particularly important for pursuing this tribal segment's interests in the conflict-ridden environment of Ṣaʿdah. After this new shaykh – predictably – came into violent clashes with the Ḥūthīs who finally displaced almost the entire shaykhly line, his firstborn (also exiled) brother began to grow into the role of the segment's shaykh. At the time of their father's death this firstborn son was not taken into consideration when the new shaykh was selected, because he had the reputation of being harmony-oriented and avoiding conflicts (*la yuḥibb mashākil*), in other words: too conciliatory. These character traits, however, regained crucial importance after the shift of the power structures in Ṣaʿdah in 2011 in favor of the Ḥūthīs and in particular during the National Dialogue[15], which in part seeks to encourage contact and reconciliation between Ḥūthīs and their (tribal, political, and denominational) contenders. Hence, the firstborn brother became a National Dialogue delegate, representing not only his tribal segment but rather the displaced tribes and tribal elites of Ṣaʿdah in their entirety during the protracted and extremely difficult negotiations with Ṣaʿdah's new Ḥūthī suzerains. In the long run it can be expected that the Ḥūthīs as the new shadow government in Ṣaʿdah will try to influence the succession within this shaykhly line and to enforce the election of a candidate who is receptive and responsive towards their positions and interests. Since the positions of the Ḥūthīs and this shaykhly line still remain utterly incompatible, Ḥūthī pressure may even be harder and lead to the marginalization of this shaykhly line and the empowerment of another, more cooperative one.

By the interplay of selection and succession, it is usually impossible that someone is elected as the successor of a shaykh without descending from the same genealogical line. Once on a track, shaykhly clans are

[15] The National Dialogue, which started in March 2013, aims to set in motion a process of national transition. By bringing together the different groups in Yemen it will address a range of issues related to the transition process. If successful, the dialogue will lead to renew a vision for a "civil state", presidential elections 2014, and the drafting of a new constitution. If the dialogue stalls, state failure and the danger of a new civil war will loom ominously as a likely outcome.

extremely difficult to derail. The deselection of a shaykh, as observed by Dostal among the Banī Ḥushaysh, actually occurs only in rare cases when a shaykh proves extremely incapable (Dostal 1985: 238). This is also due to the fact that shaykhly lines usually inherit important tribal documents and contracts whose knowledge and handling is essential for the performance of the shaykhs duties and responsibilities (Gingrich 1989a: 131-132; Weir 2007: 101). This explains why many shaykhly lines of Upper Yemen could, despite all historical vicissitudes and rivalries, maintain their positions throughout centuries.

The longevity of shaykhly lines and the principle of dynastic succession are reflected by the continuous reference to the eponymous lineage ancestors through the use of the affix *ibn* or *bin* (son of). Upon inauguration, each newly elected office holder of a long-standing shaykhly line receives this affix – e.g. Ibn Muqīt, Bin al-Aḥmar, etc. – which identifies him as the agnate of the historical founder of this particular shaykhly line. The title remains his "term of address" and "term of reference" throughout his tenure, and under this common name all shaykhs of the same line operate and have done so in some cases for over a thousand years. Thus the official name of the shaykhs from long-standing shaykhly lines is a genealogical designation, which declares the agnatic legitimacy of its bearer (Gingrich 1989a: 134).

These are the basic principles of tribal leadership as they can be observed throughout Upper Yemen and in similar forms elsewhere in south-western and southern Arabia, and to a certain extent also among many other tribal societies of North Africa and the Near and Middle East, notwithstanding important regional and social differences. Turning to the substance of this chapter, in the following I shall examine – on the basis of the commonalities outlined so far – different concepts of leadership prevailing among the tribes of Khawlān b. ʿĀmir and Hamdān. The distinct features of these tribes become clear if one looks at the layers of authority in tribal leadership which these tribes have developed — specific orders of precedence which correspond more, or less, with the internal structures of the respective tribes. These specificities in hierarchy and precedence become particularly evident by close consideration of two key responsibilities of tribal leaders: representation and jurisprudence (arbitration).

REPRESENTATION

Clans, sections, tribes and confederations are, as demonstrated, the principal entities of tribal organizations in Upper Yemen. These have corporate identities that transcend generations, and normally (but not always) each of these entities has at its apex a shaykh. The shaykhs are arranged in a more or less hierarchical order, i.e., they form layers of authority and of corresponding responsibilities in respective sub-fields of chiefly authority. These layers of authority are not automatically synonymous with a power structure; rather they indicate the position of shaykhs within the internal organization of the tribe or the confederation. These layers of authority and their function differ from confederation to confederation, and often even from tribe to tribe.

Before we consider the layers of authority and orders of precedence among the shaykhs in regard to their responsibilities of representation, we should examine their distribution within the tribal structures. The Khawlān b. ʿĀmir case allows an examination of the relation between tribal structure, position of shaykhs and layers of authority more readily than one can in most other tribes. One will rarely find a tribal confederation in which the relationship between these aspects is as orderly and stable as among Khawlān b. ʿĀmir.

The confederation of Khawlān b. ʿĀmir is, as we have seen, distinguished into the moieties of Furūd and Yahāniyyah. The tribes of the Yahāniyyah moiety include Rāziḥ, Khawlān, Jumāʿah, Fayfāʾ, and Banī Mālik. The tribes of the Furūd moiety include the tribes Saḥār, Munabbih, and Balghāzī. Each of these eight member tribes of the confederation subdivides into tribal moieties, and the tribal moieties further subdivide into numerous segments, sub-divisions, and clans.[16]

From the smallest to the largest groups, almost every one of these groups is represented by a shaykh. The shaykhs are, according to tribal internal organization, hierarchically ranked. The order of precedence among the shaykhs of Khawlān b. ʿĀmir corresponds to the structural order of the tribes and the confederation as

[16] Bipartite structures are also proven for the other constituent tribes of the Khawlān b. ʿĀmir confederation: Munabbih subdivides into the Shaʿshaʿ and ʿAliyyin moieties (Gingrich 1989a: 185-191, 1994: 25-26; Chelhod 1985: 56), Rāziḥ into Aḥlāf and Jihwaz (Chelhod 1985: 56; Weir 2007: 130-135), and Saḥār into Kulayb and Mālik (Chelhod 1985: 56; Gingrich & Heiss 1986: 170 n. 120; Lichtenthäler 2003: 41). The same applies to the member tribes on the Saudi side of the confederation.

a whole. On every level of the tribal structure, except the clan level, the tribal groups and their shaykhs are linked by a *shaykh al-shaml* (Gingrich 1989a: 105-124, 1994: 101; Weir 2007: 129-30). The term *shaml* is derived from the Arabic term *shamila*, meaning "uniting or gathering together", equivalent to the ancient Arabic term *mujammiʿ*, the "uniter" (Serjeant 1977: 228-229, 1982: 14). The *shaykh al-shaml* "gathers" (*yashmil*) the members of his tribe or tribal group as well as their particular shaykhs as a body against others and allows them to act as a unit in so far as he "gathers the word of all". The principal task of the *shaykh al-shaml*, whether at the level of tribal segments, tribal moieties, member tribes, confederation's moieties, or the whole confederation, consists in the representation of his respective tribal entity and the representation of the entity's interests towards third parties, be it other tribal units or the government (Gingrich 1989: 105). The *shaykh al-shaml* is a higher tribal representative and diplomatic authority than his coequal peers or colleague shaykhs of the same structural level within the tribal hierarchy. The representative function of the *shaykh al-shaml* is always associated with a well-defined tribal group that forms the addition of his title, for instance, *shaykh shaml al-ʿAbdīn*, *shaykh shaml Saḥār*, *shaykh shaml Furūd*, or *shaykh shaml Khawlān b. ʿĀmir*, and these titles indicate that the *shaykh shaml* of Saḥār has a higher rank in regard of tribal representation than the *shaykh shaml al-ʿAbdīn* because al-ʿAbdīn is a segment of Saḥār, etc.

This order of precedence can be demonstrated with the example of the *shaykh shaml Khawlān b. ʿĀmir*, the highest representative of the confederation. Jumāʿah tribe consists of twelve sections: Banī ʿUthmān, al-Baytayn, Banī Ḥudhayfah, Banī Shunayf, Ilt al-Rubayʿ, Āl Talīd, Majz, al-Maʿārīf, Banī ʿUbbād, Banī Suwayd, Āl Jābir, and Qaṭābir (Brandt i. pr.). Six out of these twelve sections belong to the tribal moiety of Naṣr, and each of these sections is further divided into sub-divisions, clans, etc. The Banī ʿUthmān section has three sub-divisions (Āl Thawbān, Banī al-Ḥārith, and Banī al-Khuṭāb), and each of these sub-divisions is gathered and represented by its *shaykh al-shaml*. Ibn Muqīt, the *shaykh al-shaml* of Āl Thawbān, gathers and represents all sub-divisions of Banī ʿUthmān, whereas the other two shaykhs only represent their own sub-divisions. Banī ʿUthmān and the five other sections constitute the Naṣr moiety. Also the Naṣr moiety is gathered and represented by Ibn Muqīt, who therefore occupies the position of *shaykh shaml qabāʾil Naṣr*. The sections of the other tribal moiety, the Aḥlāf, are represented by Ibn Ḥadabah. The senior shaykh of the Naṣr moiety, Ibn Muqīt, is also structurally superior to the senior shaykh of the Aḥlāf moiety and therefore occupies the position of the *shaykh al-shaml* for the whole Jumāʿah tribe. On this hierarchical level, he has within the Yemeni Khawlān b. ʿĀmir tribes four coequal peers, and within the whole Federation of Khawlān b. ʿĀmir in Yemen and Saudi Arabia, seven coequal peers, namely the *shuyūkh al-shaml* of the other seven tribes of Khawlān b. ʿĀmir confederation: Ibn al-ʿAzzām of Rāziḥ, Ibn Rawkān of Khawlān, Ibn al-Fayfī of Fayfāʾ, Ibn al-ʿAthwān of Banī Mālik, Ibn Jaʿfar of Saḥār, Ibn ʿAwfān of Munabbih, and Ibn al-Ghazwānī of Balghāzī. Five of these (including Ibn Muqīt) belong to the confederation's Yahāniyyah moiety, and the other tribes belong to the confederation's Furūd moiety. The confederation's moieties are also represented by certain shaykhs; the senior representative of the confederation's Furūd moiety (*shaykh shaml Furūd*) is the *shaykh al-shaml* of Saḥār, Ibn Jaʿfar. The *Yahāniyyah* moiety is gathered by the senior shaykh of Banū Mālik, Ibn ʿAthwān. Ibn Muqīt is, however, structurally superior (albeit he does not represent one of the confederation's moieties); Ibn Muqīt is therefore the structurally highest-ranking shaykh of all tribes of the Khawlān b. ʿĀmir confederation and entitled the *shaml shumūl* or *shaykh shaml Khawlān b. ʿĀmir al-kubrā*.[17] Simultaneously, he is the head of the *majlis al-shuyūkh* (the shaykhs' council) of Khawlān b. ʿĀmir, which consists of the senior shaykhs of the member tribes of Khawlān b. ʿĀmir and which comes together on certain rare occasions (Gingrich 1989a: 127-128, 157).

Historically the position of Ibn Muqīt as the highest representative of the confederation was at some times connected with enormous tribal prestige and influence; his position is, however, not recognized by all member tribes alike.[18] His supreme position does not wield stable power; the extent of power which his office confers depends on the personal capabilities of the incumbent. Until the 1962 revolution and the subsequent civil war, the Muqīt family maintained close (but not always conflict-free) relations with the Zaydī

[17] Ibn Muqīt is not only the head of all Khawlān b. ʿĀmir tribes in Yemen and Saudi Arabia, but de jure even of tribal groups of Khawlānī stock in other countries of the Arabian Peninsula and North Africa, see Brandt (i. pr.).

[18] For reasons of inter-tribal rivalry and due to their own opposition to the royalists, the Munabbih do not recognize the authority of Ibn Muqīt to the same extent as the other member tribes of the Khawlān b. ʿĀmir confederation (Gingrich, pers. communication).

imāms which were reinforced through marriage relations with influential *sayyid* families (Gingrich 1989b). Similar to the tribes of Ḥāshid and Bakīl, the fortunes of many tribal leaders from Khawlān b. ʿĀmir were bound up with those of successive imāms, struggling with them for power and influence, and supporting or opposing them during conflicts with their rivals.[19] During the 1960s civil war, Yaḥyā Muḥammad Muqīt, the then incumbent, was a staunch royalist, who supported Imām al-Badr "with all might" (*bi-quwwah*). He is still remembered by many people in Khawlān b. ʿĀmir with tremendous admiration. During her fieldwork in Rāziḥ in the 1970s, local informants reported to Weir that Yaḥyā Muḥammad Muqīt "had to be obeyed" (Weir 2007: 137), and *sādah* from Ḍaḥyān, normally cautious about endorsing tribal shaykhs, told me with undisguised admiration that Yaḥyā Muḥammad Muqīt "was capable of ruling Yemen and what is adjacent to it" (*kāna muʾahhal li-ḥukm al-Yaman wa mā jāwrihā*). Both *sādah* and *qabāʾil* honour the family as a pillar (*rukn*) of the Zaydī order.

Due to their royalist stance during the 1960s civil war, the Muqīt family has since lost much of its former power and influence. The successor of Yaḥyā Muḥammad Muqīt, Ḥasan, accomplished the turn towards the now dominant republican power. Yet he never managed to gain the political influence of the so-called *shuyūkh al-thawrah* – those shaykhs who supported the republic during the civil war, were rewarded accordingly for their allegiances, and who did not hesitate to play off their starting advantages against their rivals. In addition to these long-term effects of intra-tribal rivalry, the assemblage of multiple and contradictory tribal, local, national and international loyalties, which arose after the 1960s civil war in the interplay between local and domestic politics, the republican Yemeni government, and Saudi Arabia make it difficult for Ḥasan Muqīt to reflect publicly unequivocal positions, although this would not be impossible, as the al-Aḥmar example of Ḥāshid shows (we shall return to this below). He rather exerts his influence through arcane diplomacy in camera and hidden from the public gaze, pursuing his tribal and political objectives through formal and informal relationships. The consequence is a certain lack of transparency that undermines the prerogatives of tribal representation. Consequently, he has been animadverted for neglecting the principle of the *shaml* (the one who gathers, represents, or unites) as a central part of his supreme title, position, and authority. This lack of representation became particularly obvious during the Ḥūthī conflict because in times of utmost threat and disruption of the confederation during the Ḥūthī wars, tribal policy towards the state and the Ḥūthīs should not have been delayed by arcane diplomacy.

The enormous stability and persistence of hierarchies and layers of authority among Khawlān b. ʿĀmir is demonstrated by the fact that the century-old system of the *shaml* remains unaffected by this ebb and flow in power and political fortune.[20] The Muqīt shaykhly line, regardless of how powerful or insignificant the respective incumbents may be, continues to provide the highest representative of Khawlān b. ʿĀmir, even if other shaykhs, who may stand far below him in regard to this order of precedence, have temporarily gained far more power, influence, and wealth. These "minor" shaykhs push their own objectives through in the tribal environment of Khawlān b. ʿĀmir; however, its ancient order of representation and its layers of formal authority are maintained and preserved.

Compared to Khawlān b. ʿĀmir, the precedence of representation among the shaykhs of the Hamdān confederation – the tribes of Ḥāshid and Bakīl – is less stable. It is to a far greater extent negotiable and alterable and subject to the assertiveness of the individual shaykh. The office of the shaykh is constantly bound to those families claiming hereditary entitlement to shaykhdom, but the order of precedence among them is subject to a bargaining process among rival tribal shaykhs from the same "nested group". This comparatively pronounced fluidity of authority contributes to a decentralisation of representation among the tribes of the Hamdān confederation. At first glance this seems surprising: since at least the early eighteenth century, the position of senior shaykh of all Ḥāshid is inherited within the al-Aḥmar shaykhly line of al-ʿUṣaymāt (we

[19] On mutual alliances and interdependences between imāms, tribes and shaykhs, see Dresch 1989: 198-230 passim; 1991b.

[20] According to local evidence, the Muqīt shaykhly line holds the position of the *shaykh al-shaml* for the whole of Khawlān b. ʿĀmir since about 600 years. The current hierarchical structure has probably evolved in medieval times to coincide with the formation of the confederation. Before that time, different local families and lineages competed for supremacy. The Muqīt shaykhly line is apparently of extreme long standing: Al-Hamdānī mentions in al-Iklīl (Iklīl 1: 130) that in the 10th century AD Banū Naṣr already had the dominion over Jumāʿah. The incumbent Ḥasan Muḥammad Muqīt can recite a pedigree of 64 ancestors (sing. *jidd*), which certainly goes back to the 10th century AD, if not further (Brandt i. pr.).

shall return to this point below). Apart from this prominent example, the precedencies of representation and leadership hierarchies among the tribes of the Hamdān confederation are far less regular and stable than among Khawlān b. ʿĀmir.

We should at first cast a glance on the overall tribal divisions of this large confederation. Hamdān consist, as we have seen, of the two independent confederations Ḥāshid and Bakīl. The constituent tribes of the Ḥāshid confederation are al-ʿUṣaymāt, ʿIdhar, Khārif, Banī Ṣuraym, Sanḥān, Bilād al-Rūs, and Hamdān Ṣanʿāʾ. The Bakīl confederation comprises Sufyān, Arḥab, Nihm, ʿIyāl Yazīd, ʿIyāl Surayḥ, al-Ahnūm, Murhibah, Banī Maṭar, Banī Ḥushaysh, Khawlān al-Ṭiyāl, and the Shākir tribes Wāʾilah and Dahm. These tribes further subdivide extensively. In some cases, not every element of the tribal structure has a shaykh of its own. For Dhū Ḥusayn (a segment of Dahm), Banī Ṣuraym, Arḥab und Khārif, such irregularities are documented. These tribes or some of their sections have either numerous shaykhs on the same structural level without any order of precedence or no shaykh at all (Dresch 1984a: 37, 1989: 90; Chelhod 1970: 71).

In contrast to Khawlān b. ʿĀmir, where a representative of tribal units and the confederation as a whole is called *shaykh al-shaml*, we are witnessing among the tribes of Ḥāshid and Bakīl the phenomenon of the *shaykh mashāyikh* (Rathjens 1951: 175; Serjeant 1967: 284-297; Dresch 1984a: 31-49). The term *shaykh al-shaml*, although by no means unknown, is used only occasionally in central Yemen (Serjeant 1977: 228-119). In English the title of the *shaykh mashāyikh* is often translated into "shaykh of shaykhs" or "paramount shaykh" and refers to those shaykhs who occupy a particularly influential position among their coequal peers, with their charisma and influence often radiating far beyond their original tribal units.

By contrast to Khawlān b. ʿĀmir among whom the position of a *shaykh al-shaml* is constantly inherited within the same shaykhly lines, among Hamdān the position of a *shaykh mashāyikh* is historically less restricted to certain shaykhly lines. Especially among Bakīl, yet not only there, it is subject to active negotiation between competing shaykhs or shaykhly lines, whose claims are disputed and occasionally even fought over.

The prestigious position of a *shaykh mashāyikh* itself is not related to coercive power over other shaykhs and tribes. However, since this position is the result of an active bargaining process among rivals, it is usually much closer to the concept of power than the position of the *shaykh al-shaml* among Khawlān b. ʿĀmir. Not all of the individual tribes of each confederation recognize a *shaykh mashāyikh* of their own, and even here the position can remain contested between different competing shaykhly lines (Dresch 1984a: 37). Where a *shaykh mashāyikh* is recognized, his position is expressed in a document, which his "brother" shaykhs in the tribe all sign (Dresch 1984a: 37, 1989: 102).

Dresch illustrates this struggle for authority and representation among the Hamdān by using the example of the homonymous member tribe of the Hamdān confederation, Hamdān Ṣanʿāʾ of Ḥāshid, which occupies a territory north and northwest of the capital Ṣanʿāʾ (Dresch 1984a: 38). Before the 1960s civil war, the position of the *shaykh mashāyikh* of Hamdān Ṣanʿāʾ was held by ʿĀṭif al-Musallī, but was then "taken over" by Muḥammad al-Ghashmī, whose brother later enjoyed a brief period as President of the Republic before being assassinated in 1978. The rivalry between the shaykhly lines of al-Musallī and al-Ghashmī persisted and repeatedly led to violent conflicts over the "paramountcy" of Hamdān Ṣanʿāʾ. A similar rivalry happened in Banī Maṭar, a Bakīl section in the mountains west of Ṣanʿāʾ; before the civil war its *shaykh mashāyikh* came from Bayt Rammāḥ, but the position was then taken by Aḥmad al-Maṭarī, whose family were previously only shaykhs of a minor section of Banī Maṭar (Dresch 1984a: 38). Dostal, too, describes this struggle for paramountcy among the Banī Ḥushaysh in the 1970s (Dostal 1985: 239). In all cases, the profound political changes during and after the 1960s civil war led to a realignment of political positions and alliances, a restructuring of power relations and, ultimately, a reshuffle of the layers of authority and the vigorously enforced rise of shaykhly lines at the expenses of others.

Until today the tribal power relations among the tribes and sections of the Hamdān confederation are continuously rebalanced. By way of example, the Wāʾilah are one of the four sections of the Shākir (Bakīl) occupying vast territories in the east and north-east of Ṣaʿdah province and to the south, in the adjacent areas of al-Jawf.[21] Wāʾilah subdivides into numerous sub-sections, and each of these sections and their subdivisions are represented by one or more shaykhs. The most prominent of them come from the shaykhly lines

[21] For more information on Wāʾilah, see Gingrich 1993 and Lichtenthäler 2003.

of al-ʿAwjarī, Shājiaʿ, Dughsān, Qamshah, al-Ithlah, Dāyil b. Fāris, al-Kaʿbī, and al-Razzāmī, just to mention a few. Depending on the changing historical and political circumstances in that region, during the past forty years, each of these shaykhly lines of Wāʾilah gained prominence and influence, which radiated beyond the borders of Wāʾilah: the al-ʿAwjarī by their staunch royalist stance during the 1960s civil war and their subsequent radical shift in favour of the republic, the Dughsān by their connections to the communists of Southern Yemen in the years after the 1960s civil war, the Shājiaʿ at the turn of the millennium by their protest against the implementation of the Treaty of Jeddah and their violent challenge of the Yemeni and Saudi states, the al-Ithlah by their ties with radical Sunnism, the al-Razzāmī and parts of the al-Kaʿbī as supporters of the Ḥūthī movement since its very beginning, and all of them as extremely successful promoters of licit and illicit cross-border trade in an environment characterized by the substantial absence of state structures. According to historical contexts, one of them is always more "visible" to outsiders than the others and hence appears publicly as *shaykh mashāyikh Wāʾilah*, but none represents Wāʾilah as a whole. A local source explained this to me in the following way: "There is no one who gathers them officially (*la yashmilhum aḥad rasmiyyān*)... there is simply one of them at each time more prominent and influential than the others". Wāʾilah is a particularly politically diverse and competitive environment, and the prevalent diversity of political positions and the violent particularism of Wāʾilah's segments and divisions indicate that the possibility for one of them to gather or to represent the others is extremely low. Depending on the political agenda of a time, one of them may appear publicly as *shaykh mashāyikh Wāʾilah* even though he is neither elected by his colleague shaykhs nor recognized as such.

By contrast, among the immediate western neighbour of Wāʾilah, Saḥār of Khawlān b. ʿĀmir, nobody would think of considering the shaykhly lines of Manāʿ or Mujallī, who gained considerable tribal influence, political power and material wealth during and after the 1960s civil war, *shaykh al-shaml* of Saḥār. The position of the *shaykh shaml Saḥār* (along with the position of *shaykh shaml Furūd*) is firmly rooted in the Jaʿfar shaykhly line, despite the fact that their royalist stance during the 1960s civil war virtually led to a continuous loss of most of their previous power and standing, resulting in a decline of influence until it eventually diminished into insignificance.[22]

This ebb and flow of political fortunes and assertiveness does not affect the persistence of tribal relations and their relevance. A *shaykh mashāyikh*, as Dresch admirably elaborated, does not forfeit his previous position, each shaykh always remains the shaykh of the section that his family comes from: "In the way that the paramountcy of a tribe or confederation changes hands one can see politics (in fact, struggles for power) intruding on the formal alignments of shaykhly houses with the tribal structure. A particular shaykhly family is identified first with a particular section but then comes to be identified also with a larger unit; often enough it then loses its grip, as it were, and reverts to being identified only with the section it comes from. The tribal structure remains largely unchanged and shaykhly houses rise and fall within it" (Dresch 1984a: 38). The rise and fall of shaykhly lines and the ebb and flow of their authority and political assertiveness are the reasons why (again, in Dresch's phrase) "the structural or formal domains of shaykhly lines do not neatly match with political significance" (Dresch 1984a: 39). In other words, among the tribes of Hamdān there is a disjunction between the tribal structure and the domains of the shaykhs' actual influence and authority.

This decentralization and fluidity of authority and representation among the tribes of the Hamdān confederation may seem surprising or even contradictory at first sight because, among the Ḥāshid, the position of the *shaykh mashāyikh Ḥāshid* has virtually been inherited since at least the early eighteenth century within the al-Aḥmar shaykhly lineage of al-ʿUṣaymāt (Dresch 1984a: 37). Their almost exclusive entitlement to the high office of the *shaykh mashāyikh Ḥāshid* is due to the fact that the various holders of this position have all been men of great influence, who boosted (and helped to overthrow) imāms and who decisively influenced governments. Until his death in December 2007, ʿAbdullah al-Aḥmar had been the most prominent representative of tribal Upper Yemen, at times even called *shaykh mashāyikh al-Yaman* (i.e., paramount shaykh of [all tribes of] Yemen). Since the beginning of the revolution in 1962, he had held important political offices (Koszinowski 1993; Dresch 2000 passim), and after the 1960s civil war he was so influential that his marriage

[22] On the political marginalization of the Jaʿfar shaykhly line, see Lichtenthäler 2003: 57.

policy even transgressed the traditional social strata in Yemen.[23] After his death, the position of the *shaykh mashāyikh Ḥāshid* was transferred to his firstborn son, Ṣādiq.

Yet this position of the *shaykh mashāyikh* of Ḥāshid is, so to speak, an exception to the rule among Hamdān, and it raises more questions than answers. What exactly is the "paramountcy" of the al-Aḥmar family? Not all of Ḥāshid are equally under the al-Aḥmars' sway. Under the aegis of ʿAbdullah al-Aḥmar, the tribes al-ʿUṣaymāt, Banī Ṣuraym and Khārif formed a remarkably cohesive unit, yet other Ḥāshid tribes, such as ʿIdhar, were largely beyond his influence (Dresch 1984a: 43, 1989: 104-105; Peterson 2008: 16). In the 1970s, Serjeant noted that ʿAbdullah al-Aḥmar's summons to war would even be responded to by Bakīl (Serjeant 1977: 228-229). This appreciation must be viewed in the context of its time and is certainly primarily related to ʿAbdullah's leading role during the large tribal mobilizations of the 1960s civil war and then during the so-called "Revolutionary Correctional Initiative" of President al-Ḥamdī (1974-1977), who took actions to curb the political and military power of the shaykhs in the early YAR, in particular that of the major shaykhs of the north. During the Correctional Initiative, ʿAbdullah al-Aḥmar forged a national tribal alliance, which gathered shaykhs from almost all tribes of Upper Yemen and brought them into position against al-Ḥamdī. Yet already during the 1994 civil war, the title of *shaykh mashāyikh al-Yaman* was only a phrase, which today is no longer heard of at all (Dresch 1995: 40). During the Ḥūthī conflict, the events in Sufyān have clearly shown that the tribes of Bakīl were not even remotely considering following al-Aḥmar's summons, but rather resorted to ganging-up warfare against their "cousins" from Ḥāshid.[24] At the same time the tribes of Khawlān b. ʿĀmir, too, bluntly rejected a summon attempt of Ṣādiq al-Aḥmar. However, the standing and influence of the al-Aḥmar shaykhs is certainly not confined to Ḥāshid. ʿAbdullah's death has left a vacuum in national affairs and in the effective leadership of al-ʿUṣaymāt as well as Ḥāshid, and his son Ṣādiq is unlikely to replace him as a "paramount shaykh" in the same way (Peterson 2008: 16).

The history of the other constituent confederation of Hamdān, Bakīl, has been rather different: The paramountcy of all Bakīl has shifted repeatedly, being contested between different families rather than remaining with a single family, as in Ḥāshid. During the time that the al-Aḥmar were first mentioned as heads of Ḥāshid, the heads of Bakīl were from the al-Juzaylān shaykhly line of Dhū Muḥammad (Abū Ghānim 1985: 208; al-Jirāfī 1951: 181; Dresch 1984a: 37-38). Political upheavals have always had direct repercussions on paramountcy among Bakīl. For example, during the 1960s civil war (1962-1969), two paramount shaykhs of Bakīl were active, mainly in the sense of being war-time leaders of the confederation: Amīn Abū Rās of Dhū Muḥammad, who took a firm republican stance, and Nājī al-Ghādir of Khawlān al-Ṭiyāl, whose sympathies were less clear but were in the late phase of the civil war more with the royalists (Serjeant 1977: 228-229; Dresch 1989: 271 n. 14). The claims of the two families lapsed, although Ṣādiq Abū Rās, Amīn's firstborn son and successor, is now an influential political figure.[25] For some years during the period after the 1960s civil war no one was recognized as *shaykh mashāyikh Bakīl*, but then in 1981 in a huge tribal gathering in Bīr al-Mahāshimah (in Khabb al-Shaʿf area in northern al-Jawf), Nājī al-Shāyif of Dhū Ḥusayn was pushed into the position of the *shaykh mashāyikh Bakīl*.[26] Since the end of the 1960s civil war and the assassination of Amīn Abū Rās in 1978 none has gained, or is likely to gain, the same influence over Bakīl, which the al-Aḥmar recently had over Ḥāshid.[27] This lack of representation and "decentralisation of power", as Caton puts it, is not only characteristic of many Bakīlī tribes, but for the Bakīl confederation as a whole (Caton 1990: 11).

---

[23] From Bruck 2005: 146 refers to the marriage of ʿAbdullah al-Aḥmar ("Amin") with a *sharīfah* (female descendant of the prophet); his son Hāshim is a product of that liaison. For the sāda, increasingly beleaguered since the 1962 revolution, this marriage with the influential shaykh had political reasons.

[24] On the conflict between Ḥāshid and Bakīl during the late phase of the Ḥūthī conflict, see Brandt 2013.

[25] Ṣādiq Abū Rās held different high offices, e.g., Minister of State, Minister of Agriculture, Minister of Civil Service, Minister of Local Administration, Governor of Taʿiz, and most recently the post of a Deputy Prime Minister for the General People's Congress (GPC). He was an influential person of the inner circle of the Ṣāliḥ regime and has been among those who were injured during the blast in the presidential compound's mosque in June 2011, as a result of which he lost a foot.

[26] Serjeant 1977: 228-229; Dresch 1989: 366-372; Caton 1990: 11. Nājī al-Shāyif is said to be a henchman of the al-Aḥmar clan and Saudi Arabia, who put him in place to weaken the influence of Bakīl, and in particular of Bakīl's formerly powerful Abū Rās lineage.

[27] Dresch 1984a: 38; Caton 1990: 11-12. Caton (1987, 1990) also points to the strong position of local *sādah* in Khawlān al-Ṭiyāl whose responsibilities and duties at the time of his fieldwork were comparable to those of a *shaykh mashāyikh*.

After the 1960s civil war, Ḥāshid's dominance was further enhanced by the fact that largely republican Ḥāshid was able to position themselves better in the post-revolutionary republic than most tribes of Bakīl, giving the republican government and administration a certain Ḥāshidī hue, a feature which further increased the discontent of Bakīl. Particularly, the staunch republican *shaykh mashāyikh* of Ḥāshid, ʿAbdullah al-Aḥmar, and his protégés benefited from government patronage, and later on the "gray eminences" of Sanḥān, i.e., relatives of long-time President Ṣāliḥ. During the Ṣāliḥ regime (1978-2011), the small Sanḥān tribe enjoyed tremendous access to state resources. Until Ṣāliḥ's ousting in 2011, it was mainly from members of this group, yet most of them shrouded of secrecy, that the regime's inner circle was drawn.[28] Bakīl, by contrast, did not benefit from links to the centre to the same extent as leading figures of Ḥāshid, although members of the tribal elite from Bakīl became influential power-brokers of the Ṣāliḥ regime as well. Their (real or supposed) under-representation in the republican government and segregation from the inner echelons of power is a subject of continuous dissatisfaction among the tribes of Bakīl and still generates a great deal of "bad blood" between them and their "cousins" of Ḥāshid.

The tribes of Bakīl themselves are well aware that the lack of internal cohesion and unity of the confederation is a major reason for their (perceived or real) political weakness. A number of attempts have been made at resurrecting Bakīlī cohesion, including efforts by various competing shaykhs. Among the most recent was the large gathering in November 2010, which (like the meeting of 1981, in which Nājī al-Shāyif was elected *shaykh mashāyikh Bakīl*) was convened in Khabb al-Shaʿf in the remote desert-like outskirts of the vast Empty Quarter in northern al-Jawf in order to "strengthen and re-organise the house of Bakīl" (*taʿzīz wa tartīb al-bayt al-bakīlī*).[29] The initiative for this assembly was launched by Amīn al-ʿUkaymī, a shaykh of Shawlān (Dahm) and bitter enemy of former president Ṣāliḥ, known for having little reservations in regard to pursuing alliances across the political spectrum. However, the conference did not yield the expected results, since important shaykhs of Bakīl, such as Nājī al-Shāyif, had cancelled their participation and because some tribes of Dahm blocked roads leading to the conference's venue in al-Jawf due to blood feud with other Bakīlī sections.

In June 2013, numerous Bakīlī shaykhs convened a new gathering in Ṣanʿāʾ, again, in order to "unite" the Bakīlī tribes (*min ajl tawḥīd qabīlah Bakīl*) and to address the problematic situation of Bakīl in regard to what they referred to in a joint statement as the "segregation, marginalization, exclusion and deprivation of political participation" of Bakīl during the previous decades. The meeting resulted in the establishment of a 20-point plan in order to enhance the national role of Bakīl (*Mareb Press* 2013). Their radical rhetoric indicates that they are also at odds with the Transitional Government, which replaced the Ṣāliḥ government in 2011, and that they continue to believe that other tribes and shaykhs (particularly, of course, from Ḥāshid) rather than themselves are still in receipt of government's favours. They are, however, unable to overcome their inner tensions and their prevalent particularism, which results in severe limitations of their influence and power, and their attempts to resurrect internal cohesion and alliances do not produce much.

It is evident that among Hamdān the attempt to distinguish between the concepts of authority, influence, and political power founders. Among Bakīl, this confluence of features in shaykhly positions is to some extent reflected in the title *naqīb* (pl. *nuqabāʾ*). The title *naqīb* is pre-Islamic.[30] In Yemen the title *naqīb* is used as a hereditary title for exceptionally influential shaykhly families, most of them of Bakīlī stock (Dresch 1989: 405, 2006: 13 n. 43, 115 n. 38). For instance, the shaykhly lines of Abū Rās, al-Juzaylān, al-Shāyif, al-Ghādir, Thawābah, al-Ruwayshān, etc., bear the title *naqīb* rather than shaykh. Serjeant explains that during the Prophet's lifetime, the *naqībs* of Yathrib (Medina) were tribal headmen in the sense that they "were responsible for the tribes of which they were chiefs and they acted in accordance with customary law of the particular group to which they belonged" (Serjeant 1982: 14). Among Bakīl, the title bears today further connotations. Sources among the above mentioned families gave me their differing definitions of the term. One

---

28 As elaborated by Phillips (2011: 51-53).

29 See the interesting interview given by Amīn al-ʿUkaymī (*Mareb Press* 2010).

30 Sources from Bakīl attribute the term to an ancient religious origin, referring to Surat 5: 11 which says that Allah took a covenant from the Children of Israel (meaning the direct descendants of the patriarch Jacob, also called the "Twelve Tribes") and appointed twelve captains or leaders (*athnī ʿashara naqībān*) among them. The majority of these twelve ancient tribes is now considered "lost" because most of them disappeared from biblical and all other texts after the kingdom were destroyed at about 722 BCE by Assyria and their inhabitants deported or scattered throughout the region (see, for example, Grabbe 2007: 134). The Bakīlī *naqībs* see themselves as descendants of these mythical lost tribes.

source indicated that in the tribal society of Bakīl, the title *naqīb* means someone who "thoroughly examines the people's matters" (*yanqub* [sic!] *ʿan maṣāliḥ al-qawm*), giving it a social dimension in line with the social functions of tribal leadership. Another source explained that *naqīb* is a title of honour for those shaykhs, who could promote the general interests of their tribal communities through their supra-tribal importance and close relationship with the respective state overlords. A third source linked the title *naqīb* to (military) power and associated it with leadership positions in the Popular Army (*al-jaysh al-shaʿbī*) of the imāmic times.[31] The title has numerous, often ambiguous connotations; it denotes those ancient and long-standing shaykhly lines, most of them from Bakīl, which possess considerable influence in tribal and supra-tribal (political and military) spheres. In Yemen, the *naqībs* are the most promising candidates for paramountcy over Bakīl. Any offence against a *naqīb* is, similar to the *muhajjar* shaykhs, *ʿayb* or "disgrace" for which large amends are due.[32]

Among the Khawlān b. ʿĀmir, the layers of authority are directly linked to the tribal internal organization and hierarchies. Layers of authority can only be described by reference to tribal divisions; they derive from tribal alignments or run neatly in parallel with them. The positions of the shaykhs are continually passed on within these shaykhly lines and thus transcend the generations. The formal alignment of shaykhly houses with structural hierarchies is stable, though even the extent of actual influence is very changeable.

Among Hamdān, a more pronounced tendency to decentralization prevails – any attempts to systematically combine tribal subdivisions and actual domains of shaykhs are doomed to failure. The formal alignment of shaykhly houses with tribes and sections is far less regular than in Khawlān b. ʿĀmir. The position of the *shaykh mashāyikh* is a temporary dignity, or power position, which is contested and which has to be asserted and defended against competitors. Among Hamdān, the place of shaykhs cannot be reduced to an epiphenomenon of tribal alignments as in Khawlān b. ʿĀmir. It is not conceivable that the position of the highest representative of Ḥāshid or Bakīl is held by a politically marginalized family, as it is currently the case among Khawlān b. ʿĀmir. The term *shaykh mashāyikh* identifies the temporary predominance of an individual shaykh over the other representatives of the same tribal unit, it locates those who hold power and exert influence and, so to speak, it "ranks" the shaykhs. The different terms of *shaykh al-shaml* and *shaykh mashāyikh* thus refer to differing social positions (Gingrich 1989a: 105).

JURISPRUDENCE

The ability to solve problems is one of the most important capabilities of what all shaykhs of influence are ascribed. Whereas representation is particularly directed to the "outside" – representation of a tribal group of whatever size to other tribes or the state – the legal obligations of shaykhs are directed to the inside of the tribal community, comprising the tasks of mediation and arbitration according to tribal customary law.

The legal situation in Yemen is characterized by the coexistence of different legal systems. There are three options for conflict settlement: jurisprudence according to the rules of tribal customary law (*ʿurf*), according to Islamic justice (*sharīʿah*), or the state judiciary.[33] These legal systems sometimes criss-cross; in criminal cases, for example, the resolution of situations of homicide can often go through the following steps: police intervention, transmission of the case to customary arbitration, initiation of criminal proceedings by the prosecution, conciliation determining blood money and the abandonment of formal proceedings (Dupret 2000a; al-Zwaini 2006: 9-10).

The state has so far been unable to fully exercise its judicial authority through the court system, as a result of which the tribal judicial system is the predominant arena of justice in many rural areas until now. In the rural areas of Upper Yemen, *ʿurf* and *sharīʿah* law are in many ways complementary and thus coexist. They

[31] The Popular Army or *al-jaysh al-barrānī* was a kind of paramilitary force made up of tribal levies and the non-regular wing of the imāmic military forces. It is comprised of tribesmen from the Zaydī highlands, see Fattah 2010: 27-28. Other sources of the 18th century mainly use the title *naqīb* of what look to be slave commanders, see Dresch 2006: 13 n. 43. The title *naqīb* is part of the modern Arab military nomenclature, in republican Yemen denoting the equivalent to a "captain" in British or US military ranks. For tribal militias in contemporary Yemen, see Brandt 2014.

[32] Some *shaykhs* enjoy a status of special protection (*hijrah*) among the tribes, see Puin 1984; Dresch 1989: 103-106.

[33] For an excellent overview over state law in Yemen, see al-Zwaini 2012. As a result of the codification process from the 1970s onwards, Yemeni state law incorporates elements from *sharīʿah* (Islamic law), customary/tribal law, excerpts from Egyptian and other Arab laws, and international principles.

are, however, represented by different social strata: whereas the *ʿurf* is promoted by the tribes, a *sharīʿah*-judge belongs either to a family, whose origins trace back to the Prophet (a *sayyid*), or to a family of judges (*qāḍī*, pl. *quḍāʾ*; sharīʿah law specialists of tribal stock). The *sharīʿah* is synonymous with the order which the *sādah* historically attempted to introduce in Yemen (Dresch 1989: 183-188). By virtue of their extensive knowledge of *sharīʿah*, the informal jurisprudence of these *sharīʿah* arbitrators relates almost exclusively to matters with a religious connotation, like marriage, divorce, and inheritance.

Sharīʿah law and *ʿurf* are closely interrelated with each other, although the former is seen as "divine" and the latter as "man-made". *Sharīʿah* law in part developed from pre-existing southwest and west Arabian law, and *ʿurf* was influenced by *sharīʿah* (Serjeant 1962; Messick 1993: 140, 182-184; Weir 2007: 144-147). The importance and complementarity of *ʿurf* is mainly due to the fact that it contains elaborate provisions regarding numerous issues of prime local concern, such as agriculture, trade, animal husbandry, markets, grazing and water-rights, on which *sharīʿah* law is unspecific or silent (Gingrich 1989a: 117-123; Weir 2007: 145-146; Dresch 2006; Obermeyer 1981). Nevertheless, the relationship between the representatives of *sharīʿah* and those of *ʿurf* is not free of competition; historically, the *sharīʿah* representatives often condemned *ʿurf* and designated it by pejorative terms such as *ṭāghūt* (wickedness) (Glaser 1913; Rathjens 1951: 4; Serjeant 1969: 11; Dresch 1989: 184-188; 2006: 3; Haykel 2003: 65). The relation to *sharīʿah* law differs from tribe to tribe. In Rāziḥ, for example, which historically developed a close cooperation with the local *sādah* and the respective state overlords, *ʿurf* is regarded as fully compatible with *sharīʿah* law (Weir 2007: 145-146). Among their immediate tribal neighbours, the more *sādah*-hostile and isolationist Munabbih, *sharīʿah* enforcement through the *sādah* is regarded as an unwelcome interference in tribal affairs. In such cases, a situation of rivalry and competition between *ʿurf* and *sharīʿah*, between the shaykh and the *sayyid* as an arbitrator, can emerge (Gingrich 1989a: 124-126).

Customary law is a set of principles, rules and local precedent cases that regulates the reciprocal obligations of tribesmen as well as tribal obligations towards people defined as "weak". These may be tribesmen in vulnerable situations or members of the nontribal population. It is oriented towards the peaceful settlement of conflicts. In case of conflict it is applied by way of mediation (*ṣulḥ*) and arbitration (*taḥkīm*). Only when conflict mediation fails will the disputing parties bring their case to arbitration.

For the study of tribal leadership, the consideration of tribal conflict resolution is particularly interesting because a shaykh is bestowed something very like coercive power only while he acts as arbitrator. Normally a shaykh has no formal power over the members of his tribal constituency; but this changes as soon as conflict parties turn to a shaykh and initiate the tribal system of mediation and arbitration. If the problem cannot be immediately solved, the shaykh then takes from each a pledge or surety, called *ʿadl* (e.g., guns, daggers, cash). Once the pledges are taken, the shaykh acts as "guarantor" (*shaykh al-ḍamān*, in Khawlān b. ʿĀmir the material component of this position is also called the *waḍḍān*), meaning he pays the plaintiff in his own group what is due and recovers it from the shaykh of the other section, who in turn recovers it from the culprit in his group (this is one of the reasons why material wealth can boost a shaykh's position). As long as the pledges are held, the case is said to be "on the honour" of the shaykh and he is responsible for what happens. The sum of these relations (the structure which contains a dispute) can reasonably be spoken of as a structure where power is exemplified; power which mere shaykhly standing within a group cannot generate (Dresch 1984a: 39-40; al-Dawsari 2012: 5). But again shaykhs can only perform this role upon request of the conflicting parties; after the conflict ends, their ad hoc role and authority lapse.

Among the confederations of Khawlān b. ʿĀmir and Hamdān, the appointment of arbitrators to contain and settle disputes follows distinct patterns. Whereas the hierarchic and centralized system of representation among Khawlān b. ʿĀmir simultaneously determines the course of the legal proceedings in processes and legal appeal, among Hamdān, the proceedings to contain disputes are less predefined, meaning they are more decentralised and emphasize the principles of neutrality through equidistance.

It has been demonstrated that the precedencies of representation among Khawlān b. ʿĀmir are continuously linked to the tribal internal organization of the confederation. The appointment of shaykhs in processes of arbitration and appeal follows a similar pattern: Among the tribes of Khawlān b. ʿĀmir, a *shaykh al-shaml* is normally also the juridical head of his particular tribal entity. The system roughly works as follows: If disputing persons or tribal groups are from the same tribal moiety and the dispute cannot be solved ad hoc by mediation through the shaykh of their tribal unit, the case is referred to *shaykh al-shaml* of the tribal moiety. If the disputing parties are from different moieties, usually the problematic cases are referred to the *shaykh al-shaml* of the tribe. The tribal moieties of the member tribes of Khawlān b. ʿĀmir are jural domains, and the *shaykh al-shaml* of a tribal moiety is its judge of appeal in customary law. In this role he is called *maradd* or *radd* (pl. *rudūd*), a term derived from the Arabic verb *radda*, meaning someone who "answers", or "responds', or (in Weir's phrase) "to whom one resorts for solutions and judgments".[34] The *rudūd* are higher legal instances than the other *shuyūkh al-shaml*.

If the *rudūd* of the tribal moieties cannot solve the problem, or if their verdict is not accepted, the case is referred to the *shaykh al-shaml* of Khawlān b. ʿĀmir. The *shaykh al-shaml* of Khawlān b. ʿĀmir is not only the highest representative of the confederation (*shaml shumūl*), but also the final arbiter (*radd al-radd*, *ḥākim nihāʾī*, or *munhā istiʾnāf*) and therefore the highest legal authority in all cases in tribal customary law regarding appeal (*istiʾnāf*), correction (*taṣḥīḥ*), or dismissal (*buṭlān*) of the verdicts of the lower instances, namely the *rudūd* of the tribal moieties. The head of the confederation can modify or set aside the verdicts of the lower instances and issue a new verdict. A source from the Marrān Mountains in Khawlān explained this to me as follows:

> "The *shaykh al-shaml* is simultaneously the *radd* for those whom he represents (*al-shaml radd li-man taḥta shamlihu*). If a tribesman does not agree with the verdict of his *shaykh*, he turns to the next higher *shaykh* (*lahu al-dhahāb ilā l-shaykh al-ʾarfaʿ minhu*), who either confirms or rejects the verdict, and if disagreements arise again, then the tribesman can call in the final arbiter (*al-radd al-nihāʾī*), who has the last word. For example, if the *shaykh* of Walad Yaḥyā has issued a verdict against me and I do not agree with it, and he does not accept my protest, then I have the right to go to Ibn Bishr[35] to appeal against the decision of the *shaykh* of Walad Yaḥyā. And if I am not convinced by the verdict of Ibn Bishr, too, then I go to Ibn Muqīt who is the final judicial authority (*radd al-radd*) of the whole Khawlān b. ʿĀmir."

Hence the process of tribal appeal is linked to the internal tribal structure of the tribes and the confederation, but it skips in some cases the level of the *shaykh al-shaml* of a tribe because the tribal moieties (not the tribes as such) are the jural domains of the tribes, who together comprise the larger jural domain of Khawlān b. ʿĀmir. The legal roles of the *rudūd* and the *radd al-radd* are activated from below. They cannot insist on being consulted, nor can they exert authority over tribes other than their own.

Given his elevated position, not all controversial cases are passed to the *radd al-radd*. The *radd al-radd* does not have jurisdiction to check the validity of verdicts in marriage and divorce cases and family disputes. In addition, the *radd al-radd* does not accept cases in which a verdict of a state court (*ḥukm sharʿī*) in Yemen or Saudi Arabia has already been issued. Only in exceptional cases does the *radd al-radd* issue a new verdict; in general his judgment does not differ substantially from the judgment of the lower instance, so as to avoid a loss of authority and prestige of the *rudūd*. Appeal to the *radd al-radd* should not imply a diminution of any *radd*'s sovereignty. The judgment of the *radd al-radd* is final and constitutes the end of the process of tribal appeal. During her fieldwork in Rāziḥ in the 1970s, a local informant reported to Weir that people submitted to the judgments of the then *radd al-radd*, Yaḥyā Muḥammad Muqīt, "like sheep lying down for slaughter" (Weir 2007: 137). No shaykh and no *radd* can set aside the judgment of the *radd al-radd*. Only very few famous *sayyid* arbitrators, such as from the al-Qaṭābirī family, solely and exclusively have veto rights (*naqḍ*) on the judgments of Ibn Muqīt and can renegotiate the case according to the provisions of *sharīʿah* law. Due to tribal animosities, not all the Khawlān b. ʿĀmir tribes recognize the supreme legal status of Ibn Muqīt in the same way.[36] Furthermore, the impact of the 1934 international frontier demarcation, which bisects the confederation into a Saudi and a Yemeni part, led to a disruption of the traditional chains of tribal appeal and even altered some tribal affiliations (Brandt i. pr.).

This ideal proceeding is not mandatory; in practice either shaykh can be approached (Gingrich 1989a: 126; Weir 2007: 132). This can, for example, be the case in complex inter-tribal or supra-tribal disputes with members of different tribes or even confederations being involved. In these cases, arbitrators can be found

[34] Weir 2007: 132. In Munabbih the term *radd* or *maradd* is not used (Gingrich, pers. communication). The title *maradd* is pre-Islamic, see Serjeant 1982: 14.

[35] Ibn Bishr is the head of Khawlān's Jihwaz moiety.

[36] Gingrich, pers. communication.

from elsewhere. In addition, certain *rudūd* of Khawlān b. ʿĀmir often act as arbitrators in other member tribes of the confederation. For example, the *shaykh al-shaml* of Munabbih, Ibn ʿAwfān, is continuously involved in arbitration between Fayfā' and Banī Mālik on the Saudi side of the confederation.[37] The senior shaykh of Munabbih's other tribal moiety, Ibn Miṭrī, plays a prominent role in the arbitration of the border dispute between the Saudi Āl Talīd and Yemeni Āl Thābit (both segments of Jumāʿah), which erupted in 1934 with the Treaty of Ṭā'if border demarcation and continues till now.[38]

A well-known mediator and arbitrator, who does not come from the ranks of the *rudūd,* is Fāris Manāʿ from the shaykhly line of Saḥār's al-Ṭalḥ section.[39] The Manāʿ family gained political influence during the 1960s civil war and was subsequently able to amass considerable wealth when Sūq al-Ṭalḥ, formerly a purely intra-tribal market of the Saḥār, became one of the largest weekly markets in Yemen.[40] Fāris Manāʿ is not only an internationally successful arms trader and since 2011 governor of the Ṣaʿdah province, but also a skilled and highly respected mediator with the required *haybah* (prestige) and *wazn* (weight), who in extremely precarious situations of the Ṣaʿdah wars (2004-2010), when everything was failing on the ground for the government, was one of the few persons in the region who could provide essential and neutral mediation between the government, Ḥūthīs, and tribes. Such ad hoc elevation of individual persons should, however, not be confused with institutionalized authority, or, as Weir puts it: "Temporary administrative, mediatory, or representational authority must be distinguished from permanent rights and jurisdiction over a sovereign domain" (Weir 2007: 309).

Among both Khawlān b. ʿĀmir and Hamdān the process of tribal conflict resolution consists of mediation, arbitration and a two-stage appeal. Among Hamdān, however, the process to contain disputes and the chains of legal appeal do not follow a pre-defined order of precedence (as they do among Khawlān b. ʿĀmir); rather, they are more decentralized and less orderly and emphasize the principle of neutrality through equidistance instead of the principle of jural domains.

Among the tribes of the Hamdān confederation, the process of conflict containment works as follows:[41] If two men from the same tribal section are at odds, they normally go to the *ʿāqil* (head of a tribal sub-section) of that section for mediation. If the conflicting men are from different sections, usually the shaykhs of the two conflicting sections negotiate over the differences. If the negotiations of the *ʿāqil* or the shaykhs fail, they can forward the case to another, higher shaykh, who is usually a neutral shaykh from outside the two conflicting tribes, and who deals with larger cases and with cases appealed from the *ʿāqil.* This arbitrator, called the *ghaṣṣāb,* issues a verdict. His decision should be honoured by the two conflicting parties, otherwise the conflict moves to a violent stage or they resort to the process of tribal appeal.

Among Khawlān b. ʿĀmir and Hamdān the tribal justice system gives the parties the chance to appeal twice at higher tribal arbitration levels before the verdict becomes final and binding. Appeal commences if one or both conflicting parties do not agree to the *ghaṣṣāb*'s verdict and decide to go to an "appeal arbitrator" (*munhā*). The activity of the *munhā* is only activated at the request of the conflicting parties. If the parties do not accept the verdict of the *munhā,* they can resort to a final juridical instance, namely a *marāghah* (pl. *marāghāt*). *Marāghah* (sometimes also *mardaʿ*) is the title of a judicial office; the *marāghah* is considered the specialist par excellence in customary law. Among the tribes of Hamdān, the *marāghah* is the most senior shaykh in the process of tribal appeal and his verdict is final.[42] His office is hereditary (Dupret 2000b). If a case has no precedent, if no customary rule exists, or when there is a disagreement about its interpretation, the *marāghah* has the authority to create a new rule and set a new precedent (Al-Zwaini 2006: 5). The *marāghahs*

[37] Gingrich, pers. communication.

[38] Brandt 2012: 57-58. Āl Talīd and Āl Thābit are Jumāʿah sections dwelling in the borderland area of the Yemeni-Saudi frontier. Because at this border segment the territorial demarcation of the exact course of the 1934 Ṭā'if boundary line had failed, tribal considerations came into force. Therefore the Treaty of Ṭā'if put the negotiation and demarcation of these sections of the international boundary into the hands of the borderland tribes. The shifts of the boundaries of tribal territories, primarily resulting from tribal conflict or the compensation of tribal blood debt, were henceforth tantamount to alterations of the international boundary.

[39] The incumbent shaykh of al-Ṭalḥ is Fayṣal Manāʿ, an uncle of Fāris.

[40] Niewöhner 1985: 8 according to pers. information of G. Schweizer.

[41] This section mainly draws on Dresch 1989: 88-110 and the excellent papers by al-Zwaini (2006) and al-Dawsari (2008).

[42] The *marāghah* is not a "court of cassation" as suggested by CEFAS (2003), because he does not only examine the compliance of previous verdicts with the provisions of tribal law, but rather has the power to issue a new judgment.

of Hamdān are not assigned to any predefined jural domain; either *marāghah* can be approached. However, in a conflict, a *marāghah*, who is familiar with the specific local features of *ʿurf*, will prove to be the most appropriate arbitrator; whenever a tribe is particularly attached to specific regional rules and customs, it typically has a *marāghah* of its own.

Some *marāghahs* also take on large disputes of inter-tribal nature, like wars between tribes. They are specialized in the "separation" (*faṣl*) of the parties involved in inter-tribal conflicts. For instance, if a conflict happened between, say, Wāʾilah and Nihm, both tribes represented by "their" guarantor shaykhs, they would normally approach a neutral and territorially "distant" *marāghah,* such as Ibn Ḥubaysh of Sufyān, who would then endeavour to "separate" them and settle their conflict through arbitration.

Local sources deny the existence of an order of precedence among the *marāghah*. Al-ʿAlīmī, however, mentions "lower, middle, and upper" *marāghahs,* (Dupret 2000b) probably mainly in the sense of some being more or less prominent and/or capable than the others. Well-known *marāghahs* are, for instance, Ibn Shuṭayf, Ibn al-Shiʿr and Ibn Haḍabān of Dahm, Ibn Dāyil b. Fāris of Wāʾilah, Ibn Dughsān of Āl ʿAmmār, and Ibn Ḥubaysh of Sufyān. One of the most prominent *marāghahs* is Ibn Malhabah of Dahm in al-Jawf.[43] All of them are shaykhly lines of Bakīlī stock.[44] In 1997, 25 *marāghahs* were counted among the tribes in northern Yemen (Al-Zwaini 2006: 5).

A glance at these names reveals that most *marāghahs* come from renowned, but (from the perspective of the central government) rather peripheral shaykhly lines. Whereas the authority and influence of a *shaykh mashāyikh* and *naqīb* of Hamdān usually unfolds in the power games of cooperation and challenge between shaykhs and state power, the judicial office of the *marāghah* is decoupled from government influence. The most appreciated *marāghahs* come from the areas of the "tribal wolves" (the phrase of Gellner), who are still largely beyond government control and state influence, and in whose areas tribal norms and traditions still remain largely unchanged and undiluted. This is especially the case in the eastern part of the Ṣaʿdah governorate and in the al-Jawf governorate, the province northeast of Ṣanʿāʾ that fans out from near ʿAmrān east to the Rubʿ al-Khālī and the still largely undemarcated border with Saudi Arabia beyond the eastern terminus of the 1934 Ṭāʾif line. Al-Jawf governorate was created only around 1980, and the tribally organized and still hard to reach region was the last large area of Upper Yemen to come under more than the nominal control of the state, this taking place gradually since the 1980s (Burrowes 1995: 198).

The system of conflict containment shows that, among the Hamdān neutral, third-party shaykhs become involved at an early stage of mediation and arbitration. The parties to the conflict can "activate" any arbitrator they wish. Tribal hierarchies are not as important as among Khawlān b. ʿĀmir: If two sections or tribes are at odds as wholes, then the arbitrator need not be drawn from a higher order unit that contains them (Dresch 1984a: 41). Numerous shaykhs with reputations as arbitrators are constantly called on to settle disputes throughout Upper Yemen and beyond, not just in their own tribes or confederations. The arbitrator does not have to be a member of one of the two groups involved; equidistance from the conflicting parties is preferable and necessary for an arbitrator to be acceptable to both parties. The greater the extent of a conflict and / or the longer the duration, the more distant in genealogical and/or local terms the mediator should be. In the most severe cases, it is customary that arbitration is assigned to a member of a neutral tribe whose impartiality ensures the negotiation between the parties. Also, shaykhs from outside the confederation of Hamdān are involved in processes of arbitration and legal appeal. Ibn ʿAwfān of Munabbih, for instance, historically has played a major role in arbitration in Wāʾilah.[45] The web of relations criss-crosses the tribes of Hamdān somewhat irregularly. Conversely, the author of this paper knows of no case from recent history in which shaykhs from Ḥāshid or Bakīl took more than a "supervisory" role in conflict resolution in Khawlān b. ʿĀmir.[46]

[43] "Ibn Marhaba", as mentioned by Dupret (2000b), is a spelling error.

[44] The PDCI report (2011) is wrong when it states that there was only one *marāghah* for the entire al-Jawf governorate.

[45] Gingrich 2011. In 2011, Ibn ʿAwfān opened the negotiations, which should bring the violent confrontations between Ḥūthīs and Salafīs in Dammāj and the involved tribes on both sides to a halt.

[46] ʿAbdullah al-Aḥmar took a supervisory role in the conflict settlement between the Yemeni Āl Thābit and the Saudi Āl Talīd in Jumāʿah (see above). His supervisory role is certainly due to the fact that this conflict between two tribal sections of Jumāʿah was simultaneously an international border conflict between Yemen and Saudi Arabia. Apart from that, I do not know of any involvement of Ḥāshid or Bakīl shaykhs in mediation and arbitration in Khawlān b. ʿĀmir, although such a case cannot be ruled out, especially with tribes such as Saḥār whose shaykhly lines are linked by marriage to shaykhly lines of Wāʾilah (Bakīl). The "arch-conflict"

Since most *marāghahs* come from the ranks of Bakīl, the chains of legal appeal among the tribes of Ḥāshid are even less predefined than among Bakīl. During the appeal process among Ḥāshid, everyone chooses the *munhā* whom he deems suitable (*yakhtār kull ṭarf man yarāhu munhā lahu*). Any skilled and experienced shaykh can be approached. Because of the particularly pronounced decentralization of legal proceedings and the substantial absence of hereditary *marāghahs,* members of Bakīl tend to characterize the system of conflict resolution among Ḥāshid pejoratively as "weak" (*ḍaʿīf*).

TRIBALISM IN TRANSITION

In Upper Yemen the "hardy plant of tribalism" (in Gellner's phrase) has had its golden years in the period following the 1960s civil war. The shaykhs, especially those who had fought on the side of the republic, had never been more powerful than in the decade after the civil war. The warring parties' attempts to buy off tribal loyalties and the enormous financial largesse, weapons and material support provided by the imām, the republicans, the Saudi Kingdom, and, at times, the Egyptians to shaykhs on both (royalist and republican) sides had greatly strengthened the position of the northern tribal leaders (Dresch 1984b: 169; Burrowes 1987: 31; Mundy 1995: 15; Lichtenthäler 2003: 57; Weir 2007: 283).

The enormous empowerment of tribal shaykhs at the expense of their former overlords, the *sādah,* took place in an environment that was characterized by the weakness of state structures. After the civil war, the efforts of the new republican government focused on "state formation" through the financial and political patronage of influential tribal leaders while at the same time denying the simple population access to basic public services and infrastructure. Also, the Saudi government tried to secure the loyalty and cooperation of many shaykhs (in particular the borderland shaykhs) through the provision of enormous financial resources. Consequently, it was the shaykhs who brokered government influence in the tribal areas of Upper Yemen and acted as a link between their tribal constituencies and the government.

Many shaykhs indeed had their "bell[ies] full of politics" (to repeat Dresch's phrase). Before 1992, they held the majority of the seats in the early Consultative Council (*majlis al-shūrā*). In addition to their hereditary entitlement to the office of the shaykh, after Yemeni unification, they commenced to pursue also a hereditary entitlement to parliamentary representation. Particularly in the northern areas, which were dominated by tribal norms and traditions, the influential shaykhs started to inherit political offices within their lines, such as the official function of a parliamentarian for their constituencies, and vigorously asserted their political claims. In the Ṣaʿdah governorate, for instance, after 1992, "normal" people only had the chance of becoming elected members of parliament through the *ḥizb al-ḥaqq*, which was actually the political rallying point of the *sādah.* This competition for political participation and representation between influential shaykhs and their contenders led to the eruption of deadly conflicts.

Many shaykhs doubled up as agents of a self-serving Yemeni state. The state's patronage, in turn, generated disparities in wealth and power, which are quite alien to the tribal system. Many shaykhly families have moved from their tribal constituencies to the capital, Ṣanʿāʾ, or stayed there over long periods of time, thus loosening their tribal ties and, consequently, losing their tribal influence. Throughout the countryside in Upper Yemen, tribesmen were complaining of the greatest shaykhs becoming "distant", as historically they were in Lower Yemen (Dresch 2000: 160). Consequently, many shaykhs have been animadverted for neglecting the principle of representation, which is a central part of their tribal office and authority. The Ḥāshid, for instance, have seen their "paramount" shaykh, ʿAbdullah al-Aḥmar, "transformed from a leader and representative of the Ḥāshid to a government insider with his political and financial interests centred in Ṣanʿāʾ and less with his tribesmen. His own al-ʿUṣaymāt tribe has not benefitted materially from his presence on the national scene" (Peterson 2008: 17). The same happened in many parts of Upper Yemen; local sources from rural areas complain that many shaykhs were using their shaykhdom to maximize wealth and to increase their influence and power on the national level without contributing substantially to the social welfare and development of their

of Khawlān b. ʿĀmir in the 9th century AD, however, features mediation and arbitration through a neutral party, which led to the settlement of the first Zaydī imām in Ṣaʿdah and resulted in the establishment of the Zaydī *dawlah* (see Heiss 1989, 1998, and this volume).

tribal constituencies. By comparison, an ordinary businessman from Taʿiz, Hāʾil Saʿīd Anʿam, who was not a shaykh, built hundreds of schools.

The patronage exerted by the Yemeni republic had a similar adverse impact on the system of tribal mediation and arbitration. Many shaykhs spend time between Ṣanʿāʾ and their home areas so that they stay connected to their tribes. Others, however, are more or less absent in their tribal constituencies due to their political and economic ambitions. For major problems, the tribesmen still appeal to their shaykhs, travelling to the latter's new urban homes. Smaller cases are settled locally. The void arising from the shaykh's absence is filled by others, be they "minor" shaykhs, or *sādah*, whose families have vast local knowledge and centuries of experience in mediation and arbitration of tribal conflict, or ordinary tribespeople without shaykhly status, who earned their reputation by proven service to their communities, such as conflict resolution, development services, finding jobs for members, etc. Their status depends to a large extent on level of demand for their service by community members (Al-Dawsari 2012). There are cases of individual tribesmen, who did not come from shaykhly families and who filled the vacuum arising from the shaykh's absence simply because men and women turned to them to resolve their conflicts. However, the enforcement of arbitration verdicts has become difficult due to the loss of shaykhly authority and the overall erosion of tribal traditions. Thus "absentee shaykhship" (Puin 1984: 489) has a de-tribalizing effect on society.

Tribal societies have been altered by the states whose hierarchical structures of power and patronage have penetrated them from within (an argument developed by Gellner 1981). Those of us who closely followed the recent developments in Yemen will have noticed an alarming shift in public opinion in regard to influential tribal leaders. Both simple tribespeople and city dwellers increasingly cast them as all-purpose scapegoats for many social and political problems in Yemen, making the shaykhs the bogeymen of the nation. Gellner wrote that tribal leadership truly has a "Dragon's Teeth" quality and that tribes cannot be weakened by the liquidation of their leaders (Gellner 1981: 24). Political patronage and empowerment of shaykhs as exerted by the Yemeni government, however, can corrupt and undermine tribal leadership and thus paradoxically contribute to the decline of tribalism.

CONCLUSION

The tribal structures of the confederations examined in this chapter, Khawlān b. ʿĀmir and Hamdān, are not immutable, but fairly stable over long periods of time. They consist of the same elements (clans, segments, sections, tribes), which constitute similar divisions in both confederations. The tribal internal organization of the confederations can be displayed by using tree diagrams (without adopting the socio-political implications of segmentary theory), which suggest descent from a (real or putative) common ancestor. Yet these tree diagrams fail to visualize the different modes which the tribal communities have developed to "inhabit" these actually homologous structures; the structures of tribes and confederations and the features making up their socio-political organization need to be distinguished.

This is clearly illustrated by the relationship between tribal internal organization and layers of authority in tribal leadership. To illustrate this difference, this chapter examined the layers of authority in two key areas of tribal leadership: representation and jurisprudence (arbitration) according to tribal customary law. Among Khawlān b. ʿĀmir, the layers of authority follow with great historical continuity the structural hierarchy of the confederation. Both the representative authorities and the legal domains of the shaykhs are linked to the internal structure of the confederation, and the positions of authority are continuously passed on within the patrilineal shaykhly clans. At the level of the constituent tribes, representative authority rests with the senior shaykhs (sing. *shaykh al-shaml*) of the tribal moieties and tribes. The highest representatives of the tribal moieties are simultaneously their juridical heads (sing. *radd*), since among Khawlān b. ʿĀmir, the tribal moieties are the jural domains of the confederation. Above them is the authority of the head of the confederation, who is simultaneously *shaml shumūl* (the highest representative of all tribes of Khawlān b. ʿĀmir) and *radd al-radd* (the final arbiter in all legal cases).

These layers of authority, however, are not power structures. The principle of authority refers to the capacity of tribal leaders of Khawlān b. ʿĀmir to influence events as a result of widely recognized hereditary and personal prestige, knowledge, persuasion skills, and position. In contrast, power is the ability to achieve desired goals, if necessary, without the consent of all persons affected. Some (but few) shaykhs among Khawlān b. ʿĀmir *have* power, and most of them are shaykhs from minor sections and not identical to the senior shaykhs of the confederation's hierarchical system of authority. Their power is temporary and mainly results from their political assertiveness and personal wealth derived from government patronage; yet it neither implies coercive power towards their tribal constituencies, nor does it lead to an alteration of the prevailing layers of authority. The ebb and flow of political fortune does not affect the system of legal and representative authority, which is deeply rooted in the centuries-old shaykhly lines of the senior shaykhs.

The tribal internal organization of the member tribes of the Hamdān confederation (Ḥāshid and Bakīl) resembles a nested hierarchy as well. Yet, among Hamdān, a more pronounced tendency to decentralization prevails; the attempt to combine the tribal structure and the actual domains of shaykhs founders. The formal alignment of shaykhly houses with tribes and sections is far less regular than in Khawlān b. ʿĀmir. The position of the *shaykh mashāyikh* (as the highest representatives of tribal units are called among Hamdān) is a temporary dignity, or power position, which is contested and which has to be asserted and defended against competitors, and many times the position of the *shaykh mashāyikh* remains empty. The term *shaykh mashāyikh* identifies the temporary predominance of an individual shaykh over the other representatives of the same tribal unit, it locates those who hold power and influence and, so to speak, it "ranks" the shaykhs. The different terms *shaykh al-shaml* and *shaykh mashāyikh* thus refer to differing social positions.

The system of arbitration and legal appeal among Hamdān follows similar principles: The structures to contain a dispute are less prescribed and more decentralised than among Khawlān b. ʿĀmir and emphasize the principles of neutrality through equidistance (rather than the principle of jural domains). By the greater tendency towards decentralization and transition of authority, the organization of tribal leadership among Hamdān displays more heterarchical features.[47] Power and authority, understood from the Hamdān's more heterarchical perspective, respond to changing situations and can be redistributed within each structural unit, following the needs of the system. Whereas the more pronounced heterarchy among Hamdān distributes and re-distributes power in temporary settings within the tribal structural units, among Khawlān b. ʿĀmir authority, it is continuously assigned to those members high in the structure.

This chapter has attempted to work out these basic principles of tribal leadership and hierarchy in Upper Yemen and consider them in a comparative way. In everyday life of the tribal societies of Upper Yemen, these specific differences are certainly less obvious. This is, for example, due to the fact that the tribal societies are undergoing rapid and profound changes. The four past decades have been shaped by drastic changes – society and economy have changed and so did the perceptions of tribal leaders. The patronage system of the Yemeni government, which focuses on the financial and political patronage of influential tribal leaders while simultaneously neglecting the simple peoples' needs, corrupted and jeopardized shaykhly authority within many tribal constituencies. This is due to the counterproductive effect, in terms of legitimacy and authority, that state patronage has on relations between shaykhs and their tribes, with damaging repercussions on the tribal system as a whole. This loss of shaykhly authority and reputation by no means affects all shaykhs of Upper Yemen; many of them remain esteemed and deeply rooted in their tribal constituencies. In the long run, however, the system of tribal leadership only has the option of a "renewal from below" or an overall weakening of tribal norms.

ACKNOWLEDGEMENTS

I owe special thanks to Nadwa Dawsari-Johnson (Washington DC), Marie-Christine Heinze (Bonn), and Andre Gingrich (Vienna) for their helpful comments and critiques. My overall research project is made possible by the grant of a Marie Curie Intra-European Fellowship (IEF) of the European Union.

---

[47] A heterarchy is a system of organization, which features overlap, multiplicity, and/or divergent-but-coexistent patterns of relation. Crumley (1995) defines heterarchy as the relation of elements to one another when they are unranked or when they possess the potential for being ranked in a number of different ways. Heterarchy is therefore not strictly the opposite of hierarchy, but is rather the opposite of homoarchy, which is itself defined as the relation of elements to one another when they possess the potential for being ranked in one way only. A heterarchy may be parallel to a hierarchy, subsumed to a hierarchy, or it may contain hierarchies; the two kinds of structure are not mutually exclusive.

REFERENCES

Abū Ghānim, Faḍl (1991, 1985). *Al-bunyat al-qabaliyya fī-l-Yaman bayn al-istimrār wa al-taghayyur.* Ṣanʿā': Dār al-Kalīma al-Yamaniyya.

Adra, Najwa (1982). *Qabyala: The Tribal Concept in the Central Highlands of the Yemen Arab Republic.* PhD thesis. Philadelphia: Temple University.

Adra, Najwa (2011). *Tribal Mediation in Yemen and its Implications to Development.* Vienna: AAS Working Papers in Social Anthropology, 19.

Bāfaqīh, Muḥammad (1990). *L'Unification du Yémen Antique.* Paris: Geuthner.

Blumi, Isa (2010). *Chaos in Yemen. Societal collapse and the new authoritanism.* London/New York: Routledge.

Bonte, Pierre, Conte, Édouard & Dresch, Paul (Eds.), *Emirs et Présidents: structures de la parenté et du politique en pays d'islam.* CNRS: Paris.

Brandt, Marieke (2012). Friedens-Šayḫ und Kriegs-Šayḫ: Der Übergang von Kriegsführerschaft bei den Banū Munebbih im Ḥūṯī-Konflikt in Nordwest-Jemen. *Anthropos, 107*, 49–69.

Brandt, Marieke (2013). Sufyān's 'Hybrid' War: Tribal Politics during the Ḥūthī Conflict. *Journal of Arabian Studies, 3(1)*, 120–138.

Brandt, Marieke (2014). The Irregulars of the Ṣaʿdah War: 'Colonel Shaykhs' and 'Tribal Militias' in Yemen's Ḥūthī Conflict (2004–2010). In: Helene Lackner (Ed.), *Why Yemen Matters: A Society in Transition* (105–122). London: Saqi.

Brandt, Marieke (in press). Some Remarks on the Tribal Structures Among Khawlān and Jumāʿah of the Khawlān b. ʿĀmir Confederation in the Ṣaʿdah Region, Yemen, and Their Historical Formation According to Al-Hamdānī (10th Century AD). *Anthropology of the Middle East.*

Burckhardt, John L. (1831). *Notes on the Bedouins and Wahabys.* London: Colburn and Bentley.

Burrowes, Robert (1987). *The Yemen Arab Republic: The Politics of Development, 1962–1986.* Colorado: Westview Press.

Burrowes, Robert (1995). *Historical Dictionary of Yemen.* Lanham: Scarecrow Press.

Caskel, Werner (1966). *Ğamharat an-nasab: Das genealogische Werk des Hišām ibn Muḥammad al-Kalbī. 2 Vol.* Leiden: Brill.

Caton, Steven (1987). Power, Persuasion, and Language: A Critique of the Segmentary Model in the Middle East. *International Journal of Middle East Studies, 19(1)*, 77–101.

Caton, Steven (1990). *Peaks of Yemen I Summon: Poetry as Cultural Practice in a North Yemeni Tribe. Berkeley*: University of California Press.

Centre Français d'Archéologie et de Sciences Sociales de Sanaa (CEFAS) (2003). Le règlement des conflits tribaux au Yémen. *Les cahiers du CEFAS, 4.* Sanaa: CEFAS.

Chelhod, Joseph (1985). *L'Arabie du Sud, Historie et Civilisation. Tome III: Culture et institutions du Yémen.* Paris: Editions G.-P. Maisonneuve et Larose.

Crumley, Carole (1995). Heterarchy and the Analysis of Complex Societies. *Archeological Papers of the American Anthropological Association, 7(1)*, 1–5.

Al-Dawsari, Nadwa (2008). *Annex to a paper presented in Rutgers University.* Center for Negotiation and Conflict Resolution (also presented in Minot University).

Al-Dawsari, Nadwa (2012). *Tribal Governance and Stability in Yemen.* The Carnegie Papers. Washington DC: Carnegie Endowment for International Peace.

Dostal, Walter (1974). Sozio-ökonomische Aspekte der Stammesdemokratie in Nordost-Yemen. *Sociologus, 24(I)*, 1–15.

Dostal, Walter (1979). *Der Markt von Ṣanʿā'.* (Sitzungsberichte der phil.-hist. Kl. 354, Veröffentlichungen der Arabischen Kommission 1). Vienna: Verlag der Österreichischen Akademie der Wissenschaften.

Dostal, Walter (1983). *Ethnographic Atlas of ʿAsīr.* Preliminary Report. (Schriftenreihe der phil.-hist. Kl.). Vienna: Verlag der Österreichischen Akademie der Wissenschaften.

Dostal, Walter (1985). *Egalität und Klassengesellschaft in Südarabien. Anthropologische Untersuchungen zur sozialen Evolution.* Vienna: Berger.

Dresch, Paul (1984a). The Position of Shaykhs Among the Northern Tribes of Yemen. *Man, 19(1)*, 31–49.

Dresch, Paul (1984b). Tribal Relations and Political History in Upper Yemen. In: Brian R. Pridham (Ed.), *Contemporary Yemen: Politics and Historical Background and Economy, Society, and Culture in Contemporary Yemen* (154–174). London: Croom Helm.

Dresch, Paul (1986). The significance of the course events take in segmentary systems. *American Ethnologist, 13(2)*, 309–324.

Dresch, Paul (1987). Episodes in a Dispute between Yemeni Tribes: Text and Translation of a Colloquial Arabic Document. *Der Islam, 64(1)*, 68–76.

Dresch, Paul (1989). *Tribes, Government, and History in Yemen.* Oxford: Oxford University Press.

Dresch, Paul (1991a). The Tribes of Ḥāshid-wa-Bakīl as Historical and Geographical Entities. In: Alan Jones (Ed.), *Arabicus Felix: Luminosus Britannicus: Essays in Honour of A. F. L. Beeston on His Eightieth Birthday* (8–24). Reading: Ithaca Press.

Dresch, Paul (1991b). Imams and Tribes: The Writing and Acting of History in Upper Yemen. In: Philip S. Khoury & Joseph Kostiner (Eds.), *Tribes and State Formation in the Middle East* (252–287). Berkeley and Los Angeles: University of California Press.

Dresch, Paul (1995). The tribal factor in the Yemeni crisis. In: Jamal S. al-Suwaidi (Ed.), *The Yemeni War of 1994: Causes and Consequences* (33–55). London: Saqi Books.

Dresch, Paul (2006). *The Rules of Baraṭ: Tribal Documents from Yemen.* Sana'a: Centre Français d'Archéologie et de Sciences Sociales, Deutsches Archäologisches Institut.

Dupret, Baudouin (2000a). Systèmes coutumiers, centralisme juridique de l'Etat et usage du droit. *Chroniques Yéménites, 8,* Sanaa: CEFAS, 67–68.

Dupret, Baudouin (2000b). Les procédures de la justice tribale. Extrait de Rashād al-ʿAlīmī, 'La justice tribale dans la société yéménite', traduit de l'arabe. *Chroniques Yéménites, 8*, Sanaa: CEFAS, 69–80.

Al-Enazy, Askar (2005). *The Long Road from Taif to Jeddah. Resolution of a Saudi-Yemeni Boundary Dispute.* Abu Dhabi: Emirates Center for Strategic Studies.

Evans-Pritchard, Edward. E. (1940). *The Nuer: A Description of the Modes of Livelihood and Political Institutions of a Nilotic People.* London: Oxford University Press.

Fattah, Khaled. (2010). A political history of civil-military relations in Yemen. *Alternative Politics, Special Issue, 1,* 25–47.

Gellner, Ernest. (1969). *Saints of the Atlas.* London: Weidenfeld and Nicholson.

Gellner, Ernest (1981). *Muslim Society.* Cambridge: Cambridge University Press.

Gellner, Ernest (1991). Tribalism and the state in the Middle East. In: Philip S. Khoury & Joseph Kostiner (Eds.), *Tribes and State Formation in the Middle East* (109–126). Berkeley and Los Angeles: University of California Press.

Gerholm, Thomas (1977). *Market, Mosque and Mafraj: Social Inequality in a Yemeni Town.* Stockholm: Stockholm University Press.

Gingrich, Andre (1989a). *Der Agrarkalender der Munebbih. Eine ethnologische Studie zu sozialem Kontext und regionalem Vergleich eines tribalen Sternenkalenders in Südwestarabien.* Habil. Vienna University.

Gingrich, Andre (1989b). How the chiefs' daughters marry: Tribes, marriage patterns and hierarchies in Northwest-Yemen. In: Andre Gingrich, Sylvia Haas & Gabriele Paleczek (Eds.), *Kinship, Social Change and Evolution* (75–85). Proceedings of a Symposium Held in Honour of W. Dostal. Horn: Berger.

Gingrich, Andre (1993). Tribes and rulers in northern Yemen. In: Andre Gingrich, Sylvia Haas, Gabriele Paleczek & Thomas Fillitz (Eds.), *Studies in Oriental Culture and History. Festschrift für Walter Dostal* (253–280). Frankfurt a. M.: Lang.

Gingrich, Andre (1994). *Südwestarabische Sternenkalender: eine ethnologische Studie zu Struktur, Kontext und regionalem Vergleich des tribalen Agrarkalenders der Munebbih im Jemen.* Wien: WUV-Univ.-Verlag.

Gingrich, Andre (1997). Konzepte und Perspektiven sozial- und kulturanthropologischer Forschung im Vorderen Orient. *Mitteilungen der Anthropologischen Gesellschaft in Wien,* 59–67.

Gingrich, Andre (2001a). Ehre, Raum und Körper. Zur sozialen Konstruktion der Geschlechter im Nordjemen. In: Ulrike Davis-Sulikowski, Hildegard Diemberger, Andre Gingrich & Jürg Helbling (Eds.), *Körper, Religion und Macht: Sozialanthropologie der Geschlechterbeziehungen* (221–293). Frankfurt a. M.: Campus.

Gingrich, Andre (2001). "Tribe," entry in Neil J. Smelser & Paul B. Baltes (Eds.), *International Encyclopedia of the Social & Behavioral Sciences* (15906–15909). Oxford: Pergamon.

Gingrich, Andre (2011). Warriors of Honor, Warriors of Faith: Two historical male role models from south-western Arabia. In: Maria Six-Hohenbalken & Nerina Weiss (Eds.), *Violence Expressed: An Anthropological Approach* (37–54). London: Ashgate.

Gingrich, Andre & Heiss, Johann (1986). *Beiträge zur Ethnographie der Provinz Ṣaʿda, Nordjemen.* Vienna: Verlag der Österreichischen Akademie der Wissenschaften.

Glaser, Eduard (1913). *Eduard Glasers Reise nach Marib.* (Ed. D. H. Müller, N. Rhodokanakis). Vienna: Hölder.

Grabbe, Lester (2007). *Ancient Israel: What Do We Know and How Do We Know It?* New York: T&T Clark.

al-Hamdānī, al-Ḥasan (1954/1965). *Kitāb al-Iklīl.* Vol.1. (Ed. O. Löfgren). Wiesbaden: Harrassowitz.

Haykel, Bernard (2003). *Revival and Reform in Islam: The legacy of Muḥammad al-Shawkānī.* Cambridge: Cambridge University Press.

Heinze, Marie-Christine (2010). Die Grenzproblematik zwischen dem Jemen und Saudi-Arabien. In: Conrad Schetter, Stephan Conermann & Bernd Kuzmits (Eds.), *Die Grenzen Asiens zwischen Globalisierung und staatlicher Fragmentierung* (137–178). Berlin: EB-Verlag.

Heiss, Johann (1989). War and mediation for peace in a tribal society (Yemen, 9th century). In: Andre Gingrich, Siegfried Hass, Sylvia Haas, Gabriele Paleczek (Eds.), *Kinship, Social Change and Evolution: Proceedings of a Symposium Held in Honour of Walter Dostal* (63–74). Horn: Berger.

Heiss, Johann (1997). Die Landnahme der Ḫawlān nach Al-Hamdānī. In: Roswitha Stiegner (Ed.), *Aktualisierte Beiträge zum 1. Internationalen Symposium 'Südarabien interdisziplinär' an der Universität Graz; mit kurzen Einführungen zu Sprach- und Kulturgeschichte. In Memoriam Maria Höfner* (53–68). Graz: Leykam.

Heiss, Johann (1998). *Tribale Selbstorganisation und Konfliktregelung: Der Norden des Jemen zur Zeit des ersten Imams (10. Jahrhundert).* PhD thesis. University of Vienna.

Heiss, Johann (2005). Ein Šayḫ ist ein Šayḫ, aber was für ein Ding ist ein Sayyid? In: Johann Heiss (Ed.), *Veränderungen und Stabilität: Normen und Werte in islamischen Gesellschaften* (121–136). Vienna: Verlag der Österreichischen Akademie der Wissenschaften.

al-Jirāfī, ʻAbdullah (1987, 1951). *Al-muqtaṭaf min ta'rīkh al-yaman.* Cairo: ʻĪsah al-Bābī al-Ḥalabī.

Koszinowski, Thomas (1993). Abdallah Ibn Hussain al-Ahmar (Kurzbiographie). *Orient, 34(3)*, 335–341.

Lichtenthäler, Gerhard (2003). *Political Ecology and the Role of Water: Environment, Society and Economy in Northern Yemen.* Aldershot: Ashgate.

Madelung, Wilferd (1987). Islam in Yemen. In: Werner Daum (Ed.), *Yemen* (174–177). Innsbruck and Frankfurt: Pinguin Verlag.

Mareb Press (2010). *Al-shaykh Amīn al-ʻUkaymī: lastu shaykh mashāyikh Bakīl.* [http://www.marebpress.net/articles.php?id=8253]. (Last accessed: November 2010).

Mareb Press (2013). *Mashāyikh bārizūn min Bakīl yatabannūna ru'yat li-tawḥīd kubrā al-qabā'il al-yamaniyyah.* [http://marebpress.net/news_details.php?sid=56489&lng=arabic]. (Last accessed: May 2013).

Meissner, Jeffrey (1987). *Tribes at the Core: Legitimacy, Structure and Power in Zaydī Yemen.* PhD thesis. Columbia University.

Mermier, Franck (1985). Patronyme et hiérarchie sociale à Sanaa (République Arabe du Yémen). *Peuples Méditerranées, 33, Oct.–Dec,* 33–41.

Mermier, Franck (1993). La commune de Ṣanʻā: Pouvoir citadin et légitimé religieuse au XIX siècle. In: Andre Gingrich Sylvia Haas, Gabriele Rasuly-Paleczek, Thomas Fillitz (Eds.), *Studies in Oriental Culture and History. Festschrift für Walter Dostal* (242–252). Frankfurt a. M.: Lang.

Messick, Brinckley (1993). *The Calligraphic State. Textual Domination and History in a Muslim Society.* Berkeley: University of California Press.

Mundy, Martha (1995). *Domestic Government: Kinship, Community and Polity in North Yemen.* London: Tauris.

National Democratic Institute for International Affairs (NDI) (2007). *Yemen: Tribal Conflict Management Program Research Report.* Washington, D.C.: NDI.

Niebuhr, Carsten (1792). *Travels through Arabia and other countries in the East. 2 vols.* Translated by R. Heron. Beirut: Librarie du Liban.

Niewöhner-Eberhard, Elke (1985). *Ṣaʻda: Bauten und Bewohner in einer traditionellen islamischen Stadt.* Wiesbaden: Reichert.

O'Ballance, Edgar (1971). *The War in the Yemen.* London: Faber and Faber.

Obermeyer, Gerald (1981). Ṭāghuut, manʻ, and sharīʻa: The realms of law in tribal Arabia. In: Wadad Qadi (Ed.), *Studia Arabica et Islamica: Festschrift for Ihsan Abbas* (365–371). Beirut: American University of Beirut.

Partners for Democratic Change International (PDCI) (2011). *Baseline Conflict Assessment Report; Yemen Community-Based Conflict Mitigation Program, With the Support of the Conflict Prevention Pool at FCO, UK and the Delegation of the EU in the Republic of Yemen.* February 2011.

Peterson, John E. (2008). *Tribes and Politics in Yemen.* Arabian Peninsula Background Note, APBN-007.

Philby, Harry St. John (1952). *Arabian Highlands.* Ithaca: Cornell Univ. Press.

Phillips, Sarah (2011). *Yemen: The Politics of Permanent Crisis.* London: Routledge.

Puin, Gerd-Rüdiger (1984). The Yemeni hijrah concept of tribal protection. In: Tarif Khalidi (Ed.), *Land Tenure and Social Transformation in the Middle East* (483–494). Beirut: AUB.

Rathjens, Carl (1951). Taghut gegen scheri'ah. In: *Jahrbuch des Linden-Museums*. Stuttgart: Linden-Museum.

Robin, Christian (1982a). *Les Hautes-Terres Du Nord-Yémen Avant L'Islam: Recherches sur la Géographie Tribale et religieuse du Ḫawlān Quḍāʿa et du pays de Hamdān*. Istanbul: Nederlands historisch-archaeologisch Instituut te Istanbul.

Robin, Christian (1982b). Esquisse d'une histoire de l'organisation tribale en Arabie du sud antique. In: Paul Bonnenfant (Ed.), *La Péninsule Arabique d'Aujourd'hui* (17–30). Paris: Centre National de la Recherche Scientifique.

Schofield, Richard (1999). *Negotiating the Saudi-Yemeni International Boundary. Abridged Version of His Talk to the British-Yemeni Society on 31 March 1999*. [http://www.al-bab.com/bys/articles/schofield00.htm]. (Last accessed: May 2014).

Schofield, Richard (2000). The International Boundary between Yemen and Saudi Arabia. In: Renaud Detalle (Ed.), *Tensions in Arabia. The Saudi-Yemeni Fault Line. Aktuelle Materialien zur internationalen Politik, 60(7)* (15–48). Baden-Baden: Nomos.

Serjeant, Ronald B. (1969). The Zaydis. In: Arthur J. Arberry (Ed.), *Religion in the Middle East* (285–301). Cambridge: University Press.

Serjeant, Ronald B. (1977). South Arabia. In: Christoffel A. O. van Nieuwenhuijze (Ed.), *Commoners, Climbers and Notables* (226–247). Leiden: Brill.

Serjeant, Ronald B. (1982). The Interplay between Tribal Affinities and Religious Authority in the Yemen. *al-Abhath, 30*.

Serjeant, Ronald B. (1991). *Customary and Shari'a Law in Arabian Society*. Gower House: Variorum.

Wedeen, Lisa (2008). *Peripheral Visions: Publics, Power, and Performance in Yemen*. Chicago and London: University of Chicago Press.

Weir, Shelagh (2007). *A Tribal Order. Politics and Law in the Mountains of Yemen*. Austin: University of Texas Press.

Wenner, Manfred (1967). *Modern Yemen 1918–1966*. Baltimore: The John Hopkins Press.

Al-Zwaini, Laila (2005). Mediating between Custom and Code: Dar al-Salam, an NGO for Tribal Arbitration in San'a. In: B. Dupret, F. Burgat (Eds.), *Le cheikh et le procureur: Systèmes coutoumiers et practiques juridiques au Yémen et en Égypte*. (Egypte-Monde arab series 1/3, 323–335). Cairo: CEDEJ.

Al-Zwaini, Laila (2006). *State and Non-State Justice in Yemen*. Paper for Conference on the Relationship between State and Non-State Justice Systems in Afghanistan, December 10–14. United States Institute for Peace.

Al-Zwaini, Laila (2012). *The rule of law in Yemen. Prospects and challenges*. The Hague: Rule of law quick scan series Yemen.

GALACTIC POLITIES: ANTHROPOLOGICAL INSIGHTS FOR UNDERSTANDING STATES IN YEMEN'S PRE-OTTOMAN PAST*

Andre Gingrich

The present volume provides a befitting opportunity to reflect upon Walter Dostal's insights, among many others, into one of the most complex and in fact most challenging topics of studying Yemen's past and present. This concerns the roles of the state, or rather, of states, in the region's socio-cultural past and present. Considering and assessing main scholarly orientations and tendencies in this particular sub-field of research does represent an especially sensitive endeavor in view of the violent and tragic events in which the contemporary united Yemeni post-colonial state was involved throughout the first decade of the 21st century (Brandt 2012). A moment after a presidency of more than three decades left the stage, while a fragile stalemate of opposing forces is being maintained in the Yemen at the time of writing, it is appropriate to take a step back. Whatever our respective approaches may be on those current events, most in the scholarly communities would agree that it still is far too early to subject them to any profound and balanced long-term scholarly assessment from the perspectives of present-day socio-cultural analyses and of contemporary history.

RENEWED DEBATES ABOUT CONCEPTUALIZING STATES IN YEMEN

What may be pursued instead, however, is grasping the current opportunity of raised confusion, disagreements, but also of heightened awareness about the state's roles and properties in the Yemen's present to reconsider some of the established hypotheses about states' roles in the historical and academic past. This also seems to be most appropriate in a discursive situation in which, precisely because of current and recent events in the Yemen, several experts in international relations and in political sciences have discovered the Yemen as a hot spot for their own debates on the topic of states' roles in South Arabia. This includes experts from a number of think tanks as well as some of their critics, such as Lisa Wedeen (2008) and Isa Blumi (2010).

In these debates, Lisa Wedeen has assumed a rather conventional Weberian-cum-constructivist "top- down" and capital city perspective based on the urban elites' positions. By contrast, Isa Blumi at least has tried, with some rather limited success I should add, to contribute "bottom-up" aspects to his global history approach – yet most of this is based on premises that are largely following an individualist orientation and therefore, a Western bias. To make a long story short, the models and theories proposed by political sciences today in order to assess the historical roles of Yemeni states claim to be universalist – that is, they strive at being applicable everywhere. Yet behind the friendly surface of a relatively uniform universalism looms the less friendly substance of a profound Western bias (Beck 2005). Both these US American political scientists have been rather dismissive about any relevant anthropological insights on the same issues that are discussed in these two authors' respective books on the Yemen. This gives me here the opportunity to set the record straight.

* This is the extended version of a verbal presentation at the symposium commemorating Walter Dostal (Vienna, October 8th 2012). I would like to gratefully acknowledge the comments and advice communicated to me on earlier drafts of this text by my colleagues at the Austrian Academy of Sciences' (AAS) Institute for Social Anthropology (ISA), and in particular: Marieke Brandt, Guntram Hazod, Johann Heiss, Eirik Hovden, Noura Kamal, Daniel Mahoney, Martin Slama, and in ISA's advisory board Regina Bendix (University of Goettingen). Some of the discursive environment, and of the funding for part of the research related to this volume and the symposium preceding it, were provided by the Austrian Science Fund (FWF) and its grant for the SFB project "Visions of Community" (VISCOM). In this context, I also gratefully acknowledge the input to related discussions by my VISCOM project partners Christina Lutter and Walter Pohl (both: AAS and Department for History, UVienna), as well as Helmut Krasser (AAS) (†).

Most anthropologists would agree that regional and local histories play important roles in understanding the Yemen's present. Moreover, they would consent that this also is valid for the special research topic of state and governance in Yemen's past and present. As for the main periods of regional history, their fluid and intersecting division (Donner 1998) into pre-Islamic and Islamic history is self-understood, and so are the main subdivisions of Islamic history in the region (although continuities often are equally important for historiography, see Mahoney in this volume). In Yemeni studies it would therefore count as *opinio communis* that in Islamic history, one is well advised to distinguish between pre-colonial states in the region, Ottoman and British colonial state administration, and post-colonial statehood (Daum 1987; Brunner 2005). On the basis of these or similar, relatively loose and flexible distinctions into main eras of statehood, it would then also be consensual that earlier periods always had their profound impact upon succeeding periods in the region. It is obvious that such a focus on regional history would not exclude, but on the contrary would facilitate approaches from a global history perspective as well (Gingrich & Zips 2006).

In addition, regional experts of various disciplines – e.g., historians, archaeologists, geographers, or anthropologists alike – usually would agree that *some* concept of statehood not only is useful, but also indispensable for the major pre-colonial periods of written South Arabian history. The question of how exactly pre-colonial forms of statehood are to be conceptualized, in fact, is an open research problem to be addressed in this essay. Yet as a general point of departure, an academic consent is well established upholding the view that assuming any one-to-one correspondence between early modern European states and pre-colonial statehood in southwestern Arabia would be misleading an, in fact, erroneous.

On the basis of this self-evident consensus two legacies of statehood from the pre-colonial period often have attracted particular attention within the respective research communities. These are the Rasulid state entities (also including the period of Ayyubid rulers as their immediate predecessors) to the south and the west of San'a between the late 12th and the mid-15th centuries (Varisco 1994; Smith 1974, 1996), and the Zaydi states in Sa'da province and Upper Yemen since the late 9th century (Madelung 2002; Serjeant 1969). Apart from the first introduction of Islam into Southwest Arabia, these two legacies indeed represent the most profound and lasting impact of statehood in the pre-colonial era of Yemen's Islamic history. The accompanying assumptions and hypotheses imply that legacies from both state traditions, Rasulid and Zaydi, continued to play a certain role in later eras of Yemeni history, i.e. in colonial and in post-colonial times. This provides the overall rationale why anthropological reasoning about historical states in the Yemen, and about interactions between statehood and local societies, tends to primarily relate its various insights and theories to these two pre-colonial state forms, i.e. the Rasulid and the Zaydi state versions.

In general, anthropological theories about indigenous states' roles in Yemen's past and present primarily were inspired by two main models. These may be, and actually have been combined in various ways with each other. It should be added from the outset that quite typical for anthropology, and contrary to most of political sciences reasoning, both of these models share the major advantage of largely relying on concepts derived from native Arab historiography as well, i.e. they absorb and integrate some of those older Arab scholarly concepts into their respective anthropological model.

TWO ANTHROPOLOGICAL MODELS OF STATEHOOD IN SOUTHERN ARABIA

The first among these two models is what may be labeled the functional or segmentary model. It was first exemplified for the Maghreb by the work of Ernst Gellner (1981), who thereby pursued an older research tradition established by Emile Durkheim and E. Evans-Pritchard. To an extent, Gellner's functional-segmentary model was founded on Ibn Khaldun's work (14th/15th century CE), especially on that author's "Muqaddima" (ed. Rosenthal 1958). In the Yemen, Ernest Gellner's students Shelagh Weir (2006) with her description of Razih tribalism and state influence as a self-perpetuating system, and most importantly, Paul Dresch (1993) have applied and have further elaborated the model into various directions. A few of Dostal's ethnographic writings on conflict resolution in Upper Yemen also show clear leanings towards segmentary theory (Dostal 1974), as is also true for some of the writing by Johann Heiss (1987) and by me (Gingrich 1993).

In the functional-segmentary perspective, the state primarily is conceptualized as the fragile element of mediation between opposing segmentary tribal or non-tribal local forces of similar weight and of some equivalence to each other. Again and again, however, the state center by necessity is corrupted and weakened in the pursuit of this noble task. It then loses the capacity to accomplish its main function, which is the point when the state center is being transformed into a set of "weak sheep", as Ibn Khaldun metaphorically called it. The weak center then is exposed to attacks from the periphery (which also may be a nearby periphery, if state rule loses influence there), from where "hungry wolves" (i.e. tribes that were hardly integrated) attack the "sheep", and eventually kill them/overthrow them to take their position. From here, the cycle starts all over again. The model does have further ramifications, and leaves room for more complexity, but in a nutshell, this is how it basically operates.

One of the model's main advantages, beyond its elegance and simplicity, lies in the fact that mediation indeed is a central asset and sign of the quality of good governance in medieval Yemeni state activities. The biography of the first Zaydi Imam in the history of northern Yemen argues precisely this point, by portraying al-Hadi ila 'l-Haqq Yahya b. al-Husayn as the ideal mediator among feuding tribal groups of Sa'da and Najran'. According to his biographer (van Arendonk 1960), he managed to establish peace among them by imposing the superiority of shari'a law over customary tribal law. In the long tradition of Zaydi imams in northern Yemen's history, al-Hadi in this regard certainly was seen as a role model that became integrated into the normative pantheon of good Zaydi governance (see Heiss, this volume).

There can be no doubt that the functional-segmentary model therefore has its merits and its advantages, despite its Maghrebinian origins, for Southwest Arabia. Some of this region's most important features in fact are quite adequately addressed by the model – such as, for instance, the relevance of Islamic and customary law, the significance of hierarchical layers of status and of egalitarian distinction, the state machinery's relative fragility, and so on and so forth. The model's main disadvantage, however, is its disregard for profound transformations. A priority for continuity (as opposed to discontinuity) and for domestic and internal (as opposed to wider and external) factors was largely theory-inspired in this approach, and sometimes tended to disregard empirical evidence to the contrary. The segmentary model thus is largely confined to a perspective of "Plus ca change, plus ca reste la meme chose": the more changes occur, the more the basic features nevertheless remain the same in this perspective. This is a legal mediation-based, cyclical model of the history of statehood and governance (see Heiss, this volume).

The second model also became popular because in a way, it does to an extent balance out those disadvantages of the first one. I prefer to call the second one the "cultural historical" model. It is best exemplified in the works of historian Robert Serjeant (1969; Serjeant & Lewcock 1983) and anthropologists such as Walter Dostal (1984) or Mikhail Rodionov (2007). In many ways, the second model is built on insights derived from the work of al-Hamdani (10th century CE), notably in his "Sifa" (ed. Mueller 1884-91). In the Yemen, a number of anthropologists have tended to follow this perspective, ranging from Thomas Gerholm (1977) to some of the works by Johann Heiss (Heiss 2005; Heiss & Slama 2010), Gabriele vom Bruck (2005) and myself (Gingrich i. pr.) to Bernard Haykel (2010) and others. In the second model, repetitive cycles are less important than sequences of transformation. These sequences are brought about by internal as well as by wider external forces that are less relevant in the first model. Between these internal and external forces, the state acts – and this is the crucial point – not only as a legal and diplomatic mediator, but also as cultural entrepreneur, translator, and innovator, in short as a civilizational force.

Much of Walter Dostal's work on the state in Arabia, from his early (Dostal 1964) paper on the continuities of cultural forms to his very last book (Dostal 2008), testifies precisely to these points. Profound transformations usually are brought about in periods when existing states no longer are able to absorb and accommodate new external flows and growing internal tensions.

The Khaldunian and Gellnerian functional-segmentary model does deserve respect and appreciation. Yet in my view, there are also merits and advantages in the second, i.e. in the cultural historical model – particularly so if that is combined with elements from the first model. Some of these greater advantages may be summarized as a greater appreciation for language, art, and religion, as well as a more careful consideration for profound long-term changes in history together with the impact of external flows and long-distance influences.

The second model in fact seems to have more direct empirical relevance for the Ayyubid and Rasulid state forms. These Sunni (Shafi'i) states relied from the outset on good connections along the Red Sea – for military and political reasons as much as for trading and commercial purposes. Economic innovation and scientific curiosity were much more explicitly on the agenda of Rasulid rulers, and much more effectively put into practice during their reign. In that sense, the Ayyubid and Rasulid states much more obviously functioned as "civilizational forces of transformation".

So in a certain, relative and limited way, it does make some sense to attribute the segmentary (cyclical) model more closely to main Zaydi historical forms of statehood, while associating the civilizational (transformative) model somewhat more intimately with Ayyubid and Rasulid historical states. Yet any binary reasoning would tend to lead us astray in this matter, i.e. it would be one-sided to characterize the Ayyubid/Rasulid state organization as the one with only transformative characteristics, and contrast that to Zaydi state organization as the one with nothing else but legal qualities of mediation. It is much more realistic and plausible to argue that both forms of state organization had features that are reflected in both of these two models, but each of these state organizations had somewhat different priorities.

The Zaydi state was largely operating within a wider tribal environment where addressing and mediating smaller and larger conflicts belonged to the more regular routine operation of running a government wherever it did have at least some influence. At the same time, however, the Zaydi state also did accommodate some innovation from outside, even before the Ottoman presence set in. For instance, the first introduction of growing coffee in the northern mountains seems to have taken place long before the 15th century, and for what we know today it was absorbed fairly smoothly into the Zaydi realm.

On the other hand, the Ayyubid and Rasulid state presence was situated in domains where tribal organization either was more dispersed – as in the central and southern highlands, and in the hilly parts of the coastal plain – or, alternatively, where it was mostly absent as in large parts of the coastal lowlands. From the outset, this implied that legal disputes may have been more frequent, but more often they must have taken on smaller scaled dimensions. So the role of the state, and of its representatives, in the Ayyubid and Rasulid domains could not possibly lack the functions of providing arbitration and mediation according to shari'a principles. These functions merely were less spectacular and of a smaller scale than in the Zaydi case, while the "transformative" functions were much more conspicuous and effective.

Seen against the relevant historical and empirical background to which they refer, it therefore turns out that neither one of these two models is self-sufficient. What certainly is required is a combination of both of them, and in different versions of combinations at that. For certain historical cases the segmentary model may take the lead, combined with secondary features of the cultural historical model; for other instances, a balanced combination between the two may be more appropriate; in other cases still, the cultural historical model might take the lead, and so forth. The fact that Walter Dostal used both models – in a few cases his version of the segmentary model, in many other cases, his versions of the cultural historical model – therefore testifies to this scholar's great insights into the historical anthropology of Southwest Arabia already during those early phases of research when the topic of the "state" in southern Arabian history was rarely addressed at all.

A first intermediate result of this exploratory discussion therefore is that neither of the two main models of state organization that anthropologists have been using is self-sufficient. A second intermediate result indicates that one or the other combination between both of them is at least necessary to do justice to the two main state forms in pre-colonial Yemen. Thirdly, we thus may state that such a combination may be necessary for an appropriate analysis – yet necessary is not identical with being exhaustive or sufficient. A number of important features in pre-colonial Yemeni states still remain inadequately addressed, even if we employ a combination of both models discussed so far. For instance, there is the feature of fragility – more conspicuous in the Zaydi example, but also implied in the Ayyubid and Rasulid case. The feature of relative fragility comes along with interruptions, and ruptures, in time and space, with volatile presence and disappearance, and with mobile boundaries that could expand and shrink almost anywhere and at any point in time. In short, many of those very characteristics by which medieval states in South Arabia would typically differ from the modern, postmodern, and postcolonial norm remain under-explored, if we do not consider at least a third model.

A THIRD MODEL: GALACTIC POLITIES

As already anticipated by the title of this paper, I would like to introduce a third major anthropological model of historical statehood in Asia to this discussion about the properties and roles of indigenous states in Yemen's pre-colonial past and its repercussions in the present. In addition to the existing and well established two models discussed so far, it might be worth discussing the "galactic" model of the state for the reasons specified at the end of the previous section.

Originally, this model was developed for southern Asia and South East Asia. Therefore many of those elements have to be stripped off the original model if and whenever they are specific to those regions and their religions. Still, many of the model's other core elements may then continue to remain valid for discussions about Southwest Arabia as well. The "galactic" notion was coined by the Sri Lankan expert and Harvard anthropology professor Stanley Tambiah (1977), who also relied on several indigenous historians from that part of the world to elaborate his conceptual vision. In addition, Tambiah also relied to a certain extent on insights on South East Asian kingdoms by Robert Heine-Geldern (whom he refers to in his 1977 paper), who was Walter Dostal's most important teacher and intellectual influence in Vienna during Dostal's student years.

Tambiah emphasized a galactic picture of the medieval state in mainland South East Asia, envisioning a central planet surrounded by differentiated satellites, more or less autonomous but within the center's orbit – and at the margins, other such competing minor and major planetary systems. These moving clusters of planets include dynamics of pulsation, and changing spheres of influence that are waxing and waning. The respective center has to try and entertain separate, dyadic relations with each of the satellites for the purpose of keeping them apart from each other, and at bay *in toto* (which of course has its limits, triggering off resistance). Foreign trade and a limited capacity for internal taxation and mobilization belong to the state's key assets. The concept includes the emergence and rise of certain centers, as well as crises, demise, and disappearance.

It can be clearly seen how and why these more general features and properties of the galactic state model may be fruitfully applied for Southwest Arabia, also by combining it with elements of the cultural historical (transformative) and the functional-segmentary (cyclical) models. Both main versions of medieval Yemeni states feature these movements of waxing and waning, and of spatial shifts in their central location as well as in their main realms of influence. The galactic concept also helps to address internal rivalries inside the realms of Zaydi and Ayyubid/Rasulid statehood, as much as the tension-ridden relationship between them. And, while the segmentary and the cultural historical models primarily address defining functions of statehood, as well as functional cycles or periods, the galactic model primarily is focusing on shifting spheres of power in a relational or flexible structural sense.

Lifting the galactic model to such a level of abstraction where it can be peeled out of its original Buddhist and Hindu contexts of reference is not an easy task, and will require some additional conceptualization. In a similar way, moving the model from there into the different contexts of Shafi'i Sunni and Shi'i Zaydi statehood will make additional theorizing on the relevant implications for statehood necessary. Still, at this point these tasks seem feasible and worth the effort. The infusion of the abstracted galactic model with Shafi'i- and Zaydi- oriented elements of statehood indeed suggests that the outcome of this exercise will be two Southwest Arabian versions of the galactic model. By consequence, the abstract model is perceived as cross-cutting both main versions of statehood, i.e. the Zaydi and the Ayyubid/Rasulid version – similar and complementary to the segmentary and the cultural historical models.

Again, it therefore seems appropriate to combine the galactic model with the other two models in one or the other way wherever appropriate for the historical contexts of Southwest Arabia. The advantage shared by all three models is their potential to highlight basic specificities of states in pre-colonial Asian history – specificities that often are ignored in Euro-American historians' or political scientists' discourses on states in medieval Asian history. In those discourses, the states in question often are conceptualized after the model of modern European states. For this reason, fixed territorial boundaries and hierarchical control over land and humans inside these boundaries is central to such models of medieval Asian states, similar to the precursors of modern states in European history.

In the long run, discussions like the present one can demonstrate that modeling "the state" after European-based ideals only superficially seems to be faithful to a universalist paradigm, but in fact is pursuing a profoundly Eurocentric practice. For pre-colonial Southwest Arabia (and to an extent, also for pre-colonial

South Eastern Asia), fixed territorial boundaries certainly cannot be taken as a primary criteria of functioning statehood, thereby conceiving of the states in question as "containers" that precede the container models of modern nationhood and provide the main arenas within which hierarchical control is exerted. On the contrary, the medieval Asian states we have been referring to here, display defining characteristics of clustering into major and minor systems of statehood that are always "on the move" through time and space, including fairly constant processes of territorial expansion and contraction. These aspects therefore not only apply to empires wherever the term applies, but also to smaller states in Asian pre-colonial history.

Jack Goody (1976, 1990) once quite rightly pointed out that for Africa south of the Sahara it was not so much territory but rather humans that were the primary object of pre-colonial state control. One may therefore raise the analogous question whether "control" was of any primary relevance at all for pre-colonial Southwest Arabian statehood. From the available evidence it rather seems that hierarchical "influence" was the more permanent orientation pursued by most of these state constellations on the move, to be substituted by control and physical force only when necessary. "Influence", however, requires less coercion and more persuasive efforts from above through charisma, ideology, religion, symbols, rituals, and mobilization, and – by contrast to "control" – much more identification from below (Godelier 1978). Identification from below certainly is facilitated wherever the liturgical and ritual languages are accessible for the common people because they correspond more closely to the spoken vernacular forms (Behnstedt 1985). In addition, identification from below is much more indispensable wherever the common people are constituted to a considerable extent in collective associations of free persons that include large landscapes of tribal communities and interethnic constellations.

It thereby becomes conspicuous where this analysis is taking us. In the long run, these anthropological insights inspired by Ibn Khaldun, al-Hamdani, and by South East Asian historians may combine their effects towards a more regionally grounded and less uniformly universalist approach. That element of regional grounding also includes an emphasis not only on how local scholars but also how local actors perceive of states in their own interactions and identifications.

Instead of a uniform universalism with a western bias at its core, as advocated by many political scientists in the west, anthropology therefore proposes a more diversified approach of multiple universalism that also is taking account of Asian specificities. In fact this demonstrates the continuing fertility of anthropological insights on states' roles in Southwest Arabia's past and present.

REFERENCES

al-Hamdani, Abu Muhammad. *Sifa Jazirat al-'Arab*. (Ed. David H. Mueller, 1884-91, reprint 1968, 2 Vols., Leiden: Brill).

Beck, Ulrich (2005). *Power in the Global Age*. Cambridge: Polity.

Behnstedt, Peter (1985). *Die nordjementischen Dialekte. 2 Vols.* Wiesbaden: Reichert.

Blumi, Isa (2010). *Chaos in Yemen: Societal Collapse and the New Authoritarianism* (Middle East and Islamic Studies). New York: Routledge.

Brandt, Marieke (2012). Friedens-Shaykh und Kriegs-Shaykh: Der Übergang von Kriegsführerschaft bei den Banū Munebbih im Ḥūthī-Konflikt in Nordwest-Jemen. *Anthropos, 1*, 49–69.

Brunner, Ueli (2005). Geschichte. In: Horst Kopp (Ed.). *Länderkunde Jemen* (137–158). Wiesbaden: Reichert.

Daum, Werner (Ed.) (1987). *Jemen – 3000 Jahre Kunst und Kultur des glücklichen Arabien*. Innsbruck – Munich: Pinguin-Umschau.

Donner, Fred M. (1998). *Narratives of Islamic Origins: The beginnings of Islamic historical writing. Studies in late Antiquity and early Islam, 14*. Princeton: Princeton University Press.

Dostal, Walter (1964). Zur Frage der Konstanz von Kulturformen. In: Eike Haberland, Meinhard Schuster, Meinhard & Helmut Straube (Eds.). *Festschrift fur Ad. E. Jensen* (2 Vols.) (Vol. 1, 91–101). München: Renner.

Dostal, Walter (1974). Sozio-ökonomische Aspekte der Stammesdemokratie in Nordost-Yemen. *Soziologus, 24*, 1–15.

Dostal, Walter (1984). Socio-Economic Formations and Multiple Evolution. In: Walter Dostal (Ed.). *On Social Evolution* (170–183). Vienna: WUV.

Dostal, Walter (2008). *Von Mohammed bis al-Qaida: Einblicke in die Welt des Islam (Religion und Politik 8)*. Wien: Passagen-Verlag.

Dresch, Paul (1993). *Tribes, Government, and History in Yemen*. Oxford: Clarendon.

Gellner, Ernest (1981). *Muslim Society*. Cambridge: Cambridge University Press.

Gerholm, Thomas (1977). Market, Mosque, and Mafraj: Social Inequality in a Yemeni Town. *Stockholm Studies in Social Anthropology, 5*.

Gingrich, Andre (1993). Tribes and Rulers in Northern Yemen. In: Andre Gingrich, Sylvia Haas, Gabriele Paleczek & Thomas Fillitz (Eds.). *Studies in Oriental Culture and History: Festschrift for Walter Dostal* (253–280). Frankfurt/ Main – Berlin – Bern – New York – Paris – Wien: Peter Lang.

Gingrich, Andre (in press). The Use and Abuse of 'Civilization': An Assessment from Historical Anthropology for South Arabia's History. In: Johann P. Arnason & Christopher Hann (Eds.). *Reconsidering Civilization*.

Gingrich, Andre & Zips, Werner (2006). Ethnohistorie und Historische Anthropologie. In: Aloys Winterling (Ed.). *Historische Anthropologie: Basistexte* (245–263). München: Steiner.

Godelier, Maurice (1978). Infrastructures, Societies, and History. In: *Current Anthropology, 19(4)*, 763–771.

Goody, Jack (1976). *Production and Reproduction: A Comparative Study of the Domestic Domain*. Cambridge: Cambridge University Press.

Goody, Jack (1990). *The Oriental, the Ancient and the Primitive: Systems of Marriage and the Family in the Pre-Industrial Societies of Eurasia*. Cambridge: University of Cambridge Press.

Haykel, Bernard (2010). Western Arabia and Yemen during the Ottoman Period. In: Maribel Fierro (Ed.). *The New Cambridge History of Islam, Vol. 2* (436–450). Cambridge: Cambridge University Press.

Heiss, Johann (1987). War and Mediation for Peace in a Tribal Society (Yemen, 9th Century). In: Andre Gingrich, Siegfried Haas, Sylvia Haas & Gabriele Paleczek (Eds.). *Kinship, Social Change and Evolution. Proceedings of a Symposium Held in Honour of Walter Dostal (Vienna Contributions to Ethnology and Anthropology, Vol. 5.)* (63–74).

Heiss, Johann (Ed.) (2005). *Veränderung und Stabilität: Normen und Werte in Islamischen Gesellschaften* (Sitzungsberichte der Phil.- hist. Kl. Bd. 729; Veröffentlichungen zur Sozialanthropologie Bd. 7). Wien: Verlag der Österreichischen Akademie der Wissenschaften.

Heiss, Johann & Slama, Martin (2010). Genealogical Avenues, Long-Distance Flows and Social Hierarchy: Hadhrami Migrants in the Indonesian Diaspora. *Anthropology of the Middle East, 5(1)*, 34–52.

Ibn Khaldun, Abu Zayd Abdu-l Rahman. *The Muqaddimah: An Introduction to History.* (Trans. Franz Rosenthal, 1958, 3 Vols., Bollingen series XLIII. New York: Pantheon Books).

Madelung, Wilferd (2002). Zaydiyya. In: P. J. Bearman, T. Bianquis, C. E. Bosworth, E. van Donzel & W. P. Heinrichs (Eds.). *Encyclopaedia of Islam. 2d ed., Vol. 11* (477–481). Leiden: Brill.

Rodionov Mikhail (2007). *The Western Hadramawt: Ethnographic Field Research, 1983–91 (Orientwissenschaftliche Hefte, 24)*. Universität Halle-Wittenberg.

Serjeant, Robert B. (1969). The Zaydis. In: Arthur J. Arberry (Ed.). *Religion in the Middle East: Three religions in Concord and Conflict* (Vol. 2 285–301). Cambridge: Cambridge University Press.

Sergeant, Robert. B. & Lewcock, Ronald (Eds.) (1983). *Sana: An Arabian Islamic City*. London: World of Islam Festival Trust.

Smith, G. Rex (1974). *The Ayyubids and early Rasulids in the Yemen (567–694/ 1173–1295). W. Gibb Memorial', New Series, xxvi) (2 Vols)*. London: Trustees of the E. J. W. Gibb Memorial.

Smith, G. Rex (1996). Rasulids. In: C. E. Bosworth, E. van Donzel, W. P. Heinrichs & G. Lecomte (Eds.). *The Encyclopaedia of Islam, Vol. VIII* (455–457). Leiden: Brill.

Tambiah, Stanley J. (1977). The Galactic Polity: The Structure of Traditional Kingdoms in Southeast Asia. *Annals of the New York Academy of Sciences, 293(1)*, 69–97.

van Arendonk, Cornelis (1960). *Les Débuts de l'Imamate Zaudite au Yemen. Publications de la Fondation de Goeje*. Leiden: Brill.

Varisco, Daniel M. (1994). *Medieval Agriculture and Islamic Science: The Almanac of a Yemeni Sultan*. Seattle – London: University of Washington Press.

Vom Bruck, Gabriele (2005). *Islam, Memory, and Morality in Yemen: Ruling Families in Transition*. New York: Palgrave MacMillan.

Wedeen, Lisa (2008). *Peripheral Visions: Publics, Power, and Performance in Yemen*. Chicago: The University of Chicago Press.

Weir, Shelagh (2006). *A Tribal Order: Politics and Law in the Mountains of Yemen*. Austin: University of Texas Press.

NOTES ON CONTRIBUTORS

Verena Baldwin is a scientific administrator at the Austrian Academy of Sciences' Institute for Social Anthropology. Her research interests focus on the history of science, especially on Social and Cultural Anthropology during World War II. Verena Baldwin finished her Master's degree in 2008 at the University of Vienna at the Department for Social and Cultural Anthropology on "Walter Hirschberg: Textanalyse ethnologischer Publikationen (1928 – 1945)". Verena Baldwin is also part of the Academy's team that works on the estate of Walter Dostal.

Marieke Brandt received her PhD degree in Cultural Sciences at Berlin's Humboldt University in 2004. She worked for five years in International Development Cooperation Projects in Yemen and has conducted extensive research on tribal societies of north-west Yemen. She was a DAAD fellow at the University of Science and Technology in Yemen and a Marie Curie Intra-European fellow at the Institute for Social Anthropology (ISA) of the Austrian Academy of Sciences, where she currently is holding a research position. Her main fields of interest are tribalism, tribal genealogy and history, tribal politics and tribe-state relations.

Andre Gingrich is a Member of the Royal Swedish and the Austrian Academies of Sciences. He received his doctoral degree in social anthropology with Walter Dostal as first advisor of his thesis, and worked as assistant professor with him throughout the 1980s. Gingrich's ethnographic fieldwork began in Syria, and then led him through several sojourns in Asir (with Walter Dostal and Johann Heiss) and northern Yemen (partially with Johann Heiss). In 1990, Gingrich received the venia docendi for his habilitation thesis on tribal star calendars in south west Arabia. In 1998, Gingrich succeeded Dostal as Full Professor at the University of Vienna's Department for Social and Cultural Anthropology and in 2003, as head of the Austrian Academy's "anthropology unit" which he then transformed into today's "Institute for Social Anthropology".

Siegfried Haas studied social and cultural anthropology and IT economics at Vienna University. Since 1989 he served as Secretary General of the Austrian Society for the Middle East (Hammer-Purgstall) for which Walter Dostal acted as President and later as Honorary President. Siegfried Haas organized several international academic conferences, such as "Islam in a pluralist world"(Vienna 2005) or "Family, Law and Religion"(Vienna 2009). He also edited and co-edited a number of scholarly publications in Middle Eastern Studies, such as "Zentralasien und Islam"(co-ed. with A. Strasser, G. Mangott und V. Heuberger, Hamburg 2002) or „Joseph von Hammer-Purgstall – Grenzgänger zwischen Orient und Okzident" (co-ed. H. D. Galter, Graz 2008).

Sylvia Maria Haas was the longtime administrator, copy-editor and research manager at Walter Dostal's University of Vienna chair between the mid-1980s and the late 1990s. While preparing her own thesis and doctoral degree in this field, she and her husband Siegfried repeatedly carried out ethnographic fieldwork among nomadic and sedentary groups in the Algerian parts of the Sahara. These experiences culminated in the accomplishment of her 2002 doctoral thesis on the "Bridal Woman" among the Kel Ahaggar. Before and after that, she authored and co-authored several other works, some of them with Andre Gingrich. Best known among these is the interview with Walter Dostal published in "Current Anthropology" (48/3) 2007.

Ingrid Hehmeyer, Associate Professor in the History of Science and Technology at Ryerson University, Toronto, is an agricultural engineer who specializes in human-environmental relationships in the arid regions of ancient and medieval Arabia. Her current field research focusses on the history of water technology in medieval Yemen, where she investigates technical innovations in hydraulic engineering and strategies for water management that allowed people to live under harsh environmental conditions.

Johann Heiss currently is a senior researcher at the Austrian Academy of Sciences' Institute for Social Anthropology (ISA) in Vienna. After studying Classical Philology and Arabic language he finished his study of Social and Cultural Anthropology in 1998 with a dissertation on the first imam of the Yemen and the tribal situation in the 10th century with Walter Dostal as first advisor. He carried out field research in Saudi-Arabia (together with Walter Dostal and Andre Gingrich), Yemen (together with Andre Gingrich) and Indonesia (with Martin Slama). As Director of the "Shifting Memories, Manifest Monuments" project, he addressed and scrutinized the memory of the Turks in Central Europe. This resulted in several articles and two co-edited books. In addition, Heiss served since 2011 in the Austrian Science Fund-supported Special Research Realm (SFB) "Viscions of Community (VISCOM) as ISA's senior researcher in the South Arabian part of this major project.

Eirik Hovden is a post doc researcher at the Institute for Social Anthropology (ISA) of the Austrian Academy of Sciences. Hovden is part of the FWF SFB project "Visions of Community (VISCOM)" and his research focus is on the practices of welfare and community building in medieval Zaydi Yemen. Hovden wrote his MA thesis on the management of rural rainwater harvesting structures in North western Yemen. His PhD (University of Bergen, Norway 2012) is about the history of awqaf (pious endowments) in Yemen and Zaydi-Islamic waqf law. Hovden is co-editor (with Walter Pohl and Christina Lutter) of a first major research harvest in book form (with Brill, Leiden) from the VISCOM cooperation.

Wolfgang Kraus studied in Vienna with Walter Dostal, and received his doctoral degree in 1989 with a thesis on tribal organization in the Moroccan Atlas. He carried out long-term research on tribal organization, identity and related topics such as local historical memory in central Morocco. He is Associate Professor at the University of Vienna and served (2012-14) as head of its Department of Social and Cultural Anthropology.

Helmut Lukas is a social anthropologist, senior researcher at the Institute for Social Anthropology (ISA) at the Austrian Academy of Sciences, and deputy director of ISA. He also is a lecturer with venia docendi at the University of Vienna's Department of Social and Cultural Anthropology, as well as at the Austrian Institute for China and Southeast Asia Research, Vienna. His research interests include hunter-gatherer studies, cognitive anthropology, human ecology, materialist theory, interethnic relations, indigenous knowledge, ritual and kinship, and body techniques in societies of Southeast Asia. His regional interests relate to Insular Southeast Asia but also to Continental Southeast Asia including Southern China.

Daniel Mahoney has been a researcher at the Austrian Academy's Institute for Social Anthropology since 2011 for the project "Visions of Community (VISCOM): Comparative Approaches to Ethnicity, Region and Empire in Christianity, Islam and Buddhism (400-1600 CE)." He recently finished his Phd dissertation at the University of Chicago, entitled "The political landscape of the Dhamar Plain in the central highlands of Yemen during the late medieval and early Ottoman periods." It is partly based on his participation in the Dhamar Survey Project through which he has performed archaeological fieldwork since 2006.

Roswitha G. Stiegner (a native of Innsbruck) studied in Vienna, Paris, and Graz Semitic philology and socio-cultural anthropology with an increasing specialization on the Arab peninsula, while spending several sojourns in the Arab world (e.g. Saudi-Arabia 1966-68). After her doctoral thesis with Maria Höfner she served as Assistant Professor at the University of Graz departments for Comparative Philology and for translational Science. Her field research experience gained an increasing focus on South Arabia since the late 1970s. She has edited and co-edited a number of volumes in South Arabian Studies, including a book dedicated to the memory of Maria Höfner, and also served as lecturer at the University of Vienna's Department for Middle Eastern Studies. Since 2008, she has been successfully promoting the re-establishment of a teaching and research position in Ancient South Arabian Studies at that department.

Illustrations: References

Roswitha G. Stiegner:	p. 29, 31, 35, 37
Ingrid Hehmeyer:	p. 45, 47, 49, 52
Centre Français d'Archéologie et de Sciences Sociales, Ṣanʿāʾ:	p. 50
Edward J. Keall:	p. 45
Eirik Hovden:	p. 56, 59, 60
Johann Heiss:	p. 81, 82, 83, 84, 86, 87